The Rough Guide to

21ˢᵗ Century Cinema

by Adam Smith

Contents

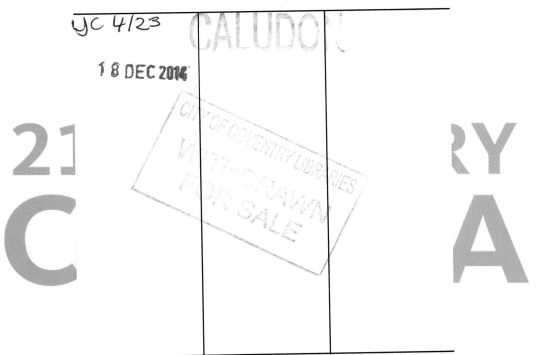

Credits

The Rough Guide to 21st Century Cinema
Editing, picture research, layout: Kate Berens
Design: Diana Jarvis and Tom Cabot
Proofreading: Samantha Cook
Production: Gemma S

Rough Guides Reference
Director: Andrew Lockett
Editors: Kate Berens, Tom Cabot, Tracy Hopkins, Matthew Milton, Joe Staines

Acknowledgements

The author would like to thank the ... the BBFC, and the ever helpful staff of the BFI library, as well as fellow critics David Parkinson, Mark ... ing, Ian ..., Ian ..., Damon Wise and Dan Jolin. Special thanks to Kate Berens for sensitive editing and what can only be de... ... Diana Jarvis and Tom Cabot for their design work, Phil Moa... at ... for supplying the ... and Samantha Cook for proofreading.

Publishing information

This first edition published October 2012 by
Rough Guides Ltd, 80 Strand, London, WC2R 0RL
Email: mail@roughguides.com
Distributed by the Penguin Group:
Penguin Books Ltd, 80 Strand, London, WC2R 0RL
Penguin Group (USA), 375 Hudson Street, NY 10014, USA
Penguin Group (India), 11 Community Centre, Panchsheel Park, New Delhi, 10017, India
Penguin Group (Australia), 250 Camberwell Road, Camberwell, Victoria 3124, Australia
Penguin Group (New Zealand), 67 Apollo Drive, Mairangi Bay, Auckland 1310, New Zealand
Rough Guides are represented in Canada by Tourmaline Editions Inc., 662 King Street West,
Suite 304, Toronto, Ontario M5V 1M7

Printed and bound by Vivar Printing Sdn Bhd, Malaysia

Typeset in Nexus and Kievit

272 pages; includes index
A catalogue record for this book is available from the British Library.
ISBN 978-1-40538-537-4

1 3 5 7 9 8 6 4 2

Introduction

There tends to be nothing the true movie fan loves more, apart obviously from the smell of popcorn in the evening, than making lists. Top tens of all time, best gangster movies, worst Westerns, goriest horrors; endless catalogues of titles to be pored over, amended, rejigged and argued about with like-minded list-makers into the wee small hours. *The Rough Guide to 21st Century* Cinema* is, then, in essence a list. Beating at its compendious heart are the 101 key films of the millennium. To warrant inclusion films not only have to be good, but distinctively 21st century: they've been in some way innovative, or marked a turning point in the development of film. So we have Judd Apatow's *Knocked Up*, an exemplar of the new raunchy relationship comedy that appeals to both sexes, as opposed to the more nineties-feeling *Bridget Jones's Diary*; and Danny Boyle's formally audacious *127 Hours* instead of his more populist, Oscar-winning *Slumdog Millionaire*.

Of course the list of cinematic casualties would make a book of its own, so apologies to fans of *Spider-Man*, *Hotel Rwanda* and Aleksandr Sokurov's one-shot masterpiece *Russian Ark*. These and many more were in at some point, and

The ultimate 21st-century summer comic-book movie, *Avengers Assemble* has Chris Hemsworth as Thor and Chris Evans as Captain America surveying the rubble they've made of New York after one of the film's extended action sequences.

all, for one reason or another, had to be sacrificed. Some omissions are bound to be controversial. Many, for instance, will be surprised to see that not a single Steven Spielberg movie made it into the canon. There is no doubt that Spielberg remains one of Hollywood's best and certainly most successful directors, but his outstanding films (so far) have been in the twentieth century. Conversely, fellow 70s icon Martin Scorsese gets two entries, one for his (first) Oscar-winning *The Departed* and another for his deliriously enjoyable homage to pulp, *Shutter Island*. (Let the arguments commence…) Also scattered throughout the book are mini-essays on subjects as diverse as the arrival (and apparent departure) of so-called "torture porn" (Cruel Intentions, p.101) and the effect of 9/11 on films (War! What movies is it good for?, p.232), as well as tasters of the kinds of films various World Hotspots have delivered in the noughties and beyond.

Alongside the key films we also take a look at some of the most important actors, actresses and directors who have defined the new millennium at the multiplex. Again, the emphasis has been on relative newcomers who show great promise, or on established talents who have made some notable new contribution in the 21st century. So while big names like Tom Cruise and Will Smith might be missing, we champion newer talents such as *Rise of the Planet of the Apes* star James Franco, *Brokeback Mountain*'s Jake Gyllenhaal and Anne Hathaway, and *The Social Network* director David Fincher. Meanwhile, Robert Downey Jr makes an appearance for staging a spectacular comeback and Werner Herzog for continuing to innovate even into his seventies.

It's traditional in movie books for the author to bemoan the state of the industry, to sagely and sadly note that films just aren't as good as they used to be. But the fact is that the ratio of good films to stinkers probably remains about the same over the years. What's certainly true of the 21st century is that there are many *more* films about. Not only has the number of films released in a given year been climbing steadily, cinephiles now have the options of DVDs and Blu-ray, streaming services such as Netflix and a plethora of digital TV channels, many of which stuff their schedules with old and lesser-known films. In this sense it is a golden age for the film fan, with seemingly almost every movie ever made available in some form or other.

And perhaps the sheer ubiquity of films in the 21st century is one source of Hollywood's current financial woes, woes that are very real. Since a peak in 2002 US ticket sales have been declining every year. The vital youth market is constantly

A note on credits
The year of release given is the UK date which occasionally differs slightly from the US date and often significantly with regards to foreign language releases. Unlike many film guides this one gives screenwriter details; where possible these are in the Writers Guild of America format, with writing teams signified by & and credits given in the order in which the participants contributed to the screenplay.

*For the purposes of this book the 21st Century is deemed to have begun on the 1st of January 2001.

Bed and awkward breakfast for Katherine Heigl and Seth Rogen in *Knocked Up*, one of the 21st century's typically raunchy comedies, aimed at audiences of both genders.

distracted by other, equally exciting ways to spend their now dwindling spare cash. Videogames are a particular worry. In 2011 the latest *Call of Duty* sold $400 million-worth of games in its first weekend on the shelves, almost twice the opening weekend of the current movie record-holder *Avengers Assemble*. And then there's film piracy, which may (or may not) be harming revenues (see p.145).

One response has been an attempt to make the movie experience more "immersive"; mainstream blockbusters such as *The Dark Knight Rises* and Ridley Scott's *Prometheus* may be presented these days in the giant IMAX format. Movies are louder and bigger and often much more expensive to make (leading occasionally to notorious and expensive flops such as Andrew Stanton's *John Carter* – see p.69). The summer is now packed with action franchises and comic-book adaptations (leaving some more mature moviegoers heaving a sigh of relief when September comes around). And of course the studios took an expensive gamble on the reinvention of a decades-old technology, 3D, to try to resuscitate sales (for more on which, see p.22).

You can understand Hollywood's desperation. But what they sometimes seem to forget is that the best kind of cinematic "immersion" is the kind of movie that transports you to that strange, unique state, almost a waking dream; a great story told with skill and sensitivity, the kind of film that spits you back blinking into the real world with the sense of having been changed in some way, however small. I hope you'll find at least 101 of them in this book.

The 101 Key
Films

127 Hours

2011, US, 94 mins, 15 (UK) R (US)

....

cast James Franco, Amber Tamblyn, Kate Mara *scr* Danny Boyle
& Simon Beaufoy (based on the book by Aron Ralston)
cin Anthony Dod Mantle, Enrique Chediak *m* A.R. Rahman
dir Danny Boyle

127 Hours begins with as much motion as can be packed into
a frame, and no one knows how to do propulsive, energized
cinema like Danny Boyle. The opening titles are a split-screen
montage of surging crowds and zooming traffic. Intercut with
all this movement a young dude rushes around his apartment,
packing hurriedly for a trip. When he arrives in the desert he hops
on a mountain bike and hurtles across the arid landscape. In a
fantastically economical bit of character establishment, when he
takes a tumble and ends up winded on the ground, half yelping,
half laughing, his first instinct is to pull out a digital camera and
take a picture of himself grinning. He meets a couple of girls; they
go diving in a sunlit pool. "I don't think we figured in his day at
all," one of the girls says as he races off again. A few minutes later
as he scampers across a crevasse, a rock gives way, he falls, and all
is suddenly very still.

　　Among the many problems that Boyle faced with *127 Hours* was
that people were talking about "that scene" before he'd shot even
a foot of film. The true story of Aron Ralston, a 27-year-old hiker
who spent five days trapped under a rock in the desert in 2003 and
finally amputated his arm to free himself, had been the subject
of a best-selling memoir, somewhat inevitably titled *Between a
Rock and a Hard Place*, and had been widely reported in the press.
How do you make a movie about a guy stuck in a crevasse for the
best part of a week, particularly since you already know that he
escapes (and the grisly details of how)? Inspired, endlessly creative
direction, and a stunning piece of virtuoso acting, it turns out, is
the way to do it.

The Rock and the Hard Place: James Franco as Aron Ralston, the real-life hiker who
found himself immovably wedged in a crevasse in an isolated part of Utah's spectacular
Canyonlands National Park.

Boyle is a master technician and deploys every trick he knows in the service of this otherwise necessarily static story: a slow reverse zoom from Ralston under the rock at the bottom of the canyon upwards to a point so high you can see the curvature of the earth, for instance, is heartstopping. Ralston's ordeal is depicted in the messages he records to himself and his family on his video camera (seen only by his close family and friends until Boyle and Franco were allowed to view them in order to recreate them in the film), which break out into sometimes surreal, sometimes touching hallucinatory sequences. We see him breaking up with his girlfriend, his family and friends occasionally watch silently from the family sofa as he struggles to free himself, Scooby-Doo makes a number of appearances. When it comes to "that scene", Boyle has set up the context so superbly that the dominant feeling is not shock or nausea but a will to see Aron succeed, though it is, of course, necessarily gruelling (sound design, superb throughout the movie, playing as much of a role as Tony Gardner's ultra-detailed prosthetics).

If there is a defining theme to Danny Boyle's otherwise disparate subjects it is an unabashed optimism and joy taken in the human spirit. He found it on the poverty-struck streets of Mumbai in his Oscar-winner *Slumdog Millionaire* (2008); he found it at the heart of the solar system in *Sunshine* (2007, p.223); and, as Aron finally pulls himself free and staggers into the sunlight, he finds it in spades here. "Choose life" was the poster tag-line for Boyle's breakthrough movie *Trainspotting* (1996). It's also a pretty good summary of the irrepressible spirit of Aron Ralston and of this unexpectedly exhilarating movie.

JAMES FRANCO
b. 19 April 1978, Palo Alto, CA, US

Novelist, scholar, model, actor and conceptual artist... is there anything James Franco can't do? Well, yes, it turns out: host the Oscars. The swoonsome polymath's inexplicably charmless stint handing out the golden statues in 2011 was a rare wrong-turn (and it may have done him more damage with Hollywood's Brahmins than perhaps he realizes), but it was a mere blip in what has been one of the millennium's most eclectic early careers. After toiling away in forgettable TV for the better part of the 1990s, Franco – who briefly found himself in trouble with the law for stealing expensive aftershave; ironically he is now the face of Gucci's men's fragrances – finally made an impact as the lead in superior TV biopic *James Dean* (2001). It got him the role of Harry Osborn, Peter Parker's betrayed pal in Sam Raimi's *Spider-Man* films (2002, 2004 and 2007). He showed an unexpected talent for comedy in *Pineapple Express* (2008), giving the best stoner performance since Sean Penn's Jeff Spicoli. He was curiously inert as scientist Will Rodman in the overrated *Rise of the Planet of the Apes* (2011), perhaps being more focused on his directorial debut *The Broken Tower* (as yet unscheduled), a black-and-white biopic of another gay poet, Hart Crane, to follow his exceptional turn as Allen Ginsberg in *Howl* (2010). He has yet to really nail the killer role that might crystallize his undoubted talents in the minds of mainstream cinema-goers, though his performance in *127 Hours* (2011) came close, and his forthcoming title role in Sam Raimi's *Oz: the Great and Powerful* (scheduled for 2013) is nothing if not intriguing. He might be wise, however, to stay away from awards ceremonies – unless he's on the receiving end.

3:10 to Yuma

2007, US, 122 mins, 15 (UK) R (US)

. . . .

cast Christian Bale, Russell Crowe, Logan Lerman, Peter Fonda, Alan Tudyk, Ben Foster *scr* Halsted Welles and Michael Brandt & Derek Haas (from a short story by Elmore Leonard) *cin* Phedon Papamichael *m* Marco Beltrami *dir* James Mangold

The received wisdom has had the Western on its deathbed for more than forty years now. But each decade seems to produce a new, if small, crop of the apparently eternal genre. The 2000s have been no exception: Kevin Costner returned to the genre he loves best with the pleasing *Open Range* (2003), Brad Pitt saddled up for *The Assassination of Jesse James by the Coward Robert Ford* (2007), and in 2011 *Iron Man* director Jon Favreau served up a Western seasoned with a slug of sci-fi to the younger crowd with *Cowboys and Aliens* (though the target audience apparently didn't understand why it wasn't called *Cowboys Vs Aliens*). But it was *Cop Land* (1997) director James Mangold, one of contemporary Hollywood's most consistently reliable helmers, who really brought home the bacon with this remake of the identically titled 1957 Glenn Ford picture. It's a classic oater of the old school, and boasts a brace of highly enjoyable performances from two stars each firing on all cylinders.

Civil War veteran Dan Evans (Christian Bale) is at the mercy of moneylenders who want to force him off his smallholding to make way for the coming railroad. Barns are burned, rivers diverted, threats are made. His teenage son William (Logan Lerman) holds him in contempt because of his perceived helplessness in the face of these bullies. But when Dan is offered a place in a posse and $200 to transport gang-leader

RUSSELL CROWE
b. 7 April 1964, Wellington, New Zealand

It's difficult to imagine a craftier example of cinematic match-making than Ridley Scott's decision to cast New Zealander Russell Crowe as the lead Maximus in *Gladiator* (2000). The movie was a roaring success and gave Hollywood perhaps its only true star of the millennium, a stardom based at least partially on an unapologetic sweaty macho appeal that had been missing from the silver screen since the pretty boys took over in the 1980s. And along with the unmediated manly movie persona came equally authentic off-screen hell-raising, enacted in bars (numerous skirmishes), hotels (telephone throwing), and award ceremonies (assaulting TV producers who cut short his poetry recitation) that no doubt delighted his personal hero and friend, the late Richard Harris. He'd come to cinephiles' attention in a blistering turn as Australian Neo-Nazi skinhead Hando in *Romper Stomper* (1993) before heading to Hollywood and being cast alongside fellow antipodean and *Neighbours* alumnus Guy Pearce in Curtis Hanson's classy *noir L.A. Confidential* (1997). An Oscar nomination was forthcoming for his performance in 2002 as schizophrenic mathematician John Nash in Ron Howard's emotionally slick *A Beautiful Mind* (his second after one for Michael Mann's much better whistleblower drama *The Insider* in 2000). Post-*Gladiator* he attempted no fewer than four times to recreate the old magic with Ridley Scott: it resolutely failed to materialize either in Provence-porn *A Good Year* (2006) or *Robin Hood* (2010), for which his accent was enthusiastically ridiculed. He had slightly better success with the thriller genre in *American Gangster* (2007) alongside Denzel Washington and *Body of Lies* (2008) with Leonardo DiCaprio. More recently he turned up as everymanish John Brennan in blue-collar thriller *The Next Three Days* (2011) and will be seen as Jor-El, Superman's dad, in *Man of Steel* (2013), a part last played by the late, and equally unpredictable, Marlon Brando.

Ben Wade (Russell Crowe) across dangerous Indian territory to meet the train to Yuma Prison, where he has an appointment with the noose, he sees a chance to both redeem himself in the eyes of his son and save his livelihood.

One of the great joys of this meticulously crafted film is its complete lack of contemporary artifice; this is a Western made like Westerns should be, with vividly sketched characters, exciting action and a robust commitment to telling a good story well. Peter Fonda chews scenery as the grizzled bounty hunter, while Ben Foster minces slightly and seems to have acquired the entire Old West's supply of eyeliner as the gang's psychotic second-in-command Charlie Prince. Crowe has a great deal of fun as the irredeemable black hat who shows an unexpected sensitive side with his delicate pencil drawings, though he's also not beyond stabbing to death a captor with a table-fork. He's a bad guy who cheerfully revels in his own villainy and invites us to do the same. "You're not all bad," says a wide-eyed William Evans, mostly, it seems, to try to justify his own increasing fascination with the excitingly dangerous outlaw. "Kid, I wouldn't last five minutes leading an outfit like that if I wasn't as rotten as hell," Ben Wade replies with no little pride. Christian Bale's performance, though, is the more subtle. Careful and guarded, he's a man who has kept his dignity intact despite fate dealing him nothing but bad hands.

Mangold delivers the required climactic shoot-out briskly and efficiently (unlike many less skilled directors of action currently plying their trade, his is gloriously coherent, making it possible to discern who is shooting at whom). *3:10 to Yuma* is made with genuine passion and respect for the genre. It's a classic tale of good sacrificing itself to conquer evil, and of a son's restored faith in the strength and courage of his father, flavoured with plenty of gunsmoke and thundering hooves. It's as solidly built and pleasingly familiar as a Dodge City coffin.

Russell Crowe as black hat Ben Wade in the custody of the posse (Luce Rains, Peter Fonda, Lennie Loftin, Christian Bale and Chad Brummett) in this meticulously crafted old-style Western.

Adaptation

2003, US, 115 mins, 15 (UK) R (US)

cast Nicolas Cage, Meryl Streep, Chris Cooper, Brian Cox, Maggie Gyllenhaal, Tilda Swinton **scr** Charlie Kaufman & Donald Kaufman (from the book by Susan Orlean) **cin** Lance Acord **m** Carter Burwell **dir** Spike Jonze

"Write what you know" is the traditional advice handed out to aspiring scriptwriters. And what Charlie Kaufman, writer of *Being John Malkovich* (1999, also directed by Spike Jonze), knew was that he was finding it impossible to adapt *The Orchid Thief*, a non-fiction bestseller by *New Yorker* journalist Susan Orlean about illegal dealers in the exotic blooms, into a shootable screenplay. So instead he delivered a screenplay about a screenwriter named Charlie Kaufman (played by Nicolas Cage) trying and failing to adapt a book about flowers, and falling in love with Orlean (Meryl Streep) from afar, while his crass but unshakeably confident twin brother Donald (also played by Cage via seamless visual effects) achieves overnight Hollywood success writing a boilerplate screenplay about a serial killer

Nicolas Cage (as screenwriter Charlie Kaufman), mired in the agonizing process of squeezing out words onto the page.

with the help of real-life scriptwriting guru Robert McKee (played by Brian Cox). To add to the giddy sense of unpredictability the action is set during the shooting of *Being John Malkovich*, and includes what must be cinema's most ambitious flashback – to "Hollywood, CA, four billion years ago" when it was a literal swamp, a cameo by Charles Darwin and an unexpected alligator attack.

Needless to say, this postmodern mélange wasn't for everyone. Some critics found it so self-referential it barely needed an audience. And certainly, with a fireworks display of intertextual tricksiness like that erupting on the screen, much depended on the central performances to anchor the movie in some kind of human reality. Happily both Nicolas Cage and Meryl Streep are at the top of their respective games: Cage's self-lacerating internal monologue concerning his own literary inadequacy, disgust at his over-padded backside and pressing need for a muffin reward for having made it through a single paragraph will be recognizable to anyone who's ever tried to write for a living. It's an exquisite agony, thrown into relief by his brother's apparently effortless success writing the kind of trashy screenplay he despises. Streep, who after a hiatus during the 1990s is rapidly re-establishing herself as one of Hollywood's premier character actresses, mines the role of author Susan Orlean for its rich comic potential: a sequence in which she brushes her teeth while feeling the oncoming effects of a new orchid-derived narcotic is as subtle a piece of pantomime as she's ever delivered.

This is a self-consciously brilliant film and occasionally too clever for its own good, finally deconstructing itself so thoroughly that all the audience has left is a vague memory of some spectacular conjuring trick having taken place before their very eyes. And the formal cleverness obscures rather than clarifies Kaufman's acute observation that humans, like orchids, must adapt to their circumstances to be truly happy. But, even if it's the kind of filmmaking that's only enjoyable in the smallest of doses, it's still an intellectually exhilarating ride handled with confidence and quiet technical skill by director Spike Jonze. And the intellectual playfulness didn't end with the credits: it emerged only after the film was released that Charlie Kaufman has no brother, twin or otherwise. Which didn't stop Kaufman dedicating the movie to his fictitious sibling's memory, and both "brothers" being nominated for an Oscar for best original screenplay – though the Academy was savvy enough to insist that should they win they would have to share a single statue.

MAGGIE GYLLENHAAL
b. 16 November 1977, New York, NY, US

It might seem an odd way to establish a career as one of the premier actresses of the new millennium: being enthusiastically (and, it should be hurriedly stated, entirely consensually) spanked by James Spader, as she was in one of the more arresting scenes in Steven Shainberg's darkly comic *Secretary* (2003), but it certainly seems to have worked for Maggie Gyllenhaal. The eldest of the Gyllenhaal siblings, she was nevertheless the last onto the screen – if by only a year, Jake beating her to it with a small role as Billy Crystal's son in 1991's *City Slickers* – with her father Stephen directing her in small roles in Graham Swift adaptation *Waterland* (1992), *A Dangerous Woman* (1993) and *Homegrown* (1998). She then ditched Dad in favour of John Waters, playing teen terrorist Raven ("I'm a Satanist and I'll be doing your make-up today!") in *Cecil B. DeMented* (2000), and subsequently her tastes remained for the most part in the indie arena. George Clooney was impressed enough to cast her in his directorial debut *Confessions of a Dangerous Mind* (2003); she was enjoyably duplicitous as a hotel manageress in convoluted scam movie *Criminal* in 2005; and she got a Golden Globe nomination for her blistering performance as an ex-con trying to rebuild her life in *Sherrybaby* (2007). Her first and so far only foray into the world of the summer blockbuster is as Assistant District Attorney and love interest Rachel Dawes in Christopher Nolan's *The Dark Knight* (2008, p.58), a part she took after Katie Holmes inexplicably declined to reprise her role from the first movie, and after assurances from Nolan that she would not just be "arm candy" for Bruce Wayne. In fact she wound up as arm candy for both Bruce Wayne/Batman and Harvey Dent/Two-Face in the movie's unorthodox love triangle, or perhaps given the fractured nature of the men's psyches, love pentagon.

WORLD HOTSPOTS #1: EUROPE

New waves ain't what they used to be…

During the first decades of the twentieth century, Europe shaped the art of cinema with Soviet montage, German Expressionism, Italian neo-realism, and French Impressionism and poetic realism. But, in the the sixty-odd years since the *nouvelle vague* sparked a radical rethink of filmmaking worldwide with films such as Godard's *A Bout de Souffle* (1960) Hollywood's commercial and technical might has reduced the impact of Europe's innovations. Americans still remade the continent's hit movies, but Europe's new waves now only caused local ripples rather than cinematic tsunamis.

Some French directors – Luc Besson, Jean-Pierre Jeunet and Michel Gondry – enjoyed success Stateside, but the auteurs of the New New Wave barely registered outside the arthouse and festival circuits. Prime examples are Olivier Assayas and François Ozon, both skilled manipulators of genre conventions. Assayas produced neo-*noir* sci-fi mash-ups like *Demonlover* (2002), as well as costume dramas, family sagas and political biopics, while Ozon pastiched Douglas Sirk in the musical whodunnit *8 Women* (2002) in between making intense melodramas and chic sex comedies. Still, the main characteristic of French-language film in the 21st century has been urban gloom, possibly best exemplified by the social realism of Belgian siblings Jean-Pierre and Luc Dardenne, whose *L'Enfant* (2006), a desperately moving tale of moral and spiritual poverty centred on an instance of child-trafficking, gained them their second Palme d'Or.

Shaken by Dane Lars von Trier and his Dogme 95 manifesto (see p.17), the northern heartland of continental miserabilism (Scandinavia, in other words) achieved a new popularity with Tomas Alfredson's tweenage vampire chiller *Let the Right One In* (2009, p.157) and the 2009 *Millennium* trilogy adapted from the crime novels of Stieg Larsson. Neither could be described as exactly cheerful, and with Austria-based Michael Haneke exporting it to France and America before returning it home to devastating effect in his account of the roots of Nazism *The White Ribbon* (2009), the tradition of northern European grimness was upheld.

Indeed, audiences in the reunified Germany became accustomed to hard-hitting dissections of the country's traumatic recent past and uncertain present. Oliver Hirschbiegel harked back to the Third Reich in *Downfall* (2005, p.75) and Hans Weingartner recalled the heyday of Baader-Meinhof terrorism in *The Edukators* (2005), while Wolfgang Becker and Florian Henckel von Donnersmarck reflected with a sour sense of "ostalgie" on life in the former East Germany in *Good Bye Lenin!* (2003, p.109) and *The Lives of Others* (2007, p.161).

The collapse of the Berlin Wall in 1989 had a profound effect on cinema in the onetime Soviet empire, too. After decades of strict censorship, filmmakers had a new freedom to discuss taboo topics. But without state sponsorship or protectionism, funding was hard to come by and it took almost a decade for the Czech and Polish industries to wean themselves off subversion and satire and begin examining the new realities of life in a democratic, free-market society. Russian cinema similarly struggled to find its voice, although in Aleksandr Sokurov, most famous for his one-take film *Russian Ark* in 2003, it boasted a master of the medium.

The most unexpected consequence of the fall of Communism, however, was the rise of Romanian film. Veteran Lucian Pintilie set the tone with *Niki and Flo* (2003), a scathing insight into the ideological chasm between the pre- and post-Ceausescu generations. Co-screenwriter Cristi Puiu continued to assess the cost of social and political change with his directorial debut *The Death of Mr Lazarescu* (2006), a pitch-black comedy that used the titular patient's endless nocturnal trekking between Bucharest hospitals, none of which will treat him, to expose the flaws in the post-Communist system. Corneliu Porumboiu further emphasized the extent to which the nation was hidebound by misplaced nostalgia, bureaucratic incompetence and social malaise in *12:08 East of Bucharest* (2007) and *Police, Adjective* (2009). But the most damning indictment was Cristian Mungiu's *4 Months, 3 Weeks and 2 Days* (2008), a dramatically unflinching account of a 1980s student's botched backstreet abortion, which won the Palme d'Or at Cannes.

Amélie

2001, Fr/Ger, 123 mins, 15 (UK) R (US)

....

cast Audrey Tautou, Mathieu Kassovitz, André Dussollier *scr* Guillaume
Laurant & Jean-Pierre Jeunet *cin* Bruno Delbonnel *m* Yann Tiersen
dir Jean-Pierre Jeunet

Jean-Pierre Jeunet's international box-office sensation is the cinematic equivalent of
one of those fancy French patisseries full of glistening syrup-glazed strawberry tarts
and barely set custards. For some it is a garden of earthly pleasures. For others, who
prefer their dessert with a little tartness, just looking in the window is enough to
send the blood sugar soaring. Cynics and cinematic diabetics beware then, for *Amélie*
is a film so sweet you feel like you should brush your teeth after the credits roll.

Audrey Tautou as the
gamine, adorable Amélie in
one of the most successful
European films of the
millennium: Parisian life
was never sweeter nor
more colourful.

As its original French title, *The Fabulous Destiny of Amélie Poulain*, indicates, this is at heart a kind of fairy tale written for adults. We first meet Amélie (Audrey Tautou) as a child being reared, we are informed by the breathless narrator (André Dussollier), by "a neurotic and an iceberg". Years later, we next encounter her at the age of 23 working with a crowd of Parisian eccentrics and oddballs at a tiny, impossibly adorable café. When she accidentally dislodges a bathroom tile and discovers a tin box containing a long grown-up small boy's treasures she determines to return them to him. His joy at the surprise is evident, and so Amélie embarks on a spree of random acts of kindness that changes lives. With the arrival of romantic interest Nino Quincampoix (doe-eyed Mathieu Kassovitz), this includes her own.

The term "gamine" could have been invented for Audrey Tautou. Wide-eyed, mischievous and, here at least, oddly sexless, she is a little reminiscent of the girls in Japanese manga, with an unearthly, waifish look accentuated in the film's poster. But as much as Tautou is the human star it is the spirit of Paris that pervades the film. Or rather a reconstituted, romanticized version of it. This is the Platonic version of the City of Light: Montmartre is blissfully free of the tourist hordes; cars have been digitally eliminated from the streets; the old Gare de l'Est has been scrubbed until it sparkles and every broken Orangina bottle and cigarette butt removed. More controversially, another kind of cleansing appears to have gone on as well. This is a Paris without a brown or black face in sight. It's particularly odd that this should be the case given the involvement of Mathieu Kassovitz, whose directorial debut *La Haine* (1995) was a shocking exposé of Parisian racial tensions. But then the idealized city is nothing new in cinema; Woody Allen's New York is hardly ethnically or economically diverse.

Amélie was snubbed by the Cannes Film Festival for being "unimportant", and some critics found its strident optimism and eccentricity a little too cloying. (It was certainly a departure in tone for director Jeunet, whose previous films included 1991's darkly witty cannibal drama *Delicatessen* and franchise misfire *Alien: Resurrection*, 1997.) This snooty cinematic puppy-kicking, of course, did nothing to damage its popular appeal and might even have helped establish it as a wildly successful audience favourite both in its home country and abroad, where it made nearly twenty times its $10 million budget, rendering it one of the most successful foreign-language films of the millennium. The world, it appears, has a very sweet tooth indeed.

Anchorman: The Legend of Ron Burgundy

2004, US, 94 mins, 12A (UK) PG-13 (US)

cast Will Ferrell, Christina Applegate, Paul Rudd, Steve Carell, David Koechner, Vince Vaughn, Fred Willard **scr** Will Ferrell & Adam McKay **cin** Thomas Ackerman **m** Alex Wurman **dir** Adam McKay

Mediocre American: Will Ferrell's Ron Burgundy checks his 70s moustache is up to muster in *Anchorman*'s perfectly realized 70s setting.

After the Rat Pack of the 50s and the Brat Pack of the 80s came the Frat Pack of the 00s: an informal band of American comedy actors with a core consisting of Will Ferrell, Vince Vaughn (key frat flick 2004's very funny *Dodgeball: A True Underdog Story*), Owen Wilson (*Zoolander*, 2001), Jack Black (whose career faded somewhat after the likeable *The School of Rock* in 2004), Luke Wilson (*Old School*, 2003), Ben Stiller (*Meet the Parents*, 2000, and its successively worse sequels) and Steve Carell (*The 40 Year Old Virgin*, 2005) usually wrangled by one of a troika of writer-directors: Adam McKay, Judd Apatow or Todd Phillips. Their comedy style has tended toward the sophomoric and man-childish, but at least for the most part avoids the gross-out oneupmanship that dominated the genre after the success of *There's Something About Mary* and its infamous hair-gel gag in 1998. *Anchorman* – the first of what McKay and Ferrell would term their "Mediocre American Man Trilogy" whose subsequent instalments include NASCAR comedy misfire *Talladega Nights: The Ballad of Ricky Bobby* (2006) and the much funnier *The Other Guys* (2010) – is in a sense the *echt* Frat Pack movie since it features almost all of them, albeit many in cameo roles. It also happens to be one of the funniest.

Set in a San Diego TV newsroom in the 1970s, the film follows the travails of Ron "The Balls" Burgundy, station anchorman and thus king of all he surveys. As a jazz-flute tooting, moustached chauvinist, his sense of self-importance is boundless ("I'm very important. I have many leather-bound books and my apartment smells of rich mahogany," he memorably announces). The only cloud on his horizon is a rival news team, headed by nemesis Wes Mantooth (Vince Vaughn). But his idyll is threatened when station manger Ed Harken (the always excellent Fred Willard) announces the appointment of – crivens! – a *female* news anchor in the shape of Veronica Corningstone (a fantastically feisty Christina Applegate). "I hear their periods attract bears" is one team member's reaction to the dreadful news.

There's something pleasingly laidback about Will Ferrell's style – a little reminiscent of fellow *Saturday Night Live* alumnus Chevy Chase – and indeed some critics wished he'd pushed the gag rate just a bit harder, though when the jokes do wear thin there are always the perfectly realized 70s decor and fashions to grin at. His great comedic achievement is to make an essentially unlikeable character somehow appealing and to efficiently milk what is not much more than a sketch idea for an hour and a half. He's aided by sterling comic work from the likes of Steve Carell, whose weather forecaster Brick Tamalad announces that "years later, a doctor will tell me that I have an IQ of 48 and am what some people call mentally retarded" (we find out that he subsequently became chief political adviser to the Bush White House), and Brian Fantana (Paul Rudd) whose vast array of aftershaves includes "London Gentleman" and "Sex Panther", which he proudly announces is illegal in nine countries. ("It smells like a used diaper filled with Indian food" is Corningstone's verdict.) Let's hope the sequel, announced by Ferrell in 2012, is as deeply silly and irresistibly funny.

WILL FERRELL

b. 16 July 1967, Irvine, CA, US

Will Ferrell began his ascent to comedy superstardom on long-running TV sketch show *Saturday Night Live* and, at his best, his easy style and air of bewildered silliness harks back to the golden era of Bill Murray or Dan Aykroyd. He studied sports broadcasting at the University of Southern California, possibly the only institution of further education at which it is possible to take such a degree, before joining LA improv group The Groundlings and subsequently serving a seven-year apprenticeship on *SNL* before leaving in 2002. He landed small parts in, among others, *Austin Powers: International Man of Mystery* (1997) and its sequel *The Spy Who Shagged Me* (1999) as one of Dr Evil's henchmen, as well as fashionista Mugatu in Ben Stiller's excellent couture comedy *Zoolander* (2001), but his big breakthrough came in 2003. That year, he starred in both Jon Favreau's surprise hit *Elf*, bringing a deft sweetness to the role of Santa's human helper Buddy, and as ageing frat-boy Frank Ricard in *Old School*, the midlife-crisis comedy whose ensemble established the core of what would become the Frat Pack. Smash-hit *Anchorman* introduced audiences to Ron Burgundy, a part for which Ferrell says he drew on his experiences sportscasting, but then NASCAR comedy *Talladega Nights: The Ballad of Ricky Bobby* (2006) failed to cross over, despite some funny moments, and *Blades of Glory* (2007), in which he played a figure skater, was underpowered and relied a little too heavily on its gay jokes. The seemingly obligatory "comedy actor in a serious role" moment was dispatched with much critical success when Ferrell played an alcoholic salesman in Raymond Carver adaptation *Everything Must Go* (made in 2010 but not released in the UK until 2011). But he was back on absolutely top comedy form in *Anchorman* director Adam McKay's underrated cop comedy *The Other Guys* (2010), in which unlikely co-star Mark Wahlberg shows an unexpected appetite and talent for dumb yucks.

Animal Kingdom

2011, Australia, 113 mins, 15 (UK) R (US)

cast James Frecheville, Guy Pearce, Sullivan Stapleton, Jacki Weaver, Luke Ford, Ben Mendelsohn, Laura Wheelwright **scr** David Michôd **cin** Adam Arkapaw **m** Antony Partos **dir** David Michôd

Cinematic neophiles were quick to declare Australian director David Michôd's scorching crime debut "the new *Goodfellas*". In fact they've been calling almost anything with guns, gore and gangsters "the new *Goodfellas*" since the early 1990s. *Animal Kingdom* certainly has plenty of all three, but otherwise the similarities are superficial. "All my life I wanted to be a gangster," Ray Liotta's Henry Hill famously intones at the beginning of Scorsese's melodrama, setting himself up to prove the old saying about more misery being caused by prayers answered than those that go unheeded. But Josh, the seventeen-year-old central character of *Animal Kingdom* (played with studied blanknesss by newcomer James Frecheville), is a very different character with a contrasting, and in many ways more satisfying story. "Kids just are wherever they are … this is where I was. After my mum died, this is just the world I got thrown into," he says towards the beginning of the film. Hill enters the jungle by choice, but Josh is trapped there from the start. His is a story not of aspiration and hubris then, but the grimmer, more vital business of survival.

Very loosely based on events in Melbourne in the mid to late 1980s, *Animal Kingdom* has Josh being looked after by a nest of criminals after his mother dies of a heroin overdose. His three uncles, tattooed thug Craig (Sullivan Stapleton), the relatively sane Darren (Luke Ford) and the randomly terrifying Pope (Ben Mendelsohn), are armed robbers. At the heart of this noxious brood is Janine "Smurf" Cody (a sweetly intimidating Jacki Weaver), a Ma Barker-style matriarch whose love for "her boys", if the way she kisses them is anything to go by, is perilously near the kind that usually turns up in Greek tragedies. Josh soon finds himself trapped in a pitched battle between the police, including a rogue element that has taken to assassinating the city's bank robbers, and his new family bent on extracting murderous revenge. The only lights in this benighted life are his girlfriend Nicky (Laura Weelwright), whom a paranoid Pope soon becomes convinced is a police snitch, and a sole uncorrupted police officer named Leckie, played with appealing understatement by the ever-reliable Guy Pearce.

In a sense *Animal Kingdom* harks back not to the 1990s but to the heyday of the gangster picture in the 40s and 50s. Pope's unhealthy relationship with his mother recalls James Cagney's with Ma Jarrett in *White Heat* (1949) and the film takes a moral line, showing the inevitable unravelling of criminal lives, that is recognizable from the crime films of the Hays Code period. But a company of extremely talented Australian actors prevents these familiar characters from slipping too close to stereotype and the setting, skilfully captured by cinematographer Adam Arkapaw, of miles upon miles of featureless, desolate suburbia, mirrors the central characters' inner bleakness. Michelôd's writing and direction are understated, the *Grand Guignol* of Scorsese or hip irony of Tarantino both completely absent. Violence is sudden, brutal and not dwelt upon; a truly gruelling sequence involving murder-by-heroin is partially obscured, and all the more distressingly effective for it. Crime movies tend to be calibrated towards action and excitement, but this is a satisfying slow burn. It's a disquieting and strangely compelling film, whose desperate atmosphere and vividly sketched characters stay with you, and it's at its best in its nicely judged ending, in which the hierarchy of the kingdom in question is surprisingly rearranged: final moments that raise as many questions as they answer.

Family ties: James Frecheville as Josh, the teenager thrust into a nest of gangsters, watched over by Jacki Weaver's matriarchal Janine "Smurf" Cody in anonymous suburbia.

Antichrist

2009, Den/Ger/Fr/Swe/Pol/It/Bel,
109 mins, 18 (UK) Unrated (US)

• •

cast Willem Dafoe, Charlotte Gainsbourg *scr* Lars
von Trier *cin* Anthony Dod Mantle *m* Kristian
Eidnes Andersen *dir* Lars von Trier

By the 2000s Denmark's most infamous auteur's
penchant for the miserable, shocking and grotesque
was well enough known to become the butt of
satirical website *The Onion*, which posted a fake set of
films featuring rape, incest and an elderly man being
forced to lick a mud-caked boot under the headline
"Denmark Introduces Harrowing New Tourism Ads
Directed by Lars von Trier". *Antichrist* did nothing
to dispel this reputation; it is a bleak, depressing,
gruelling but nonetheless highly original film, from
a director with the courage to follow his artistic
imagination wherever it leads him.

   Antichrist commences with a kind of symphonic
tragedy. Shot to the strains of a Handel aria and
in pellucid slow-motion black and white (ace
cinematographer Anthony Dod Mantle here
enthusiastically exploring the possibilities of digital
shooting), we see couple "He" (Willem Dafoe) and
"She" (Charlotte Gainsbourg) making love in the
shower, complete with the arty penetration shot that
became *de rigueur* at the turn of the millennium à
la 2000's *Baise-Moi* and Michael Winterbottom's
2004 film *9 Songs*. Intercut with this we witness
the couple's toddler escape his playpen, and as the
music swells, plunge out of an open window to his
death. Wracked by grief compounded by guilt, She
is inconsolable, despite her therapist husband's
attempts to help her. Perhaps unwisely they retreat

LARS VON TRIER
b. 30 April 1956, Kongens Lyngby, Denmark

Lars von Trier (or rather Lars Trier; he added the
von, a film school nickname) was brought up by a
father who was a Communist and a mother who
was a Social Democrat. Both were militant nudists
and his family was, as he later remembered it, a
place where "everything was permitted but feelings
and enjoyment". (To further complicate matters, his
ninety-year-old mother confessed on her deathbed
that his real father was an artist with whom she had
deliberately become pregnant to give him "artistic
genes".) Is it then any wonder that his world view is
darkly unconventional to say the least? He came to
international attention in the 1990s with Dogme 95,
a cinematic manifesto that required the forswearing
of "artificiality", including lighting and non-location
sound, and resulted in *Breaking the Waves* (1996)
and *The Idiots* (1999). By the turn of the millennium,
though, this extreme form of cinematic discipline was
apparently old hat, and he embarked on a series of
films whose common key subjects are cruelty, human
misery and America, the last often being inextricably
intertwined with the former two. His casting of Björk
in *Dancer in the Dark* (2000) was a masterstroke, the
Icelandic popstress showing great vim in a musical
that sings and dances itself all the way to the gallows.
In *Dogville* (2004), Nicole Kidman is similarly badly
treated by duplicitous American townspeople, and in
Manderlay (2006) von Trier probes the tender subject
of slavery. US critics are often hostile, bemoaning
the fact that America is a country the director has
never actually visited (among his plethora of phobias
is one of flying) – criticism he convincingly dismisses
by pointing out that Hollywood makes films about
subjects of which it is almost completely ignorant
all the time. And being declared persona non grata
while promoting his solemnly beautiful *Melancholia* at
the 2011 Cannes Film Festival (he made an ill-advised
joke about Hitler) doesn't seem to have dulled his
appetite for controversy. His next announced project
is *Nymphomaniac*, an "erotic journey" apparently
featuring a plethora of hard-core sex scenes.

to a cabin in the woods, named Eden, to continue her therapy. There the strange and surreal seem to surround them and portents of death, or rather, frustrated attempts at life, close in. He is delighted to see a deer until it turns to reveal itself trailing a stillborn calf; a baby bird covered with ants falls from its nest; a self-devouring fox announces "chaos reigns". All this is moving towards a moment of *Grand Guignol*: an act of sexual self-mutilation that had critics booing or fleeing at Cannes. (To say that von Trier asks a lot of his actors is an understatement, and both Dafoe and Gainsbourg commit themselves wholly to whatever it is he is up to.)

Made as von Trier slowly recovered from an episode of severe depression, *Antichrist* was conceived, he has said, as a horror film. It certainly has much of the genre's apparatus: as well as death and deep, dark woods, where the cabin resembles the one from Sam Raimi's *The Evil Dead* (1981), there's also strange, surreal imagery, while in its themes of grief, intimacy and sex it clearly recalls Nicolas Roeg's classic *Don't Look Now* (1973). But is there anything more to this film than an expertly made arthouse creep-out? There certainly seems to be, but pinning it down is almost impossible. Some have seen in it an attack on the inadequacies of reason: the husband's witless attempts at therapy being utterly

useless in the face of the incomprehensible tragedy experienced by the wife. The only possible response to it is a kind of self-annihilation. Or is he torturing her? Worrying her guilt with his relentless reason until she breaks and destroys both of them?

Perhaps one of the best criteria by which to judge a movie is how forgettable it is, and even if you have a feeling that *Antichrist* is, at some level, an empty amalgam of pretension and provocation, it remains difficult to shake off its strange atmosphere; it is like a nightmare that doesn't fade in the morning. Trying to find sense in its lowering imagery might be exactly the wrong thing to do, as pointless as the therapist's apparently futile attempts at curing human anguish. Deep in Lars von Triers' woods, chaos reigns.

Woodland horror movie, pretentious surrealism or both? The image of a despairing Charlotte Gainsbourg in the misty forest light is among many shots that make *Antichrist* hard to forget.

The Artist

2011, Fr/Bel, 100 mins, PG (UK) PG-13 (US)

· ·

cast Jean Dujardin, Bérénice Bejo, John Goodman, Penelope Ann Miller, James Cromwell, "Uggie" *scr* Michel Hazanavicius *cin* Guillaume Schiffman *m* Ludovic Bource *dir* Michel Hazanavicius

"I've bought a movie but you might not like it," producer Harvey Weinstein is supposed to have told his brother and partner Bob sometime in 2010. "It's black and white." Bob said he didn't mind. "It's French." Okay, said Bob. "Oh, and it's almost completely silent," Harvey added. At which point in the PG version of this anecdote Bob said he might need a bit of a sit-down. You can't really blame him. Silent cinema was thought to have gone quietly into that good night with the arrival of talkies nearly a hundred years ago. But as usual Harvey was on the right track. With Martin Scorsese's 3D tribute to silent-movie pioneer Georges Méliès, *Hugo*, being released to critical acclaim in the same year, audiences seemed in the mood to honour cinema's early days. *The Artist* is an irresistible exemplar of this new interest in old movies – and it's the sweetest present from the French to the Americans since the Statue of Liberty.

The plot, which owes more than a little to 1952's all-time classic *Singin' in the Rain*, has George Valentin (Jean Dujardin) – a silent movie star with more than a touch of both Douglas Fairbanks and, of course, Valentino about him – at the height of his stellar appeal. His megawatt smile, topped with a raffish pencil moustache, lights up picture houses and newspaper front pages. Much to everyone's delight he's permanently accompanied both on screen and off by a lively Jack Russell terrier ("Uggie", delivering the single finest performance by a canine since Rin Tin Tin hung up his collar), a mutt with whom he seems to have a closer relationship than his leading ladies, much to their entertaining displeasure, and certainly to that of his long-suffering wife (Penelope Ann Miller). But one day stogie-chomping producer Al Zimmer (John Goodman) takes him aside and shows him the latest thing: movies that *talk*. Valentin isn't impressed: "If that's the future you can keep it!" the inter-title reads. But it is indeed the shape of things to come, and unwilling to adapt to these new kind of films, he slowly sinks into poverty and despair. Meanwhile feisty flapper Peppy Miller (Bérénice Bejo), in love with Valentin since they collided on a red carpet, watches distraught as her star rises thanks to his earlier help and his falls ever farther. Can her love for him rescue the floundering star, and just why is it that he can't make it in the new world of talkies?

One of the surprising side effects of watching a silent movie a century after sound superseded them is the realization of just how many wasted words there seem to be in modern film drama. *The Artist* tells a touching story deftly but without sacrificing any complexity or emotional resonance; the suspicion that the format might be a mere gimmick is dispelled within minutes. Silent cinema purists rightly pointed out that *The Artist* is in some ways nothing like the original silent movies: cinematically, for instance, it has none of the scope or ambition of classics such as Stroheim's *Greed* (1924) or Murnau's *Sunrise* (1926). And paradoxically the movie's most inventive and enjoyable sequences come from the manipulation of sound: a nightmare sequence in which even the tiniest noise – a glass being set on a table, a car going by outside – is suddenly, terrifyingly, magnified is a highlight. But this was never meant to be a lesson in film history; rather it's a quietly graceful and irresistibly uplifting movie that it's impossible not to shout about.

Silence is golden: George Valentin (Jean Dujardin) and producer Al Zimmer (John Goodman) are all smiles for the press as Valentin signs on the dotted line.

SHATTERED GLASSES
What happened to Hollywood's 3D dream?

Like almost every development in Hollywood, the recent resurgence of 3D was powered by the twin engines of technology and money. As with the first 3D boom, which had its source in the arrival of television, Hollywood was facing stiff competition – this time from a multitude of entertainment alternatives. Rental/streaming services such as Netflix and Lovefilm, as well as the internet and videogames, not to mention vastly improved home cinema systems that, in terms of picture and sound quality, rivalled those of the cinemas themselves, all conspired to keep filmgoers away from the multiplex. In 2005 a group of tech-friendly directors, including George Lucas and James Cameron, exhorted exhibitors to improve the cinemagoing experience by re-equipping their screens with digital technology, which delivered better picture and sound. And for only $30,000 more than the $70,000 it would cost them for each screen to go digital, they could fit state-of-the-art 3D technology and charge more for a ticket, thus covering the cost of the upgrade.

The notion caught on and by 2007 DreamWorks Animation chief and Hollywood top dog Jeffrey Katzenberg, a convert to the cause, had appointed himself head cheerleader: "[3D] is the single most revolutionary change since colour pictures," he told *Business Week* in 2007. A year later his enthusiasm was undiminished. "I think in a reasonable period of time, all movies are going to be made in 3D ... 2D films are going to be a thing of the past," he said. It was easy to see the appeal; audience growth had been sluggish, if not nonexistent since 2002. And with the introduction of 3D televisions Hollywood could pipe new DVD product (and a host of newly 3D-converted classics) back into the home, helping to counteract increasing losses from the shrinking DVD retail business. As an added bonus, the process would also help prevent piracy. It seemed to be a case of win-win. And the release of James Cameron's groundbreaking *Avatar* (2009) appeared to indicate Hollywood had indeed hit paydirt. A full eighty percent of its vast audience paid a premium of up to $5 to watch the movie in the new format.

But Hollywood's dream soon began to turn sour. Post-*Avatar* some audiences began to complain that the process gave them headaches, the picture was too dark (an inevitable result of trying to cram two overlapping images onto one screen) and children found the glasses uncomfortable. To make matters worse, and despite the occasional critically acclaimed exception, including Martin Scorsese's *Hugo* (2011), the quality of 3D movies was generally poor. Films never intended to be in 3D were subject to rushed "post-conversion" (Louis Leterrier's *Clash of the Titans* in 2010 being a notorious example) by studios afraid to release action movies without 3D, egged on by exhibitors eager to cover the cost of converting their screens. Audiences, no longer sure that the extra cost of a ticket was justified, became increasingly wary. The tipping point came in the summer of 2011 with *Pirates of the Caribbean: On Stranger Tides*. While Disney had expected up to 65 percent of the US audience to pay extra to see the film in 3D, less than half actually did; the 3D audience that had represented the vast majority for *Avatar* was all of a sudden in the minority.

Katzenberg was quick to find the explanation in the poor quality of many 3D films. "We've disappointed our audience multiple times now, and because of that there is a genuine mistrust. It's really heartbreaking," he told *The Hollywood Reporter* in January 2012. "The audience has spoken, and they've spoken really loudly." Indeed they had. In 2011 total US box-office receipts declined a further 3.8 percent and ticket sales were down nearly 5 percent, its worst performance in nearly fifteen years (according to Boxofficemojo.com). The news was no better for 3D television, with sales of 3D sets declining and manufacturers blaming the lack of compelling 3D content, including movies, as part of the problem. Some commentators speculated that poor 3D films and high ticket prices had actually driven people away from the multiplexes. The very thing that was supposed to rescue the industry might be helping to kill it: catastrophic news in any dimension.

Avatar

2009, US, 162 mins, 12A (UK) PG-13 (US)

••

cast Sam Worthington, Zoë Saldana, Sigourney Weaver, Michelle Rodriguez, Stephen Lang, Giovanni Ribisi *scr* James Cameron *cin* Mauro Fiore *m* James Horner *dir* James Cameron

The one thing that almost everybody knew about James Cameron's otherwise mysterious sci-fi epic before it was released was that it was an almost sure-fire flop. Rumours of a spiralling budget (officially quoted as somewhere north of $230 million) and that Cameron's revolutionary 3D system made test-screening audiences violently nauseous swirled around the movie press. And when some images of his digitally rendered aliens, the Na'vi, emerged, they appeared to be twelve-foot-tall blue cats.

But of course *Avatar* not only was an outrageous hit, raking in a record-breaking $2.5 billion at the international box office, it ushered in digital 3D, the key technological revolution of the decade (see box, opposite), and set the stage for two sequels, currently being shot back to back. Pinning down the source of its appeal is not, however, as easy as you might think. The story is efficient but hardly inspiring: in 2154 paraplegic marine Jake (Sam Worthington) is sent to alien moon Pandora to attempt to persuade the cobalt-coloured natives to make way for interstellar strip-mining. (Cameron's eco-streak is much in evidence, as is its concomitant have-his-cake-and-eat-it attitude to technology: it's evil but hell, look how *cool* it is.) Jake inhabits an "avatar", a copy of a Na'vi body, giving him the ability to sprint through the planet's verdant forest and, vitally, to fall for one of its inhabitants (Zoë Saldana) – and then try to save them from ecological catastrophe in the shape of Col. Miles Quaritch (Stephen Lang, chewing scenery as enthusiastically as his mining machines). The 3D is subtly and inventively used, but it's worth noting that a good percentage of its delighted audience members saw the film without 3D and didn't seem to miss it. So what was it that sent fans flocking, often multiple times, to Cameron's "doomed" project?

Perhaps the answer lies not in the characters (underwritten) or the story (boilerplate), but in the *place*. Pandora is a gorgeously detailed jungle utopia, the result of a fertile imagination deployed on an industrial scale. Halfway through, when Cameron eases off on the plot and just lets Jake, and entranced audiences, see, experience, nearly *feel* Pandora's astonishing, lushly colour-saturated and occasionally gravity-defying forest-scapes, in these moments the film achieves a kind of alien bucolic ecstasy. It should come as no surprise that the director's favourite film is *The Wizard of Oz*, which similarly enchanted audiences in the Depression-struck 1930s (the then revolutionary three-strip Technicolor process playing the role of Cameron's digital-pokery). Like Victor Fleming and co's classic, *Avatar* effortlessly achieved what the best of big, bold moviemaking can: it transported audiences away from the worrying realities of the everyday world by providing them with another, better one – one so richly realized, in fact, that some found themselves suffering withdrawal symptoms when booted out of the cinema into the grey mundanities of daily life. And so in a perfectly judged, bittersweet twist Cameron lets Jake do what the audience never can. He lets him stay in Oz.

The lush, edenic, CGI landscapes of Pandora, inhabited by astonishing flora and fauna and a race of tall, lithe blue humanoids: Zoë Saldana's Neytiri wins hearts and minds to the Na'vi cause.

The Bad Lieutenant: Port of Call – New Orleans

2010, US, 122 mins, 18 (UK) R (US)

....

cast Nicolas Cage, Eva Mendes, Val Kilmer, Alvin "Xzibit" Joiner, Shawn Hatosy
scr William Finkelstein *cin* Peter Zeitlinger *m* Mark Isham *dir* Werner Herzog

The bad cop himself: Terence McDonagh, played to bug-eyed perfection by Nicolas Cage, alongside Eva Mendes' hooker Frankie.

"Everybody involved should die in the same bus crash," was reportedly director Abel Ferrara's response when he heard that Werner Herzog was intent on remaking his 1992 classic about an amoral, drug-addict cop. Herzog airily responded that he had never actually seen the film or indeed heard of Abel

Ferrara. Given that both directors were at the time attending the 2009 Venice Film Festival it gave the annual bash a frisson of excitement. Maybe critics were in for an auteur smackdown of some kind? Disappointingly the two never met, and it's difficult to know whether Herzog was telling the whole truth; a fruitful way to understand this wonderfully eccentric film is to think of it not so much as a remake of Abel Ferrara's work as a response to it. While Ferrara's film was a corrosive, bleak picture of a damned, morally tormented cop, Herzog's takes the same set-up and finds in it not only a great deal of surreality but also, and most unexpectedly, a deep sense of forgiveness and humanity.

Post-Katrina New Orleans, with its foetid greys and greens, and sense that the bayou is on the verge of erupting into the city, is an entirely appropriate stamping ground for Terence McDonagh (Nicolas Cage), a druggy policeman whose murky approach to the job has him shaking down tourists and college kids for money to pay for his habit – which he shares with girlfriend Frankie (Eva Mendes), a high-class call-girl whose clients he isn't averse to blackmailing either – as well as his spiralling gambling debts. The almost redundant plot involves a drug-related murder and a key child witness, but the real joy here is watching director and star each bring their own unpredictable seasonings to this strange gumbo.

Cage and Herzog might have been made for each other. There are even shades of the director's former muse, the late Klaus Kinski, in Cage's bug-eyed, gleefully demented performance. At various points there's the giddy sensation that director and star locked eyes, grinned and plunged into sequences without much idea how they might turn out. How else do you explain a tense police surveillance operation set to Engelbert Humperdinck's "Please Release Me", during which our cocaine-addled anti-hero glances with increasing suspicion at a pair of iguanas perched on the desk, which no one else seems able to see. When a bad guy is blasted away he exclaims "Shoot him again…! His soul's still dancing!" The camera pans to reveal the dead drug-dealer enthusiastically break-dancing to the strains of Cajun harmonica. You just don't get that in Scorsese movies. Or Ferrara ones for that matter.

But the film's biggest surprise is its abiding humanity. McDonagh should be an irredeemable monster but his bad behaviour is leavened both by his essential likeability (a testament to Cage's perfectly calibrated performance) and by the continuing sense that he might, finally, be saved. In the oblique final scene McDonagh is slumped against the glass of an aquarium. Behind him exotic fish peer out at the exotic humans. "Do fish have dreams?" he asks enigmatically. His companion, a man whose life he once saved, smiles. It's a bizarre, thoroughly unexpected grace note that really shouldn't work but does, brilliantly. Typical of a director who in his fifth decade of making films is as dazzlingly unpredictable as he was in his first.

NATALIE PORTMAN

b. 9 June 1981, Jerusalem, Israel

Unlike poor Ewan McGregor and the once promising Hayden Christensen, Natalie Portman managed to escape the deathly grip of George Lucas's constipated *Star Wars* prequels with her career undamaged. She'd been a busy child-star before Lucas cast her as Queen Amidala in *Star Wars: The Phantom Menace* (1999), making her debut in Luc Besson's *Léon* (1995) as dangerously Lolita-ish pal to the titular hit man, before turning up in the likes of *Heat* (1996) and *Mars Attacks!* (1997). She began the millennium at Harvard, having enrolled to study psychology, and declared that, apart from intergalactic royal commitments, she would take no film roles while there. When she dipped her toe back in the Hollywood water with Anthony Minghella's *Cold Mountain* (2004) she was outshone slightly by the wattage of Jude Law and Nicole Kidman, but she was irresistible in *Scrubs* star Zach Braff's less starry debut *Garden State* (2004), her shaven-headed love interest Sam reminding audiences of the feisty yet vulnerable qualities buried under the lumber-like dialogue of Amidala. Mike Nichols' adaptation of Patrick Marber's hit play *Closer* (2005) divided audiences, some hailing it as a blistering account of contemporary relationships, while others detected only cynical twenty-somethings shouting at each other, but there was no doubt that Portman was fearsomely sexy as the shouting's pole-dancing catalyst Alice. She was more down to earth but no less effective as the wife of a kidnapped soldier in war-at-home drama *Brothers* (2010), alongside Jake Gyllenhaal and Tobey Maguire. Since her Oscar for *Black Swan* (2011), she has shown a worrying tendency to pick projects with little obvious to recommend them. Neither she nor James Franco could do much to save limp comedy fantasy *Your Highness* (2011), while the presence of Ashton Kutcher should have been sufficient warning that rom-com *No Strings Attached* (2011) was best avoided (the pair were curiously lukewarm together – and the fuck-buddy theme was done with more vim and genre-subverting wit anyway in *Friends With Benefits*). Kenneth Branagh's Marvel entry *Thor* (2011) in which she played an astrophysicist was more of a success; but one can only hope that the curse of Lucas is not finally exerting its evil influence.

Black Swan

2011, US, 108 mins, 15 (UK) R (US)

cast Natalie Portman, Mila Kunis, Vincent Cassel, Winona Ryder, Barbara Hershey ***scr*** Mark Heyman and Andrés Heinz and John McLaughlin ***m*** Clint Mansell ***cin*** Matthew Libatique ***dir*** Darren Aronofsky

Ballet classic *The Red Shoes* (1948) was the obvious reference point for critics writing about Darren Aronofsky's psychological horror movie, and certainly there are superficial similarities, not least its highlighting of the gruelling physical training, the bloody feet and starvation diets that ballerinas subject themselves to. But if *Black Swan* is an *hommage* to Powell and Pressburger, it's one that takes a long and eccentric detour via the likes of Italian horror maestro Dario Argento's surreal dance-themed masterpiece *Suspiria* (1976) and early Roman Polanski movies, notably *Repulsion* (1965). Set in New York in the present day, the film has a prestigious ballet company preparing a new production of *Swan Lake*. Haughty artistic director Thomas Leroy (Vincent Cassel) brutally dismisses his ageing lead ballerina (Winona Ryder) in favour of unknown but talented company member Nina (Natalie Portman). But as rehearsals continue life seems to be imitating art, particularly when rival ballerina Lily (Mila Kunis) arrives on the scene and awakens dark, jealous forces in diffident Nina…

There's more than a dash of Brian De Palma's *Carrie* (1976) to be detected too, in the repressive relationship between Natalie Portman's self-torturing dancer and her brittle, overbearing mother (a fantastic Barbara Hershey), who spends all day painting pictures of her daughter and has, for reasons of her own, taken the locks off all the doors. She might be less *obviously* loopy than Piper Laurie's devouring matriarch but she's no less succulently insane. What kind of mother, after all, buys a self-starving ballerina a cake the size of a Chevrolet to celebrate getting a part for which she will no doubt have to starve herself further? Indeed the scenes between them in their cramped apartment, oppressively packed with watchful cuddly toys and featuring, inevitably, a musical box complete

With its creepy, dreamlike imagery, *Black Swan* captures the tortured inner life of Natalie Portman's dancer, Nina.

with twirling plastic dancer (Thérèse DePrez's production design is superb, as is Matthew Libatique's skittery, mostly handheld camerawork) are among the film's creepiest and best.

Aronofsky doesn't have the seriousness of mind or narrative control to approach the genuine terrors of Polanski's existential nightmares, but then he's probably not trying to. Despite its culturally upmarket setting – which appears to have bamboozled some critics into considering this as high art of some kind – this is a movie cheerfully aware enough of its own lowbrow roots to jemmy in a sweaty lesbian sex scene halfway through (Paul Verhoeven's camp 1995 classic *Showgirls* is another movie more than a little in evidence). And then it descends, or possibly ascends, into spectacularly staged *Grand Guignol* replete with murderous ballerinas, digitally rendered black swans, blood-drenched tu-tus and Tchaikovsky turned up to 11.

It falls to Natalie Portman, who trained intensively for ten months to deliver the ballet sequences, to anchor this enjoyably over-egged confection and she does so admirably, fully deserving her Oscar. Her Nina is almost totally passive, a believable virgin at 28, and a kind of born victim. In the real world you'd probably find yourself wanting to slap her but in Aronofsky's skewed, claustrophobic universe it's impossible not to feel for Nina as she pirouettes her way to her doom in this wild, weird *Danse Macabre*.

Blue Valentine

2011, US, 112 mins, 15 (UK) R (US)

* *

cast Ryan Gosling, Michelle Williams, Mike Vogel
scr Derek Cianfrance and Joey Curtis & Cami
Delavigne *cin* Andrij Parekh *m* Grizzly Bear
dir Derek Cianfrance

Is *Blue Valentine* the ultimate anti-date movie? It's not
that it's not exquisitely made, because it is. Nor that it
doesn't feature two of recent cinema's most talented
(and, let's face it, goshdarned pretty) actors in what
are so far some of their very best, most achingly real
performances. It's just that *Blue Valentine* takes as its
subject romance and does with it what Hollywood,
with a few notable exceptions, almost never does:
it puts it through a woodchipper. There are no last-
minute rushes across New York à la *Manhattan* (1979)
here. No soaring strings and final declarations of
undying affection on railway platforms. And it has the
unmistakeable ring of biographical truth; this is love
factually.

We begin in the present with a lost dog – not a
good sign. A little girl wanders through a field calling
the pooch's name. She is picked up by her father,
Dean (Ryan Gosling), who helps look. Later he'll tell
her, as hopes for the dog and almost everything
else fade, that the pet's gone to Hollywood to be
a star, revealing the whimsy and imagination that
once made him attractive to wife Cindy (Michelle
Williams). Now, when they're not staring at each
other, mute strangers, they just argue: about the
right way to make porridge; about car seatbelts. But
then we flash back six years to the moment they first
see each other, in a care home where Cindy works,
nursing ambitions to be a doctor. The looks are tender
and playful. He believes in love at first sight, he says.

RYAN GOSLING

b. 12 Nov 1980, London, Ontario, Canada

"He's one of those rare actors that has this gift, he
can say a thousand words without saying a line...
Alain Delon and James Stewart had that," gushed
Drive (2011, p.77) director Nicolas Winding Refn of his
star. Comparing Ryan Gosling to cinema's greats has
been all the rage recently: Clint Eastwood and Steve
McQueen are rightly name-checked in many reviews
of *Drive*. But he's taken a circuitous route to stardom,
dallying in the hills and valleys of indie cinema,
perhaps only too aware of the dangers of being co-
opted into the Hollywood machine. An alumnus of
that Ivy League academy for perky teen-talent, *The All
New Mickey Mouse Club*, alongside Justin Timberlake,
he was first noticed by American indie connoisseurs
in *The Believer* (2001), an intense, uncompromising
account of a young Jew who embraces violently anti-
Semitic beliefs. But he made his mark for mainstream
audiences playing opposite Rachel McAdams in
Nick Cassavetes' upscale tearjerker romance *The
Notebook* (2004), and subsequently gained an
Oscar nod for his troubled high-school teacher in
Half Nelson (2007). Co-star Michelle Williams was
equally honoured by Oscar for her performance in
Blue Valentine (2011), though his performance was
certainly as good. His career-best performance in
Drive, a screenplay he championed to Nicolas Winding
Refn, was scandalously ignored by the Academy
but is nevertheless probably the role on which his
future career will hinge, as he niftily managed both to
appeal to mostly male fans of 1980s urban *noir* and,
perhaps accidentally, to become the thinking female
moviegoers' pin-up du jour. He embraced his inner
matinee idol, at least a little, in *The Ides of March*
(2011), a political thriller in which he played an election
manager against George Clooney's cynical politico,
though the film sadly needed a screenplay with more
heft and bite, often feeling like an extended episode of
The West Wing. But then Alain Delon, Clint Eastwood
and Steve McQueen all had their off films too.

He plays her a song on his ukulele and sings in a goofy voice while she dances. And then we flash forward…

Cinematographer Andrij Parekh captures this festival of bewilderment and pain in calm, excruciating detail. His unforgiving long lens mercilessly charts the complex topography of Cindy and Dean's unhappiness; when Cindy foolishly mentions running into her ex Bobby Ontario (Mike Vogel, bearing a name that provides the nearest thing to a laugh) and hurriedly assures Dean that he got fat (he didn't; he has the pneumatic biceps that speak of gym membership, or failing that, prison), it catches the sudden shard of anger in him and a stab of fear in her. A supposedly romance-kindling trip to a love motel becomes a lacerating argument, caught in the chilly blue light of the absurd "space suite". And yet Parekh also captures the early sparks of affection with equal truth.

Cianfrance and his co-writers' formally daring screenplay wisely gives no specific reason for the pair's dwindling affection (though Dean's hideous aviator shades might come up in couples' counselling). It just happened. Something has worn out or broken and try as they might neither can detect precisely what it is, let alone try to mend it. It's a beautifully crafted story full of small, telling details. When the two first talk, gazing at an old locket and remarking on how pretty the young couple are in it, a faint rainbow hovers above them. When Dean plays his ukulele to a delighted Cindy, the song is "You Always Hurt The One You Love". The last few minutes are a masterclass in the emotional power of precision editing. And it ends on the Fourth of July with shots of fireworks: exploding, lighting up the sky, burning out.

Love factually: Michelle Williams and Ryan Gosling offer believably heartfelt performances, shot in unforgiving detail, as Cindy and Dean in *Blue Valentine*'s agonizing account of love gone stale.

Borat: Cultural Learnings of America for Make Benefit Glorious Nation of Kazakhstan

2006, US/UK, 84 mins, 15 (UK) R (US)

....

cast Sacha Baron Cohen, Ken Davitian, Pamela Anderson *scr* Sacha Baron Cohen & Anthony Hines & Peter Baynham & Dan Mazer *cin* Luke Geissbühler, Anthony Hardwick *m* Erran Baron Cohen *dir* Larry Charles

Sacha Baron Cohen had already brought his most popular comic creation to the big screen with *Ali G Indahouse* in 2002, a film conceived as a straightforward narrative comedy without the interaction of the unsuspecting public that had defined his early work. Though occasionally moderately funny, without the high-

Star-spangled scammer: Borat's (Sacha Baron Cohen) adaptation of the States' national anthem enrages an unprepared rodeo crowd.

intensity pranking Ali himself was not much more than an unbelievable comic caricature. The movie all but flopped, but apparently Baron Cohen learned from his mistake. For Borat, a Kazakhstani journalist character he'd originally cooked up for short-lived TV sketch show *F2F* (1996) and who also featured on Channel 4's *Da Ali G Show* (2000), he took the technique that had served him so well on television, the pitiless co-opting of unwitting real people into complex, often exquisitely embarrassing comic scenarios, to new heights – and in doing so produced one of the decade's most original and funniest comedies.

Pulling off this kind of "situationist" larking requires incredible levels of planning, on the spot improvisation and nerves of steel. This last quality is abundantly evident in a sequence in which Borat sings a version of "The Star Spangled Banner", containing among other lines "Kazakhstan is the greatest country in the world/All other countries are run by little girls", in front of an increasingly enraged 10,000-strong rodeo crowd. (It was shortly after the nerve-wracking filming of this that original director Todd Phillips left, "creative differences" being cited, to be replaced with *Seinfeld* writer and director of *Curb Your Enthusiasm*, Larry Charles.)

Some of Baron Cohen's stunts are perhaps more defensible than others: what after all had the middle-class group who hosted a dinner to welcome a representative of a foreign country really done to deserve the avalanche of bizarre and upsetting behaviour, culminating in the hostess being presented with what appears to be a paper bag containing their guest's fresh excrement, and the arrival of a "prostitute"? (A trio of racist University of South Carolina frat boys are less easy to sympathize with.) But while some critics found the film insulting to Americans, playing on their perceived insularity, at least one found the film to be a celebration of their citizens' good manners and forbearance in the most trying of circumstances. The film was also accused of being sexist, homophobic and anti-Semitic ("Although Kazakhstan a glorious country, it have a problem too, economic, social, and Jew," were among Borat's remarks that caused offence), though of course this commits the "Alf Garnett" fallacy: mistaking the views of a fictional character for those of its creator.

The result was box-office success, critical praise and enraged lawsuits in about equal measure. Among those hiring lawyers were the town of Glod in Romania, which doubled for Borat's fictional home town of Kuzcek, which sued for $38 million. Most claims were dismissed and, with the film making well over $250 million worldwide (on a budget of less than $20 million), studio executives were unlikely to have lost much sleep over them. What might have worried them more was the seeming impossibility of repeating the trick. Baron Cohen's next attempt to take one of his TV creations to the big screen, *Brüno* (2009), sank without trace. They'll be hoping for better luck with *The Dictator*, released in 2012.

LONG LIVE THE NEW FLESH #1:

Ten actors who got their big break in the 21st century...

BRADLEY COOPER Big Break: *The Hangover*
Cooper has had two triumphs in recent years, the first being his role in the smash-hit comedy *The Hangover* (2009), which made $467 million worldwide, the second being voted *People Magazine*'s Sexiest Man Alive in 2011, and thus causing a protest outside the magazine's offices by incandescent Ryan Gosling supporters. Fans of both will have something to ogle in *The Place Beyond the Pines* (2012) in which he plays a stunt man alongside his nemesis Gosling.

ANDREW GARFIELD Big Break: *The Amazing Spider-Man*
Born in LA but brought up in the UK, Garfield had the bum role in *The Social Network* (2010, p.215), Facebook co-founder Eduardo Saverin having neither the slimy mendacity of Justin Timberlake's Sean Parker nor the intriguing emotional blankness of Jesse Eisenberg's Mark Zuckerberg. He'd been better used in Mark Romanek's dystopian love story *Never Let Me Go*, but his big break was his starring role in the 2012 reboot *The Amazing Spider-Man*.

TOM HARDY Big Break: *Bronson*
Dismayed Trekkers might have first spotted Hardy in franchise-killer *Star Trek: Nemesis* (2003) as baldie villain Shinzon. A brush with crack addiction threatened to put the kibosh on his career but he cleaned up his act and staged a stunning comeback first in the title role in Nicolas Winding Refn's *Bronson* (2009) and then as Eames, "The Forger", in *Inception* (2010, p.141), where he impressed Christopher Nolan enough to be cast as incomprehensible gas-mask-wearing baddie Bane in *The Dark Knight Rises* (2012).

JOSEPH GORDON-LEVITT Big Break: *Inception*
Familiar to many as alien Tommy in long-running sit-com *3rd Rock from the Sun*, after its cancellation in 2001 he began a rapid movie ascent, first turning up in quirky indie fare such as Gregg Araki's *Mysterious Skin* (2005). He gained mainstream success in *Inception* (2010, p.141), catching the eye of both Steven Spielberg, for whom he'll play the president's son in *Lincoln*, and Quentin Tarantino, who cast him in his Western *Django Unchained*, both scheduled for 2013.

SHIA LABEOUF Big Break: *Transformers*
LaBeouf had small roles in Hollywood blockbusters such as *I, Robot* (2004), but it was as appealing every-kid Sam Witwicky in Michael Bay's cacophonous *Transformers* (2007, p.238) that he made his mark. He brought the same easy charm to sidekick Mutt in Spielberg's ill-advised reboot *Indiana Jones and the Kingdom of the Crystal Skull* (2008). More promisingly he'll be seen in John Hillcoat's bootlegging drama *Lawless* alongside Tom Hardy and Gary Oldman.

ROBERT PATTINSON Big Break: *Twilight*
Something of a blessing, more of a curse might be the way Robert Pattinson views his role as soppy bloodsucker Edward Cullen in the seemingly endless *Twilight* movies. The grist to a million tweenage girls' PG-rated dreams, he attempted to break free of the character, if not with romance, with some success in *Remember Me* (2010) and *Water For Elephants* (2011), before taking the lead in David Cronenberg's *Cosmopolis* in 2012. Still, his bulging pay-packet, a rumoured $18 million in 2009 alone, must be something of a comfort.

CHRIS PINE Big Break: *Star Trek*
Hollywood always has one conventionally handsome utility-star in its back pocket: *The Fast and the Furious* (2001) lead Paul Walker had been the go-to guy in the early 2000s, until *The Princess Diaries 2* (2004) alumnus Chris Pine arrived, shoving his chiselled jaw into the role made famous by William Shatner, Captain James T. Kirk in J.J. Abrams' relaunch in 2009. He's also been easy on the eye in Tony Scott's entertaining runaway train-flick *Unstoppable* (2010) and rom-action movie *This Means War* (2012).

JEREMY RENNER Big Break: *The Hurt Locker*
Renner both impressed and repelled with his tour de force as the titular murderer in *Dahmer* (2002), before bringing a similar intensity to *The Hurt Locker* (2009, p.134). He was incendiary and insane alongside Ben Affleck in superior Boston crime flick *The Town* (2010), then stepped into Matt Damon's franchise if not his actual shoes in Bourne reboot *The Bourne Legacy* (2012). And he donned the spandex for *Avengers Assemble* (2012) – but then so, it seems, did everybody.

JUSTIN TIMBERLAKE Big Break: *The Social Network*
Hugely enjoyable as reptilian interloper Sean Parker in *The Social Network* (2010), the music megastar's cinematic choices have subsequently been a little safe. Rom-com *Friends With Benefits* (2011) played on his undoubted sex appeal and revealed a talent for light comedy which he exploited in the otherwise dire *Bad Teacher* (2011). It'll be fascinating to see him stretch himself a little in the Coen Brothers' folk-music themed *Inside Llewyn Davis* (2013).

CHRISTOPH WALTZ Big Break: *Inglourious Basterds*
Hardly a new face to Europeans, Waltz was 53 when Quentin Tarantino cast him as the malevolent Col. Hans Landa in *Inglourious Basterds* (2009, p.143). He capitalized on his new Hollywood fame with a more than adequate turn as russkie villain Chudnofsky in the otherwise disappointing *The Green Hornet* (2011) but was stunning in Polanski's chamber-piece of horrors *Carnage* (2012, p.48) before returning to Tarantino for

The Bourne Supremacy

2004, US/Ger, 108 mins, 12A (UK) PG-13 (US)

....

cast Matt Damon, Joan Allen, Brian Cox, Julia Stiles, Karl Urban *scr* Tony Gilroy
(from the novel by Robert Ludlum) *cin* Oliver Wood *m* John Powell
dir Paul Greengrass

And things had all looked so rosy for Jason Bourne. When audiences left the amnesiac spy at the end of *The Bourne Identity* (2002) he had apparently shaken off his CIA pursuers, located girlfriend Marie (Franka Potente) in a suitably sunny clime and looked set for a contented retirement from whatever it was he couldn't remember he did. But that was before the movie became a surprise hit, unexpectedly rescuing Matt Damon's then stalled career. A second instalment was duly ordered, a new director in the shape of Paul Greengrass was hired and screenwriter Tony Gilroy charged with finding a way to send the bewildered ex-CIA spook on the run again.

Gilroy solved the problem of Bourne's apparent retirement by having him framed for the murder of two CIA agents in Berlin as part of a Russian plot to disguise the previous theft of $20 million of the CIA's cash. Marie is conveniently offed in the opening minutes and Bourne is off again on a trip that takes him across Europe,

New to the franchise, director Paul Greengrass joins Matt Damon filming on the streets of Berlin.

pursued by the excellently dragonish CIA bureau head (Joan Allen) and fellow intelligence wrangler Abbot, played by the always reliable Brian Cox (who may not be all he seems).

MATT DAMON
b. 8 October 1970, Cambridge, MA, US

With his status as one of Hollywood's new aristocracy now firmly established it's easy to forget that Matthew Paige Damon's career was, if not actually stalled, spluttering somewhat at the beginning of the noughties. The Oscar-winning *Good Will Hunting* (1998) was well behind him and subsequently he had failed to deliver a concrete role with which the public could immediately identify him. That all changed in 2002 with *The Bourne Identity*. "I hadn't had a film offer in six months because I'd had a couple of movies tank," he said in 2007 referring to a brace of unexpected flops: Will Smith vehicle *The Legend of Bagger Vance* (2001) and Billy Bob Thornton's troubled Western *All the Pretty Horses* (2001). "But [after Bourne opened] I had 20 to 30 movie offers, just based on the opening weekend." His turn as the memory-wiped CIA asset touched a nerve with modern audiences hungry for a new kind of action hero and sympathetic to the notion of the government as the bad guys. He smartly exploited the franchise's success to go on to work with Hollywood's leading directors: he was enjoyably duplicitous as a bent cop in Scorsese's Boston-set gangster flick *The Departed* (2006, p.67); the Coens made use of his regular-guy appeal as straight-shooting Texas Ranger LaBoeuf in their lightweight but thoroughly enjoyable remake of *True Grit* (2011); and he collaborated with Steven Soderbergh, with whom he'd first worked on *Ocean's Eleven* (2002), on both *The Informant!* (2009) – in which as saggy, schizophrenic whistleblower Mark Whitacre he effectively played against his Bourne image – and star-throttled plague pic *Contagion* (2011). His two collaborations with Clint Eastwood, soggy death-trip *Hereafter* (2011) and true-life South African rugby drama *Invictus* (2010), have been inexplicably disappointing, and apparently sent him running back to *Good Will Hunting* director Gus Van Sant, whose ecological, fracking-themed drama *Promised Land* is scheduled for 2013.

Damon, with his slightly porcine good looks and impressive physique, was always the perfect choice for Bourne. And while British director Greengrass's background may be in left-leaning documentaries, his Hollywood instincts are sharp enough to introduce us to our hero bathed in a sheen of sweat and clad in that iconic symbol of American male potency, the wife-beater vest. But Damon's greatest asset is an impressive air of detachment as he bugs phones, beats up bad guys and engages in car chases: he moves through the film like a small, very angry black hole.

Meanwhile Greengrass proves to be an adept at this kind of sophisticated action movie, keeping the pace up and the sense of urgency taut. His car chase finale, through the snowy streets of Moscow, is a modern masterclass in the craft, though some more traditional audiences complained that his handheld shooting style, which owes a lot to his documentary roots, gave them a headache, and action purists grumbled that much of the excitement was created in the editing suite. (After a third, equally successful instalment, *The Bourne Ultimatum*, 2007, both Paul Greengrass and Matt Damon announced their retirements from the franchise to be replaced with screenwriter Tony Gilroy as director and with *The Hurt Locker*'s Jeremy Renner for *The Bourne Legacy*, scheduled for release in 2012.)

As well as outclassing Bond at his own game, and forcing 007's producers into a radical rethink of their own character (see *Casino Royale*, p.50), the success of the Bourne franchise signalled the continuing shift in cinema audiences' view of what an action hero should be. The uncomplicated Dirty Harrys, Rambos and Terminators of the 80s and 90s have been replaced with a new breed of anxious, often reluctant protagonists – alpha males with issues, for which Jason Bourne has been the poster boy.

Bowling for Columbine

2001, US/Can/Ger, 120 mins, 15 (UK) R (US)

....

m Jeff Gibbs *dir* Michael Moore

Michael Moore was already an established master of cinematic agitprop before *Bowling for Columbine*, but this was the movie that rocketed him to international recognition as the voice of despairing liberal America. Part of the reason for the success of this account of America's attitude towards firearms was its timing: eighteen months after the attacks on the Twin Towers in New York, in the febrile run-up to the war on Iraq and only two years after the Columbine high school shootings. Another was Moore's undoubted talent as a self-publicist. A decade or so later, the shortcomings of the film are perhaps more obvious, but there's still enough energy and entertaining craziness – not to say relevance – to make it worth another viewing.

With a filmmaking style as shaggy and unkempt as its director, *Bowling for Columbine* is at least thirty minutes too long, its pacing is all over the place and a few sequences (including an animated potted history of the US) simply don't work. But on the other hand Moore's use of rare archive footage is consistently interesting and there are so many individual wacky highlights you forgive it its appearance and keep watching. Moore meets the brother of one of the Oklahoma bomb plotters who sagely notes that "the pen is mightier than the sword but you always should keep a sword handy" before cocking a handgun and holding it to his own head. And you have to admit it takes a certain chutzpah to ask a stern-looking cop whether a dog, who in a bizarre incident was involved in the shooting of its owner, "knew what he was doing".

Then there are times when Moore seems guilty of bad faith: his final showdown with doddering National Rifle Association chairman Charlton Heston, which may have been misleadingly edited, comes perilously close to bullying (though admittedly Heston's showboating at an NRA convention held in Columbine days after the massacre is nothing short of nauseating) and, perhaps worse, is uninformative. Moore produces an array of alarming and eccentric oddballs but scrupulously avoids putting himself in the position of arguing with anyone capable of making a cogent case for gun ownership. And if we are going to judge Moore's reliability, it is worth pointing out that neither Dylan Klebold nor Eric Harris actually went bowling on the morning of the day they massacred twelve students and one teacher at Columbine High School in 1999.

Tools of the trade: handheld camera and, er, shotgun in hand, Moore prods at the cosy assumptions at the heart of the US establishment.

But in a country where you can get a free gun by opening a bank account and buy hollow-points in the barbers, maybe a subtle argument isn't what's needed. As a piece of celluloid polemic the film succeeds. And regardless of your position on the issues, or your views of Moore's techniques, *Bowling for Columbine* managed to put the antiquated technology of film at the centre of a furious contemporary political debate in the age of 24-hour news and the burgeoning internet – no mean feat.

Brokeback Mountain

2006, US/Can, 134 mins, 15 (UK) R (US)

....

cast Heath Ledger, Jake Gyllenhaal, Anne Hathaway, Michelle Williams, Randy Quaid *scr* Larry McMurtry & Diana Ossana (from the story by Annie Proulx) *cin* Rodrigo Prieto *m* Gustavo Santaolalla *dir* Ang Lee

"It is not a gay *cowboy* movie," *Brokeback Mountain*'s mildly irritated producer James Schamus spent much of 2005 telling anyone who would listen. "If anything it's a gay *shepherd* movie…". But regardless of the particular species of livestock that smitten ranch-hands Ennis Del Mar (Heath Ledger) and Jack Twist (Jake Gyllenhaal) are meant to be supervising, the consensus was that it was in some sense a *gay* movie. Well, perhaps, but despite its superficial unorthodoxy the most striking thing about this beautifully made, undoubtedly affecting tale of doomed love is its Hollywood conventionality. *Brokeback Mountain* is a film that has more in common with the melodramas of Douglas Sirk than the queer politics of Derek Jarman.

We first meet denim-clad ranch-hand Jack Twist eyeing up fellow cowboy Ennis as they are interviewed for a job shepherding high in the Rockies. Once there, alone amidst the spectacular scenery, the boys' contrasting characters are revealed – Jack is curious and dynamic while Ennis is taciturn and reserved. Then one cold night another aspect of their nature reveals itself, and the two, much to their respective surprise, find themselves making love. "I ain't queer!" Ennis asserts the next day. Nevertheless in the midst of this bucolic setting they continue their affair until ejected from their personal Eden by their employer

ANNE HATHAWAY

b. 12 Nov 1982, New York, NY, US

Anne Hathaway began her professional career indulging what Disney screenwriters have no doubt scientifically discovered to be every tweenage girl's dream. As Mia Thermopolis in *The Princess Diaries* (2001), she finds that she is heir to the throne of an obscure European country; pure catnip to the pre-teen crowd and tolerable even to those who have had their braces removed, mostly thanks to deft direction by past master of celluloid schmaltz Garry Marshall (he invented *Happy Days*, after all). It was an appealing, comically astute performance from Hathaway, and successful enough for Disney to churn out a sequel in 2004 in which she starred alongside Chris Pine, later to be cast as Captain Kirk in J.J. Abrams' *Star Trek* (2009). Her next outing of note was in the more classy *Nicholas Nickleby* (2003), but then it was, no doubt frustratingly for her, back to kiddie pics with *Ella Enchanted* in 2004. Her most notable serious roles to date have been in *Brokeback Mountain* and *The Devil Wears Prada* (2006), in both cases making great successes of unpromising roles. In *Brokeback*, a film in which the dramatic focus and sympathy are mainly focused on the smitten sheeppokes, she was moving as Lureen, stricken wife to Jake Gyllenhaal's Jack Twist. As a tyro journalist in *The Devil Wears Prada* she achieved the almost impossible: not being obliterated in the ferocious heat of Meryl Streep's performance as the monstrous fashion magazine editor. Subsequently she seems to have had difficulty finding roles which effectively showcase her considerable talents. A row with director Judd Apatow over the use of footage of a woman giving birth led to her being dropped from smash comedy *Knocked Up* (2007). *Get Smart* (2008), an adaptation of a cult US TV show, sank in the UK, and spooky drama *Passengers* (2008), in which she played a grief counsellor, was a similar bust, though she gained awards nominations for her role as a drug addict in Jonathan Demme's *Rachel Getting Married* (2009). In 2010 Christopher Nolan announced that he had cast her as the key villain Catwoman in *The Dark Knight Rises* (2012), a performance she revealed had been heavily influenced by 1920s superstar Hedy Lamarr.

Gyllenhaal and Ledger on top form in *Brokeback Mountain*, as the amiable Jack Twist doffs his hat to pay a visit to the tortured soul Ennis Del Mar. Heartbreaking stuff.

(Randy Quaid). But pursuing their passion against the tide of 60s Midwestern bigotry leads to misery and, finally, tragedy.

Ang Lee delivers all this with his customary delicacy. Rodrigo Prieto's cinematography is lush and crystalline; Gustavo Santaolalla's spare and haunting score is precision-deployed with little mercy for the audience's already desiccated tear-ducts, and the two leading men acquit themselves admirably – particularly the late Heath Ledger, whose depiction of an anguished soul unable to grasp the happiness that is in front of him is genuinely heart-rending. Larry McMurtry and Diana Ossana's screenplay plucks at the heartstrings with the expertise of a concert harpist. (McMurtry, a veteran of the Western genre, wrote the novels that became *Hud*, 1963, and *The Last Picture Show*, 1971.) But it is this tastefulness, a determination not to offend, that might be *Brokeback Mountain*'s biggest flaw. The famous sex scene is frankly coy by heterosexual standards and what's more the plot reinforces the depressing trope that any homosexual relationship is firstly doomed and secondly physically dangerous. This of course may be a function of the demands of melodrama rather than sexual politics, but it still undercuts the "progressive" credentials celebrated by some critics.

There is just one mildly subversive element: the introduction of homosexuality into an area of American culture considered by many to be almost sacrosanct – the resolutely macho cowboy myth. One wonders what John Wayne would have made of it all. In any case it was enough to have some Midwestern theatres boycotting the movie and various religious groups fog-horning their disapproval. Depressing really, given that, even in the supposedly laid-back 21st century, this is a film that strains so hard to avoid scaring the horses. Or sheep.

Captain America: The First Avenger

2011, US, 124 mins, 12A (UK) PG-13 (US)

••

cast Chris Evans, Stanley Tucci, Hayley Atwell, Tommy Lee Jones, Hugo Weaving
scr Christopher Markus & Stephen McFeely (from characters created by Joe
Simon and Jack Kirby) *cin* Shelly Johnson *m* Alan Silvestri *dir* Joe Johnston

There's something pleasingly earnest about Joe Johnston's entry into the
apparently endless stream of Marvel comic book adaptations (see box, p.61). Like
Richard Donner's classic *Superman* (1978) over thirty years ago, its approach to the
inherent ludicrousness of the superhero genre is not to attempt to force it into a
"realist" mode à la Christopher Nolan's Batman movies, or to slip in the sly ironies
of *Iron Man* (2008, p.146) or *The Green Hornet* (2011) but to embrace its cheerful
innocence wholesale and to honour the naive art form that the comic book, at
least in its original form, really is at heart.

Set in 1942, the year after Marvel precursor Timely Comics published the first
Captain America story, and taking the scrawny-kid-turned-musclebound-superhero
motif later to be colonized by Stan Lee's Spider-Man, this has Steve Rogers (Chris
Evans, a likeable lunk who plays both Rogers and Captain America with humility
and finesse), a ninety-pound weakling desperate to sign up for the army and get
a shot at Jerry. Sadly the army is unimpressed by his physique; but then émigré
scientist Professor Erskine (Stanley Tucci) takes pity on him, jabs him with his
patented Super-Soldier serum, and thus transforms him into something that looks
like it walked off the cover of a 1950s beefcake magazine. Even so, much to his
disappointment, he finds himself deployed in a propaganda war rather than a real
one, spending his time in a daft costume shilling war bonds in beautifully realized
Busby Berkeley numbers ("each one you buy is a bullet in your best guy's gun!").
The nearest he gets to the front is a hopeless attempt at entertaining the troops
in Italy. "For the longest time I dreamed about coming to the front line, serving
my country … finally I got everything I wanted, and I'm wearing *tights*," our
crestfallen hero laments after being tomatoed off by troops more keen to see the
dancing girls. But, after mounting a daring rescue of a group of Allied prisoners,
he soon finds himself toe to toe with Red Skull (the reliably nefarious Hugo
Weaving channelling a demented Werner Herzog), whose HYDRA organization
threatens to be, get this, even *worse* than the Nazis!

It's true to say that Johnston (who began his career directing the similarly retro-escapist *The Rocketeer* in 1991) is not the world's greatest action director, his climactic sequence falling just a little flat (which poor-quality 3D post-conversion did little to help). While this disappointed some younger fans used to super-refined octane, it was no worry to those who prefer at least a little character and humour with their spandex. Cinematographer Shelly Johnson burnishes the film with a comfortingly old-fashioned sepia sheen while co-screenwriters Markus and McFeely give the story's wholesome, corn-fed patriotism unembarrassed full shrift. Evans is perfectly cast as the masked avenger, his chisel-jawed decency recalling Christopher Reeve; Tommy Lee Jones is gruffly entertaining as Col. Chester Philips; and if the hinted-at romance between our "star-spangled man with a plan" and spunky Brit Agent Peggy Carter (Hayley Atwell) is underdeveloped, it only mimics the original stories, where girls were hurriedly shunted off-frame when there were skeletal Nazis to be beaten to a pulp. It's almost a pity that Captain America's subsequent appearance was in the present day as part of the gargantuan Avengers ensemble. It would have been nice to visit him in 1942 again – it felt like he belonged there, forever fending off dastardly foes with a vibranium shield.

Chris Evans is perfectly cast as that most patriotic of superheroes, Captain America, in a film that combines modern-day action with a suitably burnished 1942 wartime setting.

Capturing the Friedmans

2004, US, 108 mins, 15 (UK) Unrated (US)

....

cin Adolfo Doring **m** Andrea Morricone *dir* Andrew Jarecki

It was meant to be a film about clowns. In the early 2000s Andrew Jarecki was in the middle of making a documentary about New York's children's entertainers. One of his subjects was David Friedman, "New York's No. 1 Party Clown". But while interviewing Friedman, a man he noted was constantly simmering with undirected anger, he asked about his family background. David started talking. And then Jarecki's film flew off in a direction about as far removed from buckets of water and comedy noses as can be imagined.

On Thanksgiving of 1987 David's father, Arnold Friedman, a respected Long Island schoolteacher, had been arrested for possession of child pornography. Finding that Arnold ran a computer club for the local children in his basement, the police began questioning them and horrifying stories emerged of abuse, threats, "sex games" and mass rape. But not only was Arnold accused of these crimes, his eighteen-year-old son Jesse was implicated too. Both were arrested and charged. So far, so ghastly, but what makes Jarecki's unique documentary possible was that the Friedman family seemed to have an obsession with recording themselves both on video and audio tape: extended screaming matches and endless accusations that allow us to witness almost first-hand the appalling sight of a family tearing itself apart. Arnold, a diffident, passive man, deeply shamed by the revelation of his sexual tastes, seems to have a need to confess, but to what? He has the support of his sons, who turn on their mother for refusing to rule out the possibility that her husband is guilty. She, for her part, can't seem to say the word "sex" without being physically nauseated.

But we also get to see the shoddiness of the police case against both Arnold and Jesse. Children were questioned inappropriately, hypnotism produced new "memories", an atmosphere of hysteria surrounded the case and pressure was piled on Arnold and Jesse to plead guilty regardless of the truth, to avoid long prison sentences (which they finally did). The absolute dearth of any physical evidence against either man and the sheer unlikelihood of many of the increasingly lurid accusations were ignored by investigators.

Jarecki assembles his material for maximum dramatic effect, though frankly it would be hard to make a hash of such a mesmerizing story. His coups include anonymized interviews with supposed victims and their parents, many of which seem to point to the Friedmans having been falsely accused, as well as interviews with all but one of the three brothers. After seeing the film, most people's reaction is one of troubling uncertainty: have we witnessed the modern equivalent of the Salem witch trials, innocent men destroyed by hysteria? Or two child-abusers being rightfully caught and punished? (Cinema managers in the US complained that patrons would remain in their seats sometimes for hours debating the case.) This compelling film, for all its evidence and testimony, leaves us still unsure of what we have witnessed, and sceptical about the availability of "the truth" – one of the most important points the documentary genre can make.

In August 2010 the US Second Circuit Court of Appeals concluded that there was "a reasonable likelihood that Jesse Friedman was wrongfully convicted". Nassau County District Attorney Kathleen Rice subsequently announced the appointment of a review panel. It has yet to report.

Compelling stuff: the real-life, unvarnished drama of the Friedman family (Jesse, pictured left, and Arnold); there's no happy ending here.

TRUE STORIES: Ten of the best documentaries of the millennium...

The reasons for the documentary's sudden renaissance are still open to debate. Was it the availability of new cheaper digital filming opening up the form to new filmmakers or, as some have suggested, that the conventional media was not providing the kind of in-depth factual output that audiences craved? Whatever the underlying reasons this millennium has produced some of the most interesting, quirky and disturbing documentaries in recent movie-memory.

ETRE ET AVOIR (Nicolas Philibert, 2003) Philibert followed Georges Lopez, the sole teacher at a tiny French primary school in Saint-Étienne-sur-Usson, for over a year to produce this irresistibly charming, gently moving film. The children, unselfconscious in front of Philibert's camera, simply get on with the business of growing up, learning to read and count, and in one case dealing with the death of a parent – shepherded by a patient, encouraging mentor. The idyll was shattered somewhat when, after the film's massive financial success, Lopez sued for a box-office cut.

SPELLBOUND (Jeffrey Blitz, 2003) The uniquely American institution of the National Spelling Bee is the subject for this unexpectedly nail-biting film – how would you have done with "encephalon" at the age of twelve? – but underneath the competition it is a revealing account of the wildly differing experiences of childhood in America, as director Blitz follows a group of kids and their families through the triumphs and disasters of the 1999 tournament.

THE FOG OF WAR: ELEVEN LESSONS FROM THE LIFE OF ROBERT S. MCNAMARA (Errol Morris, 2004) Veteran documentarian Errol Morris used his "Interrotron", a contraption that forces the subject to look directly into the camera when speaking, for a series of extended interviews with Robert McNamara, the US Secretary of Defense blamed by many for escalating the Vietnam War. Whether Morris's machine extracts anything like the truth is up to the viewer, but this gripping film proves that one man talking, provided he's the right man, can make for captivating cinema.

SUPER SIZE ME (Morgan Spurlock, 2004) Morgan Spurlock is a kind of lower-key, and thus for some less irritating, Michael Moore, whose celluloid polemics are characterized by quirky charm rather than self-righteousness. His thesis, that if you eat nothing but McDonald's food for a month (and say yes whenever a larger portion is offered) you'll wind up fat and ill, might not be rocket science, but he also critiques other aspects of the fast-food industry and is gently amusing company.

AN INCONVENIENT TRUTH (Al Gore, 2006) Al Gore proves that what is in essence not much more than a PowerPoint presentation can fascinate an audience and cause global controversy. Whatever your views on anthropogenic climate change, Gore's calmly presented account of the story so far is a must-watch.

MAN ON WIRE (James Marsh, 2008) In August 1974 Frenchman Philippe Petit illegally strung a cable between the towers of the World Trade Center and crossed between them, thus performing one of the greatest high-wire stunts of all time. Fertile material for a documentary – apart from the fact that there is no existing footage of the attempt. That *Wisconsin Death Trip* (1999) director James Marsh managed to produce this tense, exhilarating film using dramatic reconstructions and still photographs is testament to his skills as a filmmaker.

CATFISH (Henry Joost & Ariel Schulman, 2010) New York filmmakers Joost and Schulman follow the latter's brother, Nev, as he becomes involved in an online romance with a young woman in Michigan, but all is nowhere near what it seems. Controversially called "the best fake documentary of all time" by Morgan Spurlock, it's certainly a unique one, since the filmmakers constantly discuss their filming of the events as they unfold; the making of the film becomes part of its subject matter. Numerous objections were subsequently raised as to its veracity – ideal post-movie discussion fodder.

SENNA (Asif Kapadia, 2011) Eschewing the genre clichés of talking heads and celebrity narration, this mesmerizing film, composed entirely of archive footage (director Kapadia apparently assembled over 15,000 hours' worth), tells the story of the rise and tragic death of Formula 1 champ Ayrton Senna. Vital even for non petrol-heads.

INSIDE JOB (Charles Ferguson, 2011) The complexities of the financial collapse are skilfully navigated in this gripping account of the flawed financial system and how unscrupulous bankers milked it, made billions and destroyed the world economy. The best docco so far about the most important historical event in most of our lifetimes. Narrated by go-to Hollywood liberal Matt Damon, Alec Baldwin presumably being unavailable.

CAVE OF FORGOTTEN DREAMS (Werner Herzog, 2011) More people have walked on the summit of Everest than have entered the Chauvet caves high up on a cliff in France's Ardèche region to see the astonishing ancient cave paintings discovered there in 1994. And, until Herzog, no filmmaker had been allowed to document them. Herzog makes utterly appropriate use of 3D to bring the vivid, instantly recognizable images of people and animals to life. It's perhaps the only 3D movie that demands to be seen in the format.

Carnage

2012, Fr/Pol/Ger, 80 mins, 15 (UK) R (US)

cast Jodie Foster, John C. Reilly, Christoph Waltz, Kate Winslet **scr** Roman Polanski & Yasmina Reza (from the play by Yasmina Reza) **cin** Pawel Edelman **m** Alexandre Desplat **dir** Roman Polanski

Ever since his stunning debut *Knife in the Water* (1962), through early classics such as *Repulsion* (1965) and *Cul-de-sac* (1966), Roman Polanski has made a speciality of locking his characters in confined spaces and watching them go mad or tear each other apart. In *Carnage*, his triumphant return to absolute top form, it is a quartet of superficially civilized upper-middle-class New Yorkers that Polanski pits against each other. Two couples meet in a Brooklyn apartment to discuss a fight between their sons in the park which has left one with a couple of busted teeth. The idea is to avoid nasty legal recriminations and resolve the situation between themselves: they are, after all, mature, enlightened adults. But, as the milky light of an autumn afternoon fades, their veneer of politesse doesn't so much drop as is torn to shreds; alliances of marriage, class and gender shift and rearrange themselves as what was meant to be a demonstration of the inherent civility of the middle classes degenerates into a ferocious, and blackly hilarious, orgy of rowing, recrimination, vomited on art books, shredded flower arrangements and drowned mobile phones.

Polanski's Oscar-baiting cast are all firing on full throttle. Jodie Foster is frighteningly tightly wound as Penelope, an author and expert on African politics whose brittle smile twists into

The veneer cracks: Jodie Foster (Penelope) and Kate Winslet (Nancy) turn in satisfyingly unsympathetic performances in *Carnage*.

a masque of hysteria as her values are challenged, while John C. Reilly is perfectly cast as her husband Michael, a plumbing supplies business owner who Penelope has forced into both liberal attitudes and attire, and who has, to almost everybody's disgust, just thrown his children's pet hamster out on the street. Kate Winslet is as good as she has ever been as Nancy, the emotionally dissatisfied investment broker who produces, quite literally, the afternoon's most explosive moment, while sly, slightly vulpine Christoph Waltz – whose icy misanthropy Polanski clearly relishes and to whom the screenplay gives the juiciest, most pretension-pricking lines – irritates everybody as her Big Pharma lawyer husband Alan, continually answering calls on his ill-fated cellphone.

The obvious temptation in adapting a play into a film is to open it out. If anything Polanski does the opposite. Though the movie was actually shot in Paris, a result of Polanski's well-known legal problems, Dean Tavoularis's production design perfectly renders an upscale Brooklyn apartment, exquisitely decorated and just cramped enough to keep the combatants uncomfortably close to each other. (In the opening half-hour Polanski has mischievous fun almost allowing Nancy and Alan to leave – on two occasions they make it as far as the elevator before the director sadistically reels them back into his theatre of pain; shades of Buñuel's 1962 classic *The Exterminating Angel*.) Pawel Edelman's cinematography is crisp and precise while Alexandre Desplat's score, though only heard over the opening and closing titles, thrums with a repressed menace.

The result is tremendously funny and bracingly bitter: like the best of early Woody Allen or Neil Simon but shot through with a giddy, intoxicating malevolence. Now entering his ninth decade and clearly with as much restless energy as he's ever had, Polanski never lets the pace slacken or the savage mood evaporate and effortlessly proves, as if it needed restating, that Hell is indeed other people.

KATE WINSLET
b. 5 October 1975, Reading, UK

Kate Winslet's first acting job, when she was a twelve-year-old theatre school moppet, was cavorting with the Honey Monster in an advert for breakfast cereal Sugar Puffs. Ironic really, because her subsequent choices have tended more towards the tart rather than the safely sugary: she tends to bring a sharp-eyed intelligence to her performances, as well as a sometimes earthy eroticism, and is unafraid of taking on roles that are not immediately appealing to the audience. Though a generation will, of course, always remember her clinging to the prow alongside Leonardo DiCaprio in *Titanic* (1999), her roles soon became more complex and intriguing. She was riveting as the young, uninhibited Iris Murdoch (with Judi Dench essaying the older, Alzheimer's stricken woman) in *Iris* (2002). In Marquis De Sade drama *Quills* (2001), she utilized her Rubenesque figure (she has been an outspoken critic of Hollywood's body fascism and extracted an apology from *GQ* magazine when it digitally slimmed a cover photo of her) to rumbustuous effect as the loopy libertine's laundry lady and erotic co-conspirator. Sadly Alan Parker's notorious anti-death-penalty bomb *The Life of David Gale* (2003), in which she appeared with Kevin Spacey, opened and closed so quickly that few people had a chance to evaluate her performance as journalist Bitsey Bloom (she was fine, though the script should have been strapped to the chair). Probably her most successful year so far was 2008: an Oscar was forthcoming for her perfectly calibrated performance as a woman with a number of complicated secrets in *The Reader* and subsequently she reunited with a dried-out Leonardo DiCaprio in 1950s-set *Revolutionary Road*, an emotionally harrowing, beautifully acted portrait of a marriage in terminal disarray, the dramatic tension of which was no doubt heightened by the fact that it was directed by third hubby Sam Mendes. They divorced eighteen months later. Much of 2011 was taken up with Todd Haynes' critically lauded TV adaptation of *Mildred Pierce* but she also found time to turn up in Steven Soderbergh's reinvention of the star-laden 1970s disaster flick, *Contagion* (2011).

Casino Royale

2006, UK/Cz Rep/Ger/US, 144 mins, 12A (UK) PG-13 (US)

....

cast Daniel Craig, Eva Green, Giancarlo Gianni, Mads Mikkelsen, Judi Dench
scr Neal Purvis & Robert Wade and Paul Haggis (from the novel by Ian
Fleming) *cin* Phil Méheux *m* David Arnold *dir* Martin Campbell

"Who?" was many Bond fans' initial reaction when 007 producers Barbara Broccoli
and Michael G. Wilson announced that, after the insipid *Die Another Day* (2002),
Daniel Craig was to replace Pierce Brosnan as the perennial super-spy. Given that
the bookies had been offering odds on A-listers such as Ewan McGregor, Clive
Owen and Hugh Jackman, the selection came as a surprise to say the least. Those
who had heard of Craig knew that he was a more than solid screen actor who'd
won critical acclaim and awards for his roles in Roger Mitchell's *The Mother* (2003)
and London gangland movie *Layer Cake* (2004). But he hardly had the necessary
suaveness, and look at those ears…

In fact Craig was an inspired choice, his rough-hewn physicality recalling Sean
Connery – to whom he would eventually be favourably compared – but his greatest
asset was his acting talent. He succeeded admirably in his stated aim to give the
character more reality and emotional depth. His was to be a complex, occasionally
vulnerable Bond who bruises and bleeds, who an irritated M (Judi Dench, given
more to do than usual) dismisses as "a blunt instrument".

But if Craig was a good call, hiring Martin Campbell to direct was just as
significant. He had already midwifed one tricky Bond transition with *GoldenEye*
(1995), regarded as among the best of the series. With *Casino Royale* he nodded
to the success of the Bourne franchise in the interim, giving the movie a grittier,
more mature feel – gone are most of the gadgets and the traditional flamboyant
pre-credits action – to opt for a kind of "origins" story. We meet Bond in a chilly
black-and-white sequence as he makes the two kills (one messy, the second
ruthlessly efficient) that give him his double-o status. But a subsequent botched
attempt to capture a terrorist bomber (after a spectacular free-running action
sequence) unveils a secret conspiracy to make millions by causing terrorist
atrocities and playing the subsequent market fluctuations; this is a world away
from volcanic criminal lairs and cat-stroking SPECTRE fiends.

Bond regulars Neal Purvis and Robert Wade delivered a screenplay replete with
nice touches: the lingering shot of Craig's torso emerging from the Caribbean
wryly acknowledges the tectonic shifts in gender politics since Ursula Andress

pulled the same trick in *Dr. No* (1962). And when Bond requests a martini and the barman asks shaken or stirred, "Do I look as if I give a damn?" is the tradition-shattering reply. The sadomasochistic homoeroticism that pervades Fleming's novels is even acknowledged when a naked Bond is tied to a seatless chair and walloped on the privates by villain Le Chiffre (Mads Mikkelsen). It's not the first time Bond's genitals have been menaced – think Connery on the laser cutter in *Goldfinger* (1964) – but it's certainly the most graphic.

Meanwhile Eva Green finally delivers on the oft-made promise of a "different kind of Bond girl". Her Vesper Lynd (the name a rebuke to the Pussy Galores of Bond movies past) is more than an intellectual match for 007, she gets the better of him in their flirtatious meeting, and her duplicity finally delivers an emotional punch that goes a long way to explaining Bond's subsequent attitude to love, sex and women. Appropriately enough, since this was his 21st outing, *Casino Royale* marked the arrival of a Bond for adults.

Danny Get Your Gun: Craig reinvents Bond as a gritty post-Bourne action hero, his only gadget here a pistol, in *Casino Royale*.

City of God
(*Cidade de Deus*)

2003, Bra/Fr/Ger, 130 mins, 18 (UK) R (US)

••

cast Seu Jorge, Alexandre Rodrigues, Leandro Firmino da Hora, Phellipe Haagensen, Douglas Silva, Darlan Cunha *scr* Bráulio Mantovani (from the novel by Paulo Lins) *cin* Césare Charlone *m* Antonio Pinto, Ed Cortês *dir* Fernando Meirelles & Kátia Lund

Brazilian smash-hit *City of God* arrived on international screens in a hail of bullets, spilled blood and pulsating samba, dazzling audiences, breaking national box-office records and signalling the continued resurgence of Latin American cinema. Set in the titular *favela* outside Rio, shot on authentic locations nearby, and featuring a cast of almost entirely non-professional actors, it also provoked popular outrage in Brazil at the continuing poverty and crime in these government-designed, gang-riddled shantytowns.

Critics tended to point to gangster movies like Scorsese's *Goodfellas* (1990) and Tarantino's crime oeuvre as obvious English-language influences, but while *City of God*'s directors certainly borrow stylistically from both, with their whiplash cutting, crash zooms and other assorted energizing tricks, neither Scorsese nor Tarantino has concerned themselves with the kind of social realism that is at least a part of Meirelles and Lund's project. But as well as being an angry denunciation of the moral and physical squalor to which the *favelas* condemn their inhabitants, *City of God* is simultaneously a film about childhood and youth, a time that offers its own fresh excitement and strange joy (even set against the desperation of the *favela*), as much as it is about gangsters and guns.

Based on an autobiographical novel it follows the early years of *favelaledo* Rocket (Alexandre Rodrigues), an aspiring young news photographer who, in a long voiceover, guides us through a bloodily picaresque account of growing up in the 70s and 80s in the ironically named shantytown, a hellish slum infested with violent crime, casual murder, rape and an all-pervading drug culture. The performances are uniformly stunning: Douglas Silva is terrifying as ten-year-old psychopath Li'l Dice, a pint-sized Jimmy Cagney who beams with irrepressible childish delight as he guns down his victims in cold blood, as is Leandro Firmino da Hora, who plays the same character as a teenager. But it's Rodrigues as our

narrator who provides one of the only bright lights in what could have been a relentlessly depressing picture, with his touching ineptitude both at crime and shedding his virginity.

It's hardly a perfect film, straining as alarmingly at the seams as the *favelas* themselves, and while the criticism that its rock-promo style glamorizes violent crime might be misplaced, it could be argued that another aspect of *favela* life, the relentless suffering of the honest majority under the reign of terror imposed by these thugs, is unfortunately only occasionally presented, and never with the brio with which the endless murder and bloodshed are conjured. But it's still an astonishing, visceral experience: rarely has a film that contains so much death been so teeming with life.

Alexandre Rodrigues as Rocket, armed here with a camera, is our teenage guide in this account of growing up in the hellish surroundings of Brazil's *City of God* shantytown in the 70s and 80s.

Cloverfield

2008, US, 85 mins, 15 (UK) PG-13 (US)

∙∙

cast Mike Vogel, Lizzy Caplan, Jessica Lucas, T.J. Miller, Michael Stahl-David
scr Drew Goddard *cin* Michael Bonvillain *dir* Matt Reeves

For a supposed action blockbuster *Cloverfield* has one of the most calculatedly tedious opening twenty minutes imaginable. After a brief flash of what appears to be home video of a young couple's day out at the fairground, the footage is replaced by a recording of a twenty-something's leaving do in a New York loft

apartment. But before its teenage audience began throwing their popcorn at the screen, the lights flicker out, a giant explosion rocks the city and the Statue of Liberty's head careens down the street like a gargantuan bowling ball. That, as they say, is more like it…

As its tricksy opening implies *Cloverfield* is at heart a giant gimmick, lovingly crafted by *Lost* producer J.J. Abrams (see p.226) and his TV collaborators Drew Goddard and Matt Reeves, which takes its cue from the "found footage" movies spawned by the incredible success of micro-budgeted horror *The Blair Witch Project* in 1999. In this case the tape discovered at the beginning of the movie records the unexplained arrival of some kind of ghastly, and apparently very angry, beastie in downtown New York and the desperate ex-partygoers' attempts to escape the city. With the application of a massive effects budget it answers the burning question: what would a Godzilla flick look like if it was happening for real and captured on a camcorder?

Pre-release ballyhoo was drummed up by the secrecy of the filming (it was shot under a number of bizarre pseudonyms including "Slusho" and "Cheese") and the air of mystery initially cultivated by the studio publicity department. At early press screenings very few people had any idea *what* it was about. Sadly the surprise couldn't be preserved for paying punters – you can't help but wonder how *Psycho* (1960) or *The Crying Game* (1992) would have fared in the age of the internet.

Cloverfield gave the by then almost completely clapped out "found footage" trope a new life. Keeping the brilliant digital effects work in the corner of the jerky camcorder shot gives it emphasis and director Matt Reeves follows the old but often forgotten rule that rarely showing the monster (at least in full) forces the audience to imagine it, while reactions to events in characters' faces can be more powerful than showing the events themselves (the directors of *The Blair Witch Project* were similarly faithful to these principles). The sense of immediacy was further accentuated by the the visual echoes of panicked crowds running along New York's streets that had typified 9/11 video footage.

Motion-sickness sufferers who hoped that Hollywood's appropriation of the shaky-cam style might signal its demise would be disappointed; it subsequently turned up in *Battle Los Angeles* (2011) and *The Hunger Games* (2012, p.131) among others. But *Cloverfield* proved that Hollywood is still occasionally capable of the kind of hurly-burly that would have long-departed cinematic carnival barkers like William Castle grinning from ear to ear.

Dramatic handheld "found footage" shows Beth (Odette Yustman, centre) and Rob (Michael Stahl-David, right) being escorted away from the nightmare of a New York under attack in *Cloverfield*.

Collateral

2004, US, 120 mins, 15 (UK) R (US)

••

cast Tom Cruise, Jamie Foxx, Jada Pinkett Smith, Mark Ruffalo, Peter Berg *scr* Stuart Beattie *cin* Dion Beebe, Paul Cameron *m* James Newton Howard *dir* Michael Mann

It seems that Tom Cruise has spent at least some of his recent career attempting to shed the toothsome matinee idol image he created for himself in the 80s and 90s. In *Magnolia* (2000) he played a thoroughly self-obsessed sex-help guru; in *Tropic Thunder* (2008) he cropped up balding, overweight and with dodgy dance moves. Despite this welcome new range from Cruise, *Collateral* asks of him just one simple question: can he cut it as an out-and-out movie villain?

The answer is an emphatic yes. His performance as contract killer Vincent is among the best of his career, and thankfully Cruise avoids all temptation to ironize the role or wink at the audience to gain sympathy. We first meet him at Los Angeles International Airport, which appears to be this crisply suited, salt-and-pepper bearded executive's natural habitat. But soon after he climbs into Max's (Jamie Foxx's) cab, a corpse performs a less than graceful swan dive onto the windshield and Max discovers that Vincent's business is death. His plans for the evening, he explains, involve the reluctant cabbie ferrying him from murder to murder, sticking to a cast iron schedule.

Much of the pleasure *Collateral* offers comes not only from the stylishly staged mayhem – and Mann is the acknowledged expert of the contemporary shoot-out, with a gun battle set among the writhing bodies and deafening techno of a packed club almost topping his astonishing street fight in 1995's *Heat* – but from the dialogue between Max and his passenger. These utterly contrasting characters are both, in their own way, in the thrall of their jobs. Vincent might be a raging psychopath ("You lack standard parts that are supposed to be there in most people," Max tells him) whose philosophy would give Nietzsche the blues. "Six billion people on the planet, you're getting bent out of shape cause of [me killing] one fat guy," is his response when Vincent objects to his line of work. But he is at least, he says, in control of his own destiny. By contrast Max's nervousness and lacerating self-doubt have stymied his attempts to begin a luxury limo service. His "temporary" job cab driving has lasted the better part of a decade and Vincent's unwelcome presence forces Max to seize control of his own future. Stuart Beattie's taut screenplay, written when he was a student, is filled with sinewy scenes. In one

of the best, a long conversation between Vincent and a jazz-club proprietor about Miles Davis suddenly takes an unexpected and deadly turn. It's as good an individual moment as anything from Scorsese.

But Los Angeles is as much a star as either the story or the characters. Mann was among the first directors to embrace shooting digitally rather than onto film, a risky decision and not without its problems: original cinematographer Paul Cameron left the production after three weeks citing "creative differences", to be replaced by Dion Beebe. But the results are stunning: distant skyscrapers twinkle dimly through a thin night smog; streetlights refract through shattered windshield glass; police choppers train their piercing Nightsun halogen spotlights from the air. It's a Los Angeles that's familiar in its danger and allure, yet you've never seen it quite as seductively edgy as this. With *Collateral* Mann transforms his favourite city into a festival of blood and light.

One of Hollywood's first digitally shot films, *Collateral* has Vincent (Tom Cruise) and Max (Jamie Foxx) inhabit an atmospheric nighttime Los Angeles, illuminated by burning spots of light.

HEATH LEDGER

b. 4 April 1979, Perth, Australia; *d.* 22 January 2008, New York, NY, US

Eagle-eyed connoisseurs of 1990s imported teen telly might have first spotted Heath Ledger in *Sweat* (1996), a short-lived kiddie soap set at an elite sports institute in which he played gay cyclist Snowy Bowles. A courageous choice for so early in a career, but one that would turn out to be typical for an actor who almost consistently prized adventurousness over conventionality. He'd been born to a mining engineer and a French teacher and owed his Christian name to a parental admiration of *Wuthering Heights*. He showed an early interest in theatre and eventually carried out his almost inevitable apprenticeship in soap, in his case *Home & Away*. His first Hollywood outing, the high-school-set *Taming of the Shrew* update *10 Things I Hate About You* (1999), began to establish him as a teen heartthrob, a development with which he was distinctly uneasy but which he indulged again in lighthearted comedy-romance *A Knight's Tale* (2001). Terry Gilliam's *The Brothers Grimm* was a disappointment in 2005 – though it didn't stop Ledger collaborating with the director again on his final film *The Imaginarium of Doctor Parnassus*, which was released in 2009 after his death with Johnny Depp and Colin Farrell completing his unfinished portions – and he was a likeable libertine in Lasse Hallström's fluffy *Casanova* (2006). But the two key films for which he will be remembered are Ang Lee's anguished love story *Brokeback Mountain* (2006, p.41) and as Joker in *The Dark Knight* (2008), in both cases inhabiting the roles to an uncanny extent. "How did this actor get inside my head so well? He understood more about the character than I did," marvelled *Brokeback* author Annie Proulx. In the latter case, the experience was a harrowing one. Describing the villain as a "mass-murdering, schizophrenic clown with zero empathy", he revealed that he was having difficulty sleeping. "I probably [sleep] an average of two hours a night," he told *The New York Times* during shooting. In New York on 22 January 2008 he was found dead, the cause an overdose of prescription medication, which included pain and depression treatments as well as sleeping pills. He was 28.

The Dark Knight

2008, US, 152 mins, 12A (UK) PG-13 (US)

••

cast Christian Bale, Heath Ledger, Michael Caine, Gary Oldman, Morgan Freeman, Aaron Eckhart, Maggie Gyllenhaal *scr* Jonathan Nolan & Christopher Nolan (story Christopher Nolan & David S. Goyer) *cin* Wally Pfister *m* Hans Zimmer and James Newton Howard *dir* Christopher Nolan

Christopher Nolan's *Batman Begins* (2005) had done a lot to reverse the damage wrought by Joel Schumacher's misguided attempt to return the bat franchise to its campy TV mode with his *Batman & Robin* (1997), but it was with this hugely successful sequel, incidentally the first not to include the character's name in its title, that he fully developed his vision for the winged vigilante. Making good on the promise made at the end of his first film, Nolan introduces Joker (Heath Ledger) as the movie's primary villain, eschewing the traditional origins story to present the character as a fully formed psychotic – a point emphasized by Joker's contradictory explanations of how he became the monster he is. Recruited by Gotham's criminal underworld to kill Batman and thus allow them to resume their business unhindered, he instead pursues a terrifying agenda of his own: chaos for its own sake, revealing himself to be a surrealist artist working in the media of cruelty and violence.

Nolan delivers a coolly stylish film, his fifth in collaboration with cinematographer Wally Pfister

Christian Bale returns as the Dark Knight in Christopher Nolan's sleekly visualized sequel to *Batman Begins*, but the movie is dominated by Heath Ledger's astonishing performance as Joker, a villain whose distorted exterior reflects the character within.

(who shot portions of the film in the IMAX format). His shots of the clean, gleaming lines of modern Gotham (for the most part downtown Chicago) and its buildings' light-drenched interiors bring to mind Michael Mann, and indeed Nolan later quoted *Heat* (1995) as a visual, as well as thematic, influence. His grasp of action sequences, though, is often less sure: a car chase is frustratingly incoherent. And if it occasionally wears its contemporary concerns too obviously on its sleeve – the ethics of surveillance and the possible justifications of torture among them – Nolan and his brother's well-crafted screenplay keeps the story taut throughout its extended running time.

Christian Bale's Batman remains a gravelly voiced cypher, developing the first instalment's notion of Batman's power being as much symbolic as physical. But at the film's heart is the late Heath Ledger's astonishing performance as Joker. A terrifying nexus of physical tics, his tongue flicking in and out like a lizard's, he plays the role like a villain from a horror movie – the fiendish, sadistic traps and tricks he plays on his victims call to mind Jigsaw from the *Saw* franchise, though he is an infinitely more interesting character, his mask of smeared, faded make-up indicating a truly distorted human being, if indeed he is human at all. Along with the film's relentless sense of impending violence, this horror aesthetic – intensified by subsidiary villain Harvey Dent/Two-Face's (Aaron Eckhart) gruesome make-up – led to many in the UK feeling its 12A certificate was insufficient. Questions were even asked in the House of Commons: testament perhaps to the fact that *The Dark Knight* marked the moment that the genre caught up with its comic book progenitors and, for good or ill, finally grew up.

TIGHTS! CAMERA! ACTION!
The unstoppable rise of the comic-book movie...

Of course there's nothing new in Hollywood turning to the world of comic books for inspiration. Soon after the invention of the comic in the 1930s (which itself had emerged from the popular "funnies" sections of American newspapers) the studios started cranking out versions for the big screen in the form of the Saturday-morning serials that entertained kids in the 1940s and 50s. But aside from a few marginal subsequent low-budget efforts the key event in the development of the modern comic-book movie was Richard Donner's *Superman: The Movie* in 1978, which was the first to give the format a big budget and an all-star cast.

It was followed by Tim Burton's *Batman* reinvention in 1989 and by the mid-1990s the explosion in comic-book adaptations began to hit the multiplexes. *The Crow* (1994) together with *Blade* (1996) introduced a new edge and sexiness along with explicit violence. It was an aesthetic that would last well into the next millennium with almost every new comic-book movie boasting of its superior "darkness" and pitched squarely at the studios' key demographic: 16- to 25-year-old males rather than families with children. Cynics explained this new popularity in terms of a depressing generational phenomenon of cinematic arrested development: with Gen X unable or unwilling to distinguish between low (juvenile) and high (adult) culture, they have no real desire to graduate from one to the other. But in fact the root cause for the genre's dominance may be more financial than sociological. With blockbuster budgets trending ever upwards, studio execs, themselves now of a thirtysomething generation brought up on comics, balked at investing in untried characters and stories, preferring to back projects with at least some audience recognition and success already behind them. Comic books (conveniently already a visual medium) fit the bill perfectly.

The key combatants in the subsequent battle for superhero millennial box-office supremacy were, as had been the case on the newsstands, DC and Marvel. DC, always the slightly weaker of the stables, were set back at the cinema by the relative failure of Bryan Singer's attempt to reboot the Big Blue Boy Scout with his *Superman Returns* (2006). Singer brought a nostalgic, romantic sensibility to his film, at odds with the hectic action demanded by 21st-century fans. But Christopher Nolan seemed to nail the prevailing taste, seasoning his Batman films with a modish tech-*noir* feel, an anguished central character and enough violence to worry parents. Still, the overall winners have been Marvel. Early to spot the prize that was in the offing, the company transformed itself into a fully fledged studio in 1996 (subsequently bought by Disney for $4 billion in 2009), who deployed not only their *Spider-Man* (2002) to huge

box-office success but also the full array of their Avengers characters, including *Iron Man* (2008, p.146), *Thor* (2011) and *Captain America* (2011, p.43), all of which led to their box-office record smashing superhero mash *Avengers Assemble* in 2012. Meanwhile, for those turned off by the traditional superhero comics, there were adaptations of more esoteric pulp such as Sam Mendes' *Road to Perdition* (2002), David Cronenberg's *A History of Violence* (2005, p.127) and Marjane Satrapi's affecting *Persepolis* (2008, p.191).

But with all the A-List heroes spoken for, the studios were forced to dig among the less well-known comic books with mixed results. There were some inventive and unusual films which drew on books, such as Robert Rodriguez and Frank Miller's adult *noir Sin City* (2005) and Edgar Wright's *Scott Pilgrim vs. The World* (2010), while instant cult hit *Chronicle* (2011) bolted the superhero myth to a found-footage format; all pushed the genre in new directions. Notorious misfires included Ben Affleck as blind crusader against injustice *Daredevil* (2003), Keanu Reeves as supernatural gumshoe *Constantine* (2005), Josh Brolin as the lead in the virtually unwatchable (even at 81 minutes) *Jonah Hex* (2010), Seth Rogen's *The Green Hornet* (2011) and DC's attempt to make a franchise out of *Green Lantern* with Ryan Reynolds, which foundered in 2011.

As well as barrel-scraping, the studios' other response to running out of material has been to reboot their successful franchises more and more frequently, vastly reducing gaps between the demise of one spandex iteration and the launch of the next. Ang Lee's *Hulk* (2003) had been out of cinemas for only five years before the character was re-invented with Ed Norton in the role; Sam Raimi's *Spider-Man 3* (2007) was followed by a new run at the boy-arachnid just five years later (contrast the eight years that passed between Joel Schumacher's *Batman & Robin* and Nolan's *Batman Begins* and the almost three decades between the last of the Donner-originated *Superman* films and *Superman Returns*). It's a risky strategy, diluting the sense of "event" that ideally surrounds these celluloid behemoths. Matthew Vaughn's *X-Men: First Class* (2011) was judged to suffer from its proximity to the last of the original *X-Men* movies five years earlier and an *X-Men Origins* film (*Wolverine*) only two years before; audiences tend to see a new film as simply a sequel, and sequels traditionally make ever-decreasing revenues at the box office. But nevertheless with the likes of *The Amazing Spider-Man* and *Avengers Assemble* (both 2012) still being among the most potentially profitable movies ever made, the comic book looks likely to reign supreme at the summer box office for some time yet.

Dark Water

2003, Jpn, 101 mins, 15 (UK) R (US)

••

cast Hitomi Kuroki, Rio Kanno, Mirei Oguchi *scr* Yoshihiro Nakamura and Ken'ichi Suzuki (from a novel by Kôji Suzuki) *cin* Jun'ichirô Hayashi *m* Kenji Kawai, Shikao Suga *dir* Hideo Nakata

"Water, water everywhere..." might have been a good poster tag-line for this unnerving gem of a Japanese ghost story. It drenches people in rainstorms, gushes from broken taps, spills out of baths, stains ceilings and seeps under doors. Frankly this is a haunting that doesn't need an exorcist – it needs a good plumber.

Yoshimi (Hitomi Kuroki) is a mother going through the agonies of a messy divorce. Forced to move home and to fight for the custody of her young daughter, she finds herself in a small, cramped apartment in a grim suburb. But only days after moving in, mysterious events begin to add to her woes: an inexplicable water stain begins to spread across the ceiling, a red schoolbag refuses to be thrown away and, more worrying still, Yoshimi starts to sense the presence of another little girl, one who, she finds out, vanished a year ago...

Director Hideo Nakata had initiated the Western fad for Japanese horror with *Ring* (2000) and its sequels and here again shows his great skill in investing everyday objects – that bright red school bag with a rabbit on the front, that spreading water stain on the ceiling, the agonizingly slow lift doors at the end of the shared walkway – with a palpable sense of dread. And as with *Ring* he makes good use of grainy television images, in this case the CCTV in the ever-present elevator that occasionally reveals people who really can't be there. His sense of place is perfect too, a drab, anonymous concrete apartment block beside a murky grey river, a world away from the bright neon and packed streets that Westerners at least associate with Japanese cities. (The film's occasional flashbacks are shot in a jaundiced yellow, which adds to the uneasy, corrupted atmosphere, and makes a horrific sense only at the end of the story.)

Kuroki is excellent as the brittle, terrified tenant, a woman coming apart at the seams (her almost constantly stricken expression, seemingly always moments away from tears or a scream, brings to mind Shelley Duvall in Stanley Kubrick's haunted house film *The Shining*, 1980). Also deserving of praise is Kenji Kawai and Shikao Suga's score which mixes the sounds of water dripping with echoing, creaking noises that bring to mind a decaying apartment building – or perhaps the interior of a rooftop water-tank – to cold-sweat inducing effect.

In *Dark Water*, the everyday is suffused with dread: bathtime – at least for Hitomi Kuroki – has never been quite so frightening.

After this, and perhaps Takashi Shimizu's *The Grudge* (2004), the fashion for Japanese scares petered out somewhat with the locus for international horror shifting towards Spain and Latin America (ironically, Brazilian director Walter Salles directed the workmanlike, but nowhere near as terrifying Hollywood remake of *Dark Water* in 2005 with Jennifer Connelly in the lead role). But the brief flowering of Japanese horror gave cinema some top-notch scary movies, and this is amongst the best of them. *Dark Water* is a sophisticated, moving ghost story infused with a unique atmosphere of grief, sadness and longing; it's a movie where you care deeply about the characters and hence sympathize with the awfulness of their situation all the more intensely. And it's a scary movie that leaves you in need of a drink – anything, that is, except water.

The Day After Tomorrow

2004, US, 124 mins, 12A (UK) PG-13 (US)

....

cast Jake Gyllenhaal, Dennis Quad, Emmy Rossum, Ian Holm *scr* Roland Emmerich & Jeffrey Nachmanoff *cin* Ueli Steiger *m* Harald Kloser and Thomas Wanker *dir* Roland Emmerich

Audiences had a choice of two contrasting movies when it came to the millennium's most pressing environmental issue: climate change. One featured a slightly paunchy middle-aged man in a suit delivering a PowerPoint presentation. The other had helicopter crashes, gargantuan tornadoes tearing up Greater Los Angeles, and a 150-foot tsunami inundating the Statue of Liberty. And wolves. Lots of wolves.

Al Gore's worthy documentary *An Inconvenient Truth* (2006) was surprisingly successful given its lack of cinematic ooomph (see box, p.47), but Roland Emmerich's epic disaster flick was the one audiences flocked to – ever since he blew up the White House in the trailer for *Independence Day* (1996), the German-born director has been hailed a master of crowd-pleasing cinematic scale, if not subtlety. Here it's the whole planet he gets to menace, employing Industrial Light & Magic's biggest computers to stunning effect. The slimline plot has climatologist Jack Hall (Dennis Quaid) warning of oncoming disaster only for the weather to go kerflooey much more suddenly than even he predicted. Tokyo is pounded by grapefruit-sized hailstones, the US freezes and Jack's son Sam (Jake Gyllenhaal) finds himself trapped in the flooded New York Public Library, burning the world's classics to keep warm as dad negotiates vast ice floes to save him. Meanwhile the population of North America flees south to warmer climes, only to be turned away at the border by unsympathetic Mexicans in one of the film's few flashes of humour.

All disaster movies exploit spectacle at the expense of character, but Emmerich seems particularly prone to this: his films often have a cold, mechanical feel, entirely appropriate since they are mainly the product of computers. Here, though, the chill is effectively offset by likeable performances, particularly from Gyllenhaal in his first attempt at an action hero, while the presence of veteran Ian Holm as a phlegmatic scientist adds a certain dignity to the proceedings. Of course the real *raison d'etre* of movies like this are the effects sequences, and here Emmerich excels once again, digital technology delivering with near perfect photo-realism scenes of chaos and destruction that would have been impossible a few short years earlier: giant crevasses rip open in Arctic ice sheets, airliners plunge to the ground and a Russian oil-tanker floats down Fifth Avenue. In fact, the incredible clarity of these sequences can sometimes be a little disconcerting, thanks to a psychological phenomenon called the Uncanny Valley effect: as digital effects manage to synthesize reality more and more closely without ever quite matching it, there comes a point at which the spectator inevitably finds themselves attempting to spot the flaws and hence distanced from the imagery rather than drawn in.

As for Emmerich's claim that *The Day After Tomorrow* educated the goggle-eyed public on the dangers of global warming? Well, perhaps. After all who could fail to be moved by a message as stark as "humanity – change your ways, or the movie star gets it"?

Escape from New York: Sam (Jake Gyllenhaal) negotiates the flooded streets of the metropolis in Roland Emmerich's effects-laden *The Day After Tomorrow*.

The Departed

2006, US, 151 mins, 18 (UK) R (US)

....

cast Jack Nicholson, Matt Damon, Mark Wahlberg, Leonardo DiCaprio, Martin Sheen, Ray Winstone, Vera Farmiga, Alec Baldwin
scr William Monahan (adapted from *Infernal Affairs* by Alan Mak and Felix Chong) *cin* Michael Ballhaus *m* Howard Shore
dir Martin Scorsese

By the start of the 21st century it was looking more and more like Martin Scorsese, then approaching his sixties, might be in line to repeat Alfred Hitchcock's unfortunate achievement of ending a stunning Hollywood career without having won a best director Oscar, despite receiving no fewer than six nominations. So it might not be a coincidence that during the first decade of this millennium his films seemed to be calibrated for mainstream success and awards glory, rather than demonstrating the kind of edgy boldness of his early work. *Gangs of New York* (2002) plucked gently at American sentiment post-9/11 while *The Aviator* (2004) was a lush biopic of Howard Hughes, an American legend with deep Hollywood connections, but as far as Oscar was concerned, it was all to no avail.

It's hard then, to see *The Departed* as anything less than an all-out assault on the sensibilities of the Academy. At its heart is Jack Nicholson, one of modern cinema's living icons, as Boston Irish gang boss Costello, a spider at the centre of a web of crime that has proven impervious to the attempts of the Boston police to clean it up. This is largely because Costello has planted a rat, in the shape of apple-cheeked detective Colin (Matt Damon), in the department. But the cops have their own informant in the form of Billy (Leonardo DiCaprio), run by detectives Queenan (Martin Sheen) and outrageously foul-mouthed Dignam (Mark Wahlberg). So, a Hollywood icon, the three hottest young male leads of their generation, and a supporting cast boasting the heavyweight likes of Sheen, Alec Baldwin and Ray

A tense meeting between Jack Nicholson's malevolent Costello and Leonardo DiCaprio's fresh-faced Billy in the knot of betrayals and triple-crosses that make up Scorsese's Oscar-winning *The Departed*.

MARK WAHLBERG

b. 5 June 1971, Boston, MA, US

Mark Wahlberg's decision to abandon the world of white rap and underpants modelling in favour of an acting career was greeted by most critics as a bad joke. But by 2011 *The New York Times* was only half kidding when it suggested that he might be the most under-appreciated actor of his generation. He was born in working-class Dorchester, Boston, just a few miles from leafy Cambridge where Matt Damon, alongside whom he would star in Scorsese's *The Departed* (2006), was raised. If Wahlberg would rather forget the early years of gangs, racially aggravated assault and prison, numerous profile writers seem unwilling to let him, but his early movies showed that he was more than the pneumatic torso and ingratiating grin showcased by those iconic posters for Calvin Klein. He was genuinely scary as every father's worst nightmare, psycho boyfriend David McCall, in *Fear* (1996), before delivering his career-making performance as Dirk Diggler, human appendage to a record-breaking penis in Paul Thomas Anderson's *Boogie Nights* (1998). One of the paradoxes of his career is that he is usually at his worst in the kind of action films he would seem to identify with – *The Corruptor* (1999), *Shooter* (2007), *Max Payne* (2008) – but almost consistently convincing and skilful in the kinds of movies you get the feeling he might not rush out to watch. His ongoing collaboration with director David O. Russell on Iraq war satire *Three Kings* (2000), heart-it-or-hate-it *I* ❤ *Huckabees* (2004), and *The Fighter* (2011, p.95) must be one of the most unexpected in movie history, but has produced some of Wahlberg's most interesting movies; his work with James Gray on sophisticated, character-driven crime dramas *The Yards* (2000) and *We Own the Night* (2007), alongside Joaquin Phoenix, is equally impressive. He and Phoenix were early casting choices for Ang Lee's *Brokeback Mountain* (2006, p.41), but the sex scenes were for Wahlberg a step too far – "they creeped me out," he told one interviewer. More recently he revealed unexpected comedic skills in *The Other Guys* (2011), alongside Will Ferrell, and in *Ted* (2012), starring alongside a foul-mouthed teddy bear. It's all a long way from hawking knickers for a living.

Winstone, all in a gangster flick – the director's home turf. Frankly you got the feeling that if this didn't get Scorsese a golden statue he might just pack up his clapperboard and go home.

Of course none of this is to deny that *The Departed* is a gripping, expertly made crime thriller. The plot (adapted from 2002's Hong Kong hit *Infernal Affairs* – only the second time Scorsese has indulged in a remake, the first being *Cape Fear* in 1991) sets up a Gordian knot of betrayal, paranoia and triple crosses that Scorsese navigates with his customary technical aplomb: orchestrating slo-mo, flash cutting, iris zooms and a new trick, punctuating the final gun battle with almost imperceptible freeze-frames – all the while making good use of his vast record collection. Meanwhile, veteran editor Thelma Schoonmaker's razor editing propels us through the not inconsiderable running time without ever letting the pace slacken.

The main dramatic attraction, though, is Scorsese directing Nicholson for the first time: a pairing irresistible to any fan of modern American cinema. Scorsese conjures from Nicholson that unique, delicious, dangerous *schtick* halfway between mischief and uncompromising malevolence. "How's your mother?" he asks a barfly after smashing Billy's already broken arm with the young cop's own boot. "I'm afraid she's on her way out," is the reply. "Aren't we all," he grins. "Act accordingly."

In 2007 Martin Scorsese finally climbed the podium at LA's Kodak Theatre and accepted the Academy Award for best achievement in directing for *The Departed*. And everyone heaved a sigh of relief.

OOPS! FLOPS, FARRAGOS AND FANDANGOES

Ten millennial movies everyone would rather forget...

ROLLERBALL (John McTiernan, 2002)
How the mighty have fallen. *Die Hard* director John McTiernan, once the king of the action flick, made an inexplicable dogs' dinner of this redundant remake, sinking *American Pie*'s Chris Klein's hopes of making it as an action star. McTiernan was subsequently given a jail term for his involvement in the Pellicano case – he should have asked for *Rollerball* to be taken into consideration.

THE ADVENTURES OF PLUTO NASH (Ron Underwood, 2002)
Widely considered to be the greatest box-office flop of all time, making a paltry $7 million from a budget of well over $100 million, this comeback vehicle for one-time comedy superstar Eddie Murphy had him as a club owner fending off the mafia. On the moon.

SWEPT AWAY (Guy Ritchie, 2002)
Guy Ritchie's cinematic love-letter to his wife had Madonna as an irritating, filthy-rich, spoiled socialite, a part which she was inexplicably unable to play convincingly. The finished film snagged an impressive five Razzies and both Ritchie and his ex would no doubt rather it be swept under the carpet.

GIGLI (Martin Brest, 2003)
Bennifer vehicle that marked the end of the media's love affair with the superstar couple, this bomb-com was unanimously panned, played for just three weeks and made a paltry $6 million from a $75 million budget. Ben and Jen separated soon afterwards.

THE WICKER MAN (Neil LaBute, 2006)
Utterly misconceived remake of the Brit horror classic with Nicolas Cage as the copper done for by nutty pagans in a sequence involving a mask of live bees, a fate marginally less painful than sitting through this film.

SUPERMAN RETURNS (Bryan Singer, 2006)
The *X-Men* (2000) director's long-cherished remake has a more than acceptable Brandon Routh as the Big Blue Boy Scout but Singer's romantic tone and religious metaphors, as well as a perceived a lack of action, sadly doomed it for the multiplex hordes. The studio rebooted the franchise as *Man of Steel* with Zack Snyder directing.

THE HAPPENING (M. Night Shyamalan, 2008)
The Sixth Sense (1999) director M. Night Shyamalan's already stalling career came to a shuddering halt with this barking mad eco-horror, which had humankind attacked by killer trees, no doubt furious at the number of their kind sacrificed for this woeful script.

THE LOVE GURU (Marco Schnabel, 2008)
Mike Myers had been one of the comedy superstars of the 90s with franchises such as *Austin Powers: International Man of Mystery* (1997) but having flamed out in the 2000s after a falling out with the studio, this inept farce was his disastrous attempt at a comeback. Neither wise nor loveable.

JACK & JILL (Dennis Dugan, 2012)
Adam Sandler's sex-swap comedy was dismally unfunny even for him, managed to generate an almost unprecedented 3% score on Rotten Tomatoes, won a record-breaking ten Razzies, and left *TIME Magazine*'s critic memorably observing that "it is 24 hours since I saw *Jack & Jill* and I still feel dead inside".

JOHN CARTER (Andrew Stanton, 2012)
Pixar golden boy and *WALL-E* (2008, p.249) director Stanton's first foray into live-action blockbuster territory suffered from a confusing marketing campaign (the rest of the original title, "Of Mars", was dropped early on, leaving many uncertain of what the movie was about) as well as a general lack of enthusiasm for its tale of a nineteenth-century human's adventures on the red planet. Though it was moderately well reviewed, audiences stayed away and the film was humiliatingly beaten at the box office by *21 Jump Street*, a comedy remake of the cheesy 80s teen TV series. Disney ruefully announced that the film's failure would leave a $200 million hole in the company's finances and led to the resignation of Disney head Rich Ross.

District 9

2009, NZ/US/S. Afr, 112 mins, 15 (UK) R (US)

....

cast Sharlto Copley, David James, Jason Cope, Vanessa Haywood *scr* Neill Blomkamp & Terri Tatchell *cin* Trent Opaloch *m* Clinton Shorter
dir Neill Blomkamp

District 9 begins with news footage of a vast flying saucer gliding into view above Johannesburg. At first the mind turns to the violent invasions of *Independence Day* (1996). But when nothing happens, and months later humans finally enter the still hovering ship, they find not an invading army but thousands of shivering, malnourished interstellar refugees. With nowhere for them to go, and apparently unable to pilot their own spacecraft, they're settled in an outlying area, District 9, which twenty years later has become a slum. Nicknamed "Prawns" by the locals, they soon become socially reviled. "No Aliens" and "Humans Only" signs start to go up and, under pressure, the government agrees to move them to a new "home" (in fact an internment camp) miles out of the city. It outsources the job to Multi-National United and field-operative Wikus Van De Merwe (Sharlto Copley) is despatched to implement the move. But when he is infected with an alien virus and begins to grow a Prawn-like claw (shades of Kafka's *Metamorphosis* in this sharply written film) he begins to fully grasp what it is like to live as an oppressed, despised minority.

Debut director Neill Blomkamp shoots partly in mockumentary format, generating a sense of immediacy by mixing faux TV news with to-camera interviews and fake advertising, and the integration of the CGI aliens (designed by *Lord of the Rings* FX house Weta) into conventionally photographed action is seamless. But key to the movie's success is Sharlto Copley's performance as the hapless, David Brent-ish Wikus Van De Merwe (the surname is a common butt of jokes in South Africa). He's too sharp an actor to paint Wikus as a thoughtless bigot; instead he's a somewhat helpless, self-aggrandizing middle-manager doing his best to impress his craven bosses, while Blomkamp and Terri Tatchell's screenplay is clever, often funny, and doesn't shy away from the complexities of any of the issues it raises. Sure, the South African authorities are corrupt and prejudiced, but then the aliens are a pretty unpleasant lot too – they spend much of their time fighting, urinating in the street and arguing over tins of cat food (an unlikely alien delicacy). You begin to wonder if this might be why their planet has foisted them on Earth in the first place.

As well as being state-of-the-art in terms of its effects, *District 9* deployed a state-of-the-art viral marketing campaign. Mysterious posters appeared with no explanatory text but the "No Aliens, Humans Only!" logo, insinuating the idea of the movie in the curious moviegoer's mind long before anyone actually knew what it was about. Telephone hotlines were set up to to "report alien sightings" while ingeniously designed websites, fake blogs and tweets by "alien dissidents" popped up. The days of film marketing consisting of not much more than posters and a trailer after the "For Future Presentation" music are, it seems, long gone.

Given South Africa's history of apartheid the subtexts are hardly difficult to spot; even the title is a nod to District 6, an area of Cape Town from which 60,000 blacks were forcibly evicted in the 1970s. But *District 9*'s theme is not confined to the past, nor is it geographically specific. The aliens are really interplanetary asylum-seekers, bringing with them all the attendant problems and social tensions. It all makes for a pungently political blockbuster, one that marshalls its ideas as expertly as its action.

Illegal alien: Wikus Van De Merwe (Sharlto Copley) flashes his ID badge as he tries to enforce the so-called Prawns' eviction from the slums of *District 9*.

Donnie Darko

2002, US, 113 mins (director's cut 134 mins), 15 (UK) R (US)

··

cast Jake Gyllenhaal, Jena Malone, Drew Barrymore, Maggie Gyllenhaal, Noah Wyle, Patrick Swayze *scr* Richard Kelly *cin* Stephen Poster *m* Michael Andrews *dir* Richard Kelly

If you were over 25 in 2002, then writer-director Richard Kelly's stunning debut film may well have passed you by. Imagine *Back to the Future* (1985) rewritten by Franz Kafka and shot by David Lynch and you might come up with something a bit like *Donnie Darko* – though even that pair might have balked at the giant demonic talking bunny. For the younger crowd, though, it rapidly established itself as being as generation-defining as *Rebel Without A Cause* (1955). If James Dean had spoken to the repressed youth of the 1950s and Ferris Bueller had been the poster-boy of the brashly optimistic 80s, Donnie (Jake Gyllenhaal in the career-making title role) was a child born of noughties millennial anxiety.

A teenage somnambulist and former arsonist, Donnie is tormented by visions of a sinister talking rabbit, whose eerily calm, synthesized voice informs him that the world is about to end. When an aircraft engine plummets into his bedroom he narrowly escapes death, only to become convinced that time travel is possible

Jake Gyllenhaal as Donnie, with Jena Malone (Gretchen), pondering time-travel paradoxes and giant decaying rabbits in the dark, dreamlike and seductively strange *Donnie Darko*.

JAKE GYLLENHAAL

b. 19 December 1980, Los Angeles, CA, US

When your dad's a director (Stephen Gyllenhaal), your mum's a screenwriter (Naomi Foner) and you were taught to drive by a movie icon (Paul Newman), it's almost inevitable that you'll eventually hear the siren call of the film set. So it was for Jake Gyllenhaal, who arrived on our screens bearing one of modern cinema's most egregious smirks as the eponymous, hood-lidded hoodie in Richard Kelly's surreal, labyrinthine *Donnie Darko* (2002) and – once the world had learned to pronounce his name (it's Jillenhaal) – has had good reason to smile ever since. His main strength, apart from his undoubted good looks, has been an impressive taste in directors and material: in a few short years he has worked with Sam Mendes on Iraq War movie *Jarhead* (2006), David Fincher on *Zodiac* (2007), and with Jim Sheridan in "war at home" movie *Brothers* (2010), alongside Tobey Maguire and Natalie Portman, where he gave the film's best performance. And he is still probably best known to a generation as homosexual farmhand Jack Twist in Ang Lee's fiercely sentimental adaptation of Annie Proulx's *Brokeback Mountain* (2006, p.41). The only role in which he looked genuinely uncomfortable was as the leather-vested lead in Jerry Bruckheimer's stalled videogame action franchise *Prince of Persia: The Sands of Time* (2010), the relative failure of which sent him scurrying back to more interesting films, such as romance *Love and Other Drugs* (2010) and superior sci-fi flick *Source Code* (2011). Bad news for his bank account maybe, but better news for fans of the kind of varied, mature American cinema that seems to be his natural home.

and that it might be possible to see the future. At school, meanwhile, traditional teaching is giving way to a bizarre self-help cult run by Jim Cunningham (a mischievously cast Patrick Swayze). Sci-fi, then, meets teen movie meets a kind of existentialist neo-*noir* in an exhilarating genre mash-up. If it sounds a heady concoction that's because it is.

Kelly's screenplay channels some of the acidity of the blacker teen movies of the late 1980s and early 90s, such as *Heathers* (1989) and *Pump Up the Volume* (1991), though venturing into even more bizarre territory. He further strengthens these resonances by setting the movie in the late 1980s and adds echoes of *Blue Velvet* (1986), with its depiction of idyllic American suburbia concealing something if not rotten, at least deeply weird, at its core.

For the most part subjecting movies to post 9/11 critical analysis is as predictable and tiresome as insisting that every 70s slasher movie with a masked man and a chainsaw was a Vietnam allegory. But with *Donnie Darko*, which was released in the US only weeks after the Twin Towers were attacked, the approach might be more rewarding, particularly in explaining its instant appeal to the young. After all, Donnie is a boy troubled by what he perceives as the coming apocalypse, his obsession with time travel and escaping his destiny symptomatic of the key desire to put an incomprehensible world into some kind of order. It's not unreasonable to suggest that many of the younger Americans that this enigmatic, funny, and finally heartbreaking film spoke to might have some sympathy with his plight.

Donnie Darko was also a salutary lesson in the dangers inherent in a brilliant debut. After delivering the now *de rigueur* director's cut in 2004 (neither better nor worse, just a bit longer), Richard Kelly seemed unable to repeat his initial success: his second film, *Southland Tales* (2006), was a production debacle that didn't receive a US release, while *The Box* (2009) was at least coherent but, compared with his first movie, unambitious. Like its protagonist, *Donnie Darko* seems to have been a glorious one-off.

Downfall

2005, Ger/Aus/It, 155 mins, 15 (UK) R (US)

cast Bruno Ganz, Alexandra Maria Lara, Ulrich Matthes, Corinna Harfouch, Juliane Köhler **scr** Bernd Eichinger (adapted from books by Joachim Fest and Traudl Junge & Melissa Müller) **cin** Rainer Clausmann **m** Stephan Zacharias **dir** Oliver Hirschbiegel

Oliver Hirschbiegel's gripping account of Hitler's last days in the Berlin bunker begins with a short extract from another film, André Heller and Othmar Schmiderer's 2002 documentary *Blind Spot: Hitler's Secretary* (itself a mesmerizing

End of the Third Reich: Juliane Köhler as devoted, enigmatic Eva Braun with Bruno Ganz's brooding Hitler in the dictator's bunker.

experience and well worth seeking out), in which Traudl Junge, then in her late seventies and terminally ill, wonders how it happened that she, like so many other Germans, was drawn towards Hitler and his poisonous creed. We get a hint of the answer in the prologue that follows. It is 1943 and in the middle of the night a group of anxious-looking women, candidates for the post of Hitler's secretary, are ushered in to an interview with the Führer. Having picked Junge (Alexandra Maria Lara), Hitler begins dictation. Understandably nervous, she makes a mess of the typing, and hearing her stop the Führer comes over and surveys her work. "I think we had better start again," he says, with the fatherly concern of a man who knows his presence can have a dramatic effect on people. It's a human side of a man, in other respects a monster, that is rarely depicted.

Things have changed, though, by April 1945. Holed up in his Führerbunker, the Russian artillery pounding the devastated city, Hitler is on the verge of defeat. The late Swiss actor Bruno Ganz delivers a tour de force as the harried leader: pacing the tiled corridors of his lair, hunched, brooding and on the cusp of outright insanity, he rants and raves and orders imaginary armies to defeat the oncoming enemy. Ulrich Matthes is excellent as the cadaverous Joseph Goebbels, a man who seems even more interested in the Führer's place in history than is his boss, while his wife Magda (Corinna Harfouch) is portrayed as a cold, ruthlessly devoted fellow traveller; the scene in which, horrified at the idea of them living in a world without Hitler or National Socialism, she calmly poisons her own children is the film's most chilling moment.

Hirschbiegel is masterly in his depiction of the growing sense of surreality, hysteria and panic in the bunker in the final days and hours. Generals bicker, soldiers get roaring drunk. Eva Braun, artfully played by Juliane Köhler, is an enigma. Flirtatious, effortlessly likeable, she attempts to keep spirits up, in one bizarre scene dancing wildly on a table before the windows of the above-ground ballroom are blown in; but you begin to realize she is aware, sanguine and unrepentant about the fate that awaits her. Particularly powerfully evoked is the devotion that many still felt to the Nazi cause – and Hitler personally – even when they were plainly defeated.

Downfall is the first German film about Hitler and the Third Reich since the end of the war to make an international impact. It's probably not surprising then that it's somewhat buttoned up, a film on its best behaviour that takes few artistic risks. But as an honest, sober and compelling account of the last moments of one of history's darkest periods it's unlikely to be bettered any time soon.

Drive

2011, US, 100 mins, 18 (UK) R (US)

••

cast Ryan Gosling, Carey Mulligan, Albert Brooks, Ron Perlman, Bryan Cranston *scr* Hossein Amini (from the novel by James Sallis) *cin* Newton Thomas Sigel *m* Cliff Martinez *dir* Nicolas Winding Refn

The story might be set in the Los Angeles of the present, the attitude neon-drenched neo-*noir* and the style pilfered from the 80s, but at its heart *Drive* is pure spaghetti western, with perhaps a nod to *Shane* (1953). By day our nameless hero (Ryan Gosling, credited in the titles only as "Driver") is a movie stunt-driver, rolling police cruisers and careening into buildings. By night he makes his real money as a top-flight getaway driver. "I'm yours for five minutes," he informs his clients. "A minute before or after that and you're on your own." When his pretty neighbour Irene (Carey Mulligan, who does what she can with an underwritten role) and her young son find themselves in trouble he falls for them and tries to help, only to become drawn into a war of vengeance with a group of local gangsters.

Gosling, an actor who had been showing promise in offbeat indies for a decade (he took the title roles in both *The United States of Leland*, 2005, and *Lars and the Real Girl*, 2008), as well as setting more than a few hearts aflutter in Nick Cassavetes' *The Notebook* (2004), may have finally found the vehicle that rockets him to the A List. His "Driver" is the epitome of movie cool: sporting a bizarre satin jacket emblazoned with a yellow scorpion (perhaps a nod to Kenneth Anger's cult 1963 short *Scorpio Rising*, as well as the fable of the scorpion and the frog), which could only look hideous on anyone else, and with a toothpick

CAREY MULLIGAN

b. 28 May 1985, London, UK

Think what you like about Carey Mulligan, you can't accuse her of not being a ferociously determined self-starter. When she was rejected by no fewer than three drama colleges, the seventeen-year-old wrote to actor/screenwriter Julian Fellowes, who had spoken at her school, asking for a meeting and career advice. After Fellowes put her in touch with a casting director she attracted the attention of up-and-coming director Joe Wright who, no doubt struck by her classically gamine features (which have provoked instant and unavoidable comparisons to Audrey Hepburn), cast her in his debut film *Pride & Prejudice* (2005). It looked like she might be trapped in corsets forever, subsequently turning up in a string of TV period adaptations including *Bleak House* (2005) and *Northanger Abbey* (2007), but in 2009 she found her star-making role, bringing an incandescent appeal to Jenny, a precocious sixteen-year-old girl who embarks on an ill-advised affair with an older man (Peter Sarsgaard) in Lone Scherfig's adaptation of Lynn Barber's memoir *An Education*. Hollywood finally took notice, though the early roles were not promising. She had a small role in Johnny Depp gangster flick *Public Enemies* (2009) and served as proxy for Oliver Stone's daddy issues opposite Shia LaBeouf and Josh Brolin in the curiously flat sequel *Wall Street: Money Never Sleeps* (2010). She fared better in indie movies, particularly Mark Romanek's *Never Let Me Go* (2011), with fellow rising British star Andrew Garfield, and Steve McQueen's *Shame* (2012), in which she managed to make an impact alongside co-stars New York and Michael Fassbender's penis. She'll next be seen opposite Leonardo DiCaprio in Baz Luhrmann's much anticipated 3D adaptation of *The Great Gatsby*. It's all testament to Mulligan's impressive versatility, and frankly anyone who can boast a cinematic dance card marked with both a Coen Brothers movie – *Inside Llewyn Davis*, in which she'll play opposite Justin Timberlake, scheduled for 2013 – and an as yet untitled Charlie Kaufman and Spike Jonze project isn't going to be needing to call anyone for career help anytime soon.

constantly wedged between his teeth, he brings to mind Steve McQueen in *Bullitt* (1968) or even Clint Eastwood in one of his "no name" roles. His face remains a study of (undeniably handsome) impassivity, whether he's ferrying Los Angeles's criminal fraternity to and from jobs or reducing a thug's cranium to a bloody mulch with his boot.

Danish director Nicolas Winding Refn (known for his *Pusher* series of films as well as *Bronson*, 2009) proves himself expert at creating tension, particularly in the early heist scenes – which are not traditional car chases but brilliantly staged games of automotive cat and mouse in which the precision of the editing mirrors that of the driving – punctuated by staccato bursts of extraordinarily staged violence, which is mostly brief but extremely bloody even by 21st-century standards. But his boldest gambit is to lard the movie with a kind of synthetic 80s look accompanied by obscure electronic pop. It could have been appallingly kitsch; instead it channels the ultra cool of urban *noirs* such as William Friedkin's *To Live And Die In L.A.* (1985) and Walter Hill's *The Warriors* (1979). Like those directors he has been accused of peddling style over substance. Well maybe, but when he can deliver style like this, who really cares?

A real hero: the quietly enigmatic, unnamed driver (Ryan Gosling) waiting five minutes in Nicolas Winding Refn's supercool, 80s-styled *Drive*.

LONG LIVE THE NEW FLESH #2: Ten actresses who got their big break in the 21st century...

JESSICA CHASTAIN Big Break: *The Tree of Life*
A relative latecomer to actorly fame and fortune, Juilliard alumnus Chastain toiled in upscale telly including *ER* and *Law & Order* before Terrence Malick cast her in his 2011 philosophical film-poem, in which she was positively ethereal as Brad Pitt's wife and the embodiment of human grace. She had a smaller role in civil rights drama *The Help* (2011) and has completed work with Malick again on a forthcoming as yet untitled project.

ZOOEY DESCHANEL Big Break: *500 Days of Summer*
The daughter of legendary cinematographer Caleb Deschanel, Zooey had been turning up in Hollywood roles of varying prominence and quality – in Cameron Crowe's *Almost Famous* (2001), Matthew McConaughey vehicle *Failure to Launch* (2006) – before she was tragically cast in a starring role in M. Night Shyamalan's *The Happening* (2008). Thankfully she survived that catastrophe to really make her mark as the female half of a workplace love affair gone wrong in *500 Days of Summer* (2009), a fizzy, intelligent indie rom-com labelled by some as this generation's *Annie Hall* (1977).

REBECCA HALL Big Break: *Vicky Cristina Barcelona*
Theatrical pedigrees don't come much more distinguished than Rebecca Hall's (her dad is Sir Peter) so perhaps it's no surprise that she's quickly established herself as one of Britain's most promising actresses. Cinemagoers should be most grateful for her role in Woody Allen's *Vicky Cristina Barcelona* (2009), a movie that marked the beginning of Allen's recent revival, but she was also effective as a hostage/love-interest in Ben Affleck's crime drama *The Town* (2010), and as a spook-hunter in classy 1920s-set British ghost story *The Awakening* (2011).

SALLY HAWKINS Big Break: *Happy-Go-Lucky*
Sally Hawkins had been one of Britain's busiest actresses up until her international arthouse breakthrough in Mike Leigh's *Happy-Go-Lucky* (2008) as irrepressible schoolteacher Poppy, turning up in films as varied as gangster flick *Layer Cake* (2004), abortion-and-tea drama *Vera Drake* (2005), and Woody Allen's abysmal *Cassandra's Dream* (2008) alongside fellow millennial breakthrough Hayley Atwell. (Maybe she'll have better luck in Woody's as yet untitled San Francisco-set film where she is to play "a neurotic who's ... fun and rough around the edges", tentatively scheduled for 2013.)

MILA KUNIS Big Break: *Black Swan*
Ukrainian-born Kunis first shot to public attention in the sitcom *That 70s Show* as on-off girlfriend of Ashton Kutcher, but her key film role was as jealous hoofer Lily, opposite Natalie Portman, in Darren Aronofsky's enjoyably over-egged *Black Swan* (2011). She also seems to have made a speciality of starring in rom-coms alongside studly ex-pop pin-ups, turning up with Justin Timberlake in *Friends With Benefits* (2011) and then with Mark Wahlberg and a foul-mouthed stuffed toy in *Ted* (2012).

JENNIFER LAWRENCE Big Break: *The Hunger Games*
Before landing one of the most sought-after roles of the millennium, Kentucky-born Lawrence had turned up as mutant shapeshifter Raven/Mystique in *X-Men: First Class* (2011), but laid the groundwork for *The Hunger Games* (2012) with a stunning, physically gruelling performance in gritty family drama *Winter's Bone* (2010), for which she learned to skin rabbits and gained an Oscar nomination. As well as the *Games* sequels, she's set to appear in an *X-Men* film scheduled for 2014.

ELLEN PAGE Big Break: *Juno*
It would be nice to say that Ellen Page's big break came with 2004's *I Downloaded A Ghost* simply because it's one of the best TV movie titles of all time, but this was just one of the forgettable telly outings she endured before turning up as Kitty Pryde/Shadowcat in *X-Men: The Last Stand* (2006), and then in her star-making role as the eponymous knocked-up schoolgirl in 2008. Subsequently she injected a note of welcome scepticism as the only girl in Leo's gang in *Inception* (2010, p.141).

SAOIRSE RONAN Big Break: *Atonement*
Having been bounced on none other than Brad Pitt's knee as a baby (her actor dad appeared with him in *The Devil's Own* in 1997), it was perhaps no wonder that Irish-born Saoirse Ronan would succumb to the acting bug. Joe Wright spotted her for precocious Briony Tallis in his 2007 Ian McEwan adaptation, for which she got an Oscar nomination. A couple of misfires, including Peter Jackson's misjudged *The Lovely Bones* (2010) followed, before Wright rode to the rescue and cast her in his superb thriller about a naive hit-girl, *Hanna* (2011, p.117).

ZOË SALDANA Big Break: *Avatar*
The eagle-eyed might have spotted Saldana in blink-and-you'll-miss-them roles in *Pirates of the Caribbean: The Curse of the Black Pearl* (p.193, 2003) and Spielberg's *The Terminal* (2004), but it was in 2009 as lithe, eight-foot alien Neytiri that she wowed audiences. She was more recognizable as intergalactic phone operator Uhura in J.J. Abrams' slick *Star Trek* (2009) and will be seen again manning the switchboard in its 2013 sequel.

EMMA STONE Big Break: *Easy A*
Having established herself as a highly promising comedy actress alongside Jonah Hill in the excellent *Superbad* (2007), Stone continued to plough the comedy furrow with the likes of *Ghosts of Girlfriends Past* (2009) and the much better *Zombieland* (2009) alongside Woody Harrelson. Her sparkling performance in *Easy A* (2010), a high-school comedy which, like *Clueless* (1995), adapted Classic Lit. 101 for the teen crowd (in this case Hawthorne's *The Scarlet Letter*) was good enough to get her the role of Spidey's main squeeze Gwen Stacy in *The Amazing Spider-Man* (2012).

Eden Lake

2008, UK, 91 mins, 18 (UK) R (US)

••

cast Michael Fassbender, Kelly Reilly, Jack O'Connell *scr* James Watkins *cin* Christopher Ross *m* David Julyan *dir* James Watkins

British horror underwent a minor renaissance during the noughties, taking its inspiration from the distinctly British themes of domestic cult movies such as *The Wicker Man* (1973) with its "old religion", as well as from the paranoid 70s US horror typified by Wes Craven's *The Hills Have Eyes* (1977), rather than the campery of the Hammer movies that had thus far been its high point. Neil Marshall was key to the revival with his effective werewolf movie *Dog Soldiers* (2002) and spelunking shocker *The Descent* (2005), likewise Ben Wheatley with his contemporary pagan-themed *Kill List* (2011). But none of them cut quite as close to the bone as James Watkins did with *Eden Lake*. This is a nightmare movie located slap-bang in the middle of contemporary culture, a gruelling horror ripped right from the headlines.

British class anxiety, fear of kids gone feral and the gaping generation gap are the subtexts that debut writer/director Watkins (who went onto a gentler but no less skilfully wrought style of horror with Daniel Radcliffe starrer *The Woman in Black* in 2012) mines in his tightly wound ordeal movie. In the tradition of John Boorman's *Deliverance* (1972), *Eden Lake* begins with a vacation: yuppie-ish couple Steve (Michael Fassbender) and girlfriend Jenny (Kelly Reilly) head off to the countryside for a romantic break, during which he intends to propose. While sunbathing at the titular lake (we learn from a signpost that before its recent gentrification it was the slightly less paradisaical Slapton Quarry, hinting at the class

MICHAEL FASSBENDER

b. 2 April 1977, Heidelberg, Germany

"He's so perky, it drives you crazy," lamented director David Cronenberg of his star in *A Dangerous Method*. "One day, I found him out in the sun with this big smile. I said, 'Michael, why are you smiling like that?' He said, 'I don't know … life.' I said, 'It's so irritating that you're happy all the time.'" It has to be said that in the year in question, 2011, Fassbender had a lot to smile about. He had paraded around in the altogether for much of Steve McQueen's audience-dividing tale of sexual addiction *Shame* and was showered with awards for it (though Oscar balked at the nudity), had the fanboys purring in *X-Men: First Class* as the soon-to-be Magneto, and delighted the more conservative crowd as Rochester in *Jane Eyre*. But the German-born Irishman's sudden ubiquity was the result of hard graft and a decade of actorly poverty and false starts. An early role in the Steven Spielberg-produced miniseries *Band of Brothers* (2001) led, to his great disappointment, to nothing; and by 2004 he was more famous for being the guy in the Guinness ad who swims to New York than for any non-stout-related projects. But that was all to change in 2008 with his astonishing performance as self-starving IRA prisoner Bobby Sands in artist Steve McQueen's debut movie *Hunger*: a mesmerizing performance that included a seventeen-minute conversation shot in a single take and for which he went through the method initiation ritual of a crash diet, losing three stone in ten weeks. Subsequently he's made good use of his Irish charm and undeniable looks, establishing himself as arthouse totty in the likes of *Fish Tank* (2009, p.98) and as Carl Jung in Cronenberg's *A Dangerous Method* (2012). The same year sees him star in Ridley Scott's massively anticipated *Alien* prequel *Prometheus* and he's scheduled for another collaboration with muse McQueen in 2013, period drama *Twelve Years a Slave* which, given their history, is critic bait. It looks like those German/Irish eyes are going to be smiling for a long time yet.

tension that underpins much of the horror to come) they are interrupted by a crowd of loud youths. Steve intervenes and a sequence of events begins that will feature Stanley knives, petrol, mobile phones and much running and screaming. "Where are the parents?" is of course the unspoken question. When Jenny staggers out of the woods hours later, bloodied, covered in mud and, it has to be said, distinctly unbetrothed, she finds out. She'll wish she hadn't.

Watkins's technical achievements are impressive: he makes a great deal out of his location, turning a scrappy patch of woodland and a disused quarry into a threatening and virtually inescapable landscape, and coaxes a terrifying performance from Jack O'Connell as the gang's leader. And he's genre-savvy enough to provide ample shock moments to satisfy gore-hounds, but it is his exploitation of

Fall from grace: Jenny (Kelly Reilly) and Steve (Michael Fassbender) discover the lakeside woods are not as green and pleasant as they seem in James Watkins' terrifying *Eden Lake*.

current concerns – the collapse of authority (tellingly, Jenny is a teacher), as well as an unspoken, liberal middle-class fear of a violent underclass who are strangers to the values these tourists take for granted – that give *Eden Lake* its ferocious bite.

Eden Lake made more than a few headlines itself. Many felt that it was not much more than a splenetic *Daily Mail* editorial extended over an hour and a half ("A contemptible right-wing tract" was typical language from one of the movie's enraged critics). Perhaps so, but horror, at its best, doesn't just provide the safe scares of the fairground rollercoaster, but gives vent to buried fears and anxieties not readily expressible in polite company; it disquiets and disturbs. And whatever your political take on *Eden Lake*, a quiet weekend away in the country will never be quite the same again.

Elephant

2004, US, 81 mins, 15 (UK) R (US)

··

cast Alex Frost, Eric Deulen, Timothy Bottoms, John Robinson, Elias
McConnell, Nathan Tryson, Carrie Finklea *scr* Gus Van Sant *cin* Harris Savides
dir Gus Van Sant

In Gus Van Sant's dreamy, almost unbearably sad meditation on the Columbine
massacre of 1999, his camera drifts unhurriedly around the playing fields and
hallways of an ordinary American high school like a sorrowful ghost. It pauses for
what seems like an age to observe the rhythms of a touch-football game; in a long
tracking shot it follows a good-looking boy in a lifeguard sweatshirt through the

halls as he peacocks in front of admiring girls. On its travels it picks up snatches of adolescent life: the blond-haired kid phoning his brother to come pick up their drunken dad and thus getting a detention for being late; the troika of Queen Bees endlessly debating the relative merits of boyfriends and best friends over lunch before retiring to the bathroom to throw up. It tells the small dramas of being at school with more honesty than any teen movie. And knowing what is about to happen, it drinks in all this ordinariness with greed.

The title is borrowed from British dramatist Alan Clarke's 1989 TV play about the violence in Northern Ireland, which featured brutal murder after brutal murder with no context or story. The horrific fact of this relentless violence was the eponymous elephant in the room, the glaring truth no one would mention. Van Sant's style has always been similar to the one Clarke employed in his 1989 film, with its long Steadicam sequences and languid pacing, but here Van Sant applies it to just a single moment of horror: the Tuesday in April 1999 when two high-school boys murdered twelve students and one teacher in Columbine, Colorado, before killing themselves. *Elephant* is not meant to be an exact re-creation: apart from the two killers, the characters bear no relation to the dead of Columbine and the dialogue was mostly improvised by a non-professional cast (the work of the late, legendary casting director Mali Finn, known for trawling high-school drama clubs and youth offender programmes rather than Beverly Hills zip codes and thus discovering Edward Furlong and Brad Renfro, among others). The result, though, is achingly real.

But what exactly is Van Sant's elephant in the room? Perhaps it is the same thing that offended many critics when the film won the Palme d'Or at the Cannes Film Festival. This film is utterly silent on the motives of Dylan Klebold and Eric Harris, and on what might be done to prevent a recurrence. We see their dopplegängers at home, slouching and sleeping like normal teenagers. Sure, one lazily plays a violent video game, but his friend plays Beethoven's *Moonlight Sonata* on the piano surprisingly beautifully. They watch a television programme about Nazism, but not with any great enthusiasm. Van Sant refutes the comforting notion that there is something that can be done; that this will never happen again. They buy assault rifles on the internet, something that could be prevented. But even then, he seems to say, horror is part of the fabric of the world. His film contains studied images of brightly coloured plastic dinner trays neatly stacked in the cafeteria, as they have been every day for years, and of a teenage boy bleeding to death on a classroom floor, and treats them with the same impassivity. It marvels that these two things exist in the same universe.

Alex Frost in the school cafeteria, a study of ordinariness in *Elephant*, Gus Van Sant's meditation on the Columbine massacre.

Enter the Void

2010, Fr/Ger/It/Can, 143 mins (director's cut 161 mins),
18 (UK) Unrated (US)

....

cast Nathaniel Brown, Paz de la Huerta, Cyril Roy, Olly Alexander *scr* Gaspar
Noé and Lucile Hadzihalilovic *cin* Benoît Debie *m* Thomas Bangalter
dir Gaspar Noé

You get the feeling that if a device was invented that reached out of the screen
and randomly punched cinema-goers in the face no one would employ it with
more enthusiasm than Gaspar Noé. After all, the ageing *enfant terrible*, a key
member of the movement that has been termed New French Extremism, does
seem to do everything in his considerable cinematic power to drive them away.
In *Irréversible* (2002) he subjected them to a story told backwards that featured
both an unspeakably graphic sequence of a man having his head stoved in with a
fire extinguisher and a nine-minute rape, shot from a fixed camera, that was, for
more than a few viewers, quite literally unwatchable. Now with *Enter the Void* he
delivers a barely coherent, drug-drenched hallucination which, among other firsts,
includes an explicit sexual penetration shot from the point of view of the vagina.
A brave experiment, pushing cinema to its very limits and beyond? Or porn and
provocation dressed up as art: the ultimate bad trip? Well, probably both.

Loosely influenced by notions of reincarnation taken from The Tibetan Book
of the Dead, *Enter the Void* begins with a botched drug deal at a Tokyo nightclub
(The Void), in which small-time American dealer Oscar (Nathaniel Brown) is shot
by cops while trying to flush his stash down a filthy squat toilet. Subsequently his
soul rises out of his body and floats above the pulsating, roiling city, observing its
inhabitants and their lives, particularly that of his sister (Paz de la Huerta), who
came to Tokyo at his behest only to find employment as a stripper and is now in
an exploitative relationship with a sleazy pole-dancing-club owner.

The screen becomes a cauldron of light and the visuals Noé conjures from it
are indescribably strange and occasionally alarming: luminous fractal patterns
coalesce and converge, strobing light seems to reveal shadowy human shapes
burned in one's retina as an after-image, at one point the whole city throbs and
pulses with a jaundiced yellow light. The edges of cars, buildings and people
bleed Kirlian hues. In one of his loopier contrivances, when prostitutes and their
clients fuck – and they do so to excess in this film – their genitals emit a golden

ectoplasm. It's a symphony of psychedelic sleaze: Hieronymus Bosch daubed in neon. All the while the camera, representing Nathaniel's soul's endlessly shifting point of view, drifts, twists and zooms above, around and beneath his nightmarish vision of Tokyo, through strip joints, love hotels, drug dens and abortion clinics. Buried in this incredible visual excess is a stark human tragedy. Observing his childhood we see that Oscar and his sister were orphaned in a car crash (horrifically staged and repeatedly shown), and that their lives have slowly unravelled from that point onwards. In the midst of all this impressionism the sequence in which a screaming five-year-old girl is dragged from her brother by social workers recalls *Cathy Come Home* (1966) in its gut-wrenching misery.

Recommending *Enter the Void* without a slew of caveats would be critically reckless: it assaults the senses, tries the patience, occasionally upsets the stomach and suffers from acting that might, charitably, be described as uncertain. But if you watch closely, and with the kind of sympathy for these children lost in a DayGlo nightmare that Noé brings to this unique, uncompromising film, it's also one that might break your heart.

Neon nightmare: Tokyo seen through the hallucinatory camera of Gaspar Noé in *Enter the Void*.

Eternal Sunshine of the Spotless Mind

2004, US, 108 mins, 15 (UK) R (US)

....

cast Jim Carrey, Kate Winslet, Kirsten Dunst, Mark Ruffalo, Elijah Wood, Tom Wilkinson *scr* Charlie Kaufman (story Charlie Kaufman, Michel Gondry, Pierre Bismuth) *cin* Ellen Kuras *m* Jon Brion *dir* Michel Gondry

As Joel, Jim Carrey shows a less familiar serious side in his relationship with quirky Clementine (Kate Winslet), in Michel Gondry and Charlie Kaufman's inventive collaboration.

Ever since Jerry Lewis's revelatory turn in Scorsese's *The King of Comedy* in 1983 popular American comedians have been lining up to show their more serious sides, and presumably garner what they consider to be artistic credibility. In recent years Robin Williams investigated his darker depths to great effect in *Insomnia* and the excellent *One Hour Photo* (both 2002), while Adam Sandler played it straight in *Punch-Drunk Love* (2003, p.197). Jim Carrey, the most successful film comedian of the 1990s (he broke records with his $20 million pay cheque for *The Cable Guy* in 1996), had dabbled with a more serious side in Peter Weir's prophetic *The Truman Show* (1998) and Milos Forman's Andy Kaufman biopic *Man on the Moon* in 1999. But it was with this dazzling, labyrinthine, ideas-stuffed film that he really showed that he had the chops to make it as a compelling, serious actor.

Not so much downplaying his trademark zaniness as obliterating it under layers of mumbles and diverted glances, Carrey is Joel Barish, a profoundly lonely man who one day impulsively ditches work and heads to Montauk on Long Island where he wanders the almost deserted beach. There he catches sight of a young woman, Clementine (Kate Winslet) who, on the train back, begins to talk to him. They appear ideally suited, her zestiness bringing him out of his shell, and the two embark on an affair. But after a row Joel finds that Clementine has employed the services of Lacuna Inc, a brainwashing service, and has had all trace of him obliterated from her memory. Angry, Joel decides to do the same, but lying unconscious in his apartment hooked up to Lacuna's jerry-rigged contraptions he changes his mind. Thus for the bulk of the film Joel chases the fading Clem through his faltering memory. Of course, when memory is unreliable, *was* that in fact the first time they met? And might they be doomed, *Groundhog Day* style, to keep trying to remain together, only to fail and repeat the experience?

One of the strangest things about films written by Charlie Kaufman is that critics usually wind up talking about the screenplay rather than the director. He is perhaps the only writer in Hollywood who is discussed in auteur terms. Here director Michel Gondry matches the apparently endless flow of ideas with visual invention: sets seem to bleed into one another, street signs subtly erase themselves during dialogue scenes, buildings age and crumble to dust, and he cleverly uses dimming light and shadow to represent fading recollection. (And he increases this sense of time out of joint by placing the opening credits a full eighteen minutes after the start of the movie.) But this is predominantly a film of ideas. It's probably impossible to distil a single point from all these conceptual pyrotechnics: the obvious question is even if it were possible to erase bad memories, should we? Would we just be doomed to repeat them? And do memories change of their own accord anyway, fading, losing their edge, protecting us from constantly reliving painful past moments?

Winslet is on feisty form as the impulsive Clem (though with her mood changing as unpredictably as her hair colour, it's difficult to imagine anyone lasting long with her) but it's Carrey who really convinces as a man trapped in himself; he lends the character of Joel an affecting melancholic air. Sadly he subsequently seemed unable or uninterested in capitalizing on this real promise. Instead recently we find him extracting cheap laughs from flatulent CGI penguins in *Mr. Popper's Penguins* (2011), a cinematic first that, perhaps, we'd all pay to forget.

MARK RUFFALO

b. 22 Nov 1967, Kenosha, WI, US

"Survivor" is probably as good a description as any when it comes to Mark Ruffalo. Not only did he struggle through a decade or so of mediocre movies and TV in the 90s only to invent himself in the 2000s as one of America's most versatile and reliable character actors, he survived a brain tumour which at one point looked like it might put an end to his career before it had begun to flower. He'd almost broken through to the mainstream in 1999 with roles in Ang Lee's Civil War drama *Ride with the Devil* and the flawed but still more than watchable *Studio 54*, both of which underperformed. But it was a couple of years later, with *You Can Count on Me* (2001), a painfully honest examination of sibling relationships in which he played with uncanny sensitivity a wayward brother trying to reconnect with his older sister (Laura Linney), that he caught the eye of indie audiences and various festival awards panels. He had to drop out of M. Night Shyamalan's *Signs* (2002) when he fell ill to be replaced by Joaquin Phoenix at the last minute. His too-frequent attempts at rom-com have been non-starters with both *View From the Top* (2003), co-starring Gwyneth Paltrow, and *13 Going on 30* (2004) with Jennifer Garner failing to ignite the screen or box office. Character-driven drama seems to be his natural home and he excelled as friend of a dying Sarah Polley in cancer drama *My Life Without Me* (2003). He provided solid support to Robert Downey Jr and Jake Gyllenhaal as a homicide detective in David Fincher's compelling serial killer flick *Zodiac* (2007), and performed the same task alongside Leonardo DiCaprio in *Shutter Island* (2010, p.207), with whom he had almost equal screen time (and watching the film a second time reveals his to be the much more complex and enjoyable performance). He's been generally wary of the summer blockbuster but excelled as Bruce Banner/The Hulk in *Avengers Assemble* (2012), a gutsy move given that both Eric Bana and Ed Norton had failed to launch the character in recent films. Perhaps more interestingly, he's scheduled to appear in *Now You See Me* – Louis Leterrier's promising thriller about a group of illusionist thieves pursued by the FBI, with a dream cast including Woody Harrelson, Michael Caine, Morgan Freeman and James Franco's younger brother, Dave.

Far From Heaven

2003, US/Fr, 107 mins, 12A (UK) PG-13 (US)

••

cast Julianne Moore, Dennis Quaid, Dennis Haysbert, Patricia Clarkson *scr* Todd Haynes *cin* Edward Lachman *m* Elmer Bernstein *dir* Todd Haynes

Todd Haynes' decision to revisit what were dismissed at the time as "women's pictures" – the lush melodramas produced by, among others, Douglas Sirk in the 1950s, with shamelessly overwrought titles such as *All That Heaven Allows* (1955) and *Written on the Wind* (1956) – might seem quixotic at first. After all,

despite their recent critical reappraisal, what could these ancient Technicolor artefacts have to say to modern audiences? But what emerged was no dusty museum piece or pointless theoretical exercise, but a powerfully acted, beautifully made and emotionally wrenching drama, and a picture of the agonies of repression and shame in matters of race and sex that are, thankfully, at least mostly behind us.

Things look almost perfect for the Whitakers, an upper-middle-class couple living in leafy Hartford, Connecticut. Frank (Dennis Quaid) is the ultimate company man, an executive at TV manufacturers "Magnatech", where comments about the female employees' dresses are welcomed, not grounds for an employment tribunal, and his secretary's first duty in the morning is to take his coat and hat and hand him his coffee (into which we see him sneak a slug of whiskey, the first intimation that things may not be as rosy with Frank as they seem). Meanwhile Cathy (a radiant Julianne Moore), her couture perfectly colour co-ordinated with the blazing New England fall, spends her time wrangling her perfectly behaved children ("That's not the kind of language

we use in this house!" she exclaims when the boy lets fly with a "Gosh Darn!"), organizing social functions and sipping afternoon daiquiris with the gals (notably the splendid Patricia Clarkson as best friend and acid gossip Eleanor). But when she discovers hubby in a shocking lip-lock with another man, Cathy's world shatters and she finds herself tempted by her own forbidden love for handsome young black gardener, Raymond (Dennis Haysbert playing the kind of genre-appropriate "saintly black" role that Sidney Poitier made his own). In the repressed, racist world of 1950s Connecticut, heartbreak and social catastrophe are the inevitable result.

The values and attitudes of that time are now so alien to us that the greatest risk Haynes ran was the danger of pastiche, of the film inadvertently turning into a snarky period spoof, a kind of low-wattage version of *The Brady Bunch Movie* (1995). But Haynes' control and commitment to his characters effortlessly dispel any notion of this as crass satire. Technically the film is a joy: production designer Mark Friedberg and costumier Sandy Powell meticulously re-create the styles of the times while veteran composer Elmer Bernstein's score (his last before his death in 2004) swoons and soars. Quaid, a consistently underestimated actor, shows here what he's capable of – given the material – as the shame-wracked husband whose visit to a psychiatrist in order to help him "beat this thing" is one of the film's disconcerting highlights. But at *Far From Heaven*'s shattered heart is Julianne Moore's captivating performance as Cathy, a woman whose essential decency and courage shine through, and which in the way of true tragedy, are finally her undoing. Devotees of Sirk pictures will know that the genre does not lend itself to happy endings: now, as then, bring Kleenex.

Haute couture: a stunningly costumed Julianne Moore descends the staircase in Todd Haynes' impeccably detailed period piece *Far From Heaven*.

PATRICIA CLARKSON
b. 29 December 1959, New Orleans, LA, US

"[Her] performances stand out in current American film like crisp martinis in a soda fountain," was *The New York Times* columnist Ben Brantley's verdict on "Queen of the Indies" Patricia Clarkson, a name that, go on admit it, you're having difficulty putting a face to, back in 2004. To push the boozy metaphor a little further: her style is often dry and understated but her performances slowly reveal their depth – in her turn as a grieving mother in Thomas McCarthy's *The Station Agent* (2004, p.220), or as a dying woman in 2004's *Pieces of April*, for which she was Oscar nominated. These, then, are performances that are not shaken but carefully stirred. But equally she can inject a champagne fizz of glamorous wit in the likes of George Clooney's Edward R. Murrow biopic *Good Night, and Good Luck* (2006) or *The Scarlet Letter* update *Easy A* (2010), in which she played an eccentric mother (mums being something of a speciality). After toiling through the 80s and 90s in theatre, small film roles and television, she made something of a cinematic breakthrough in 1999 with Lisa Cholodenko's tale of a druggily destructive lesbian relationship *High Art*, for which she garnered rave reviews. Subsequently Sean Penn cast her as a grieving mother in his gloomy but excellent *The Pledge* (2001), while Lars von Trier had her as a vindictive townswoman in *Dogville* (2004). She channelled her inner Agnes Moorhead and delivered, in a single beautifully achieved reaction shot, the most heart-rending moment in Todd Haynes' melodrama *Far From Heaven*. From the mid-2000s she started alternating her independent work with bigger, showier Hollywood movies, playing the role of Rachel 2 ("a woman in a cave", as she put it) in a key scene of Scorsese's *Shutter Island* (2010, p.207), while Woody Allen cast her in both *Vicky Cristina Barcelona* (2009) and alongside Larry David in *Whatever Works* (2010). She also had great fun pawing a mostly naked Justin Timberlake as another mother, this time to Mila Kunis, in sparky rom-com *Friends With Benefits* (2011).

The best remakes...

OCEAN'S ELEVEN
(Steven Soderbergh, 2002)

The best kind of movie to remake: one that wasn't much good in the first place. Soderbergh packs his sleek and sexy heist movie with the cream of the A-List in Clooney, Damon and Pitt, seasons it with a dose of retro-cool in the shape of Elliott Gould and doesn't neglect to include what the 1960 original so obviously lacked – a plot.

THE MANCHURIAN CANDIDATE
(Jonathan Demme, 2004)

The 1962 Cold War classic is niftily transposed to a contemporary setting with giant military/industrial conglomerates replacing superpowers as the source of the film's pervasive paranoia. Liev Schreiber is fine as the brainwashed politico but it's Meryl Streep as his creepy mother (originally played by Angela Lansbury) who steals the show.

MY BLOODY VALENTINE
(Patrick Lussier, 2009)

Amidst the depressing slew of low-quality remakes of 80s slashers here's one that got it right. *Scream* (1997) editor Lussier piles on the imaginative gore and gratuitous nudity in this fanboy crowd-pleaser about a guy with a (pick) axe to grind. All in entirely genre-appropriate 3D.

LET ME IN
(Matt Reeves, 2010)

An object lesson in how to take a beautifully wrought foreign-language film (*Let The Right One In*, p.157) and translate it for American audiences. *Cloverfield* (2008, p.54) director Matt Reeves doesn't impose himself on the story, transferring the action from Sweden to New Mexico but maintaining its creepy romanticism, and adding a few subtle touches of his own.

TRUE GRIT
(Joel Coen & Ethan Coen, 2011)

The Coens had attempted a remake before with *The Ladykillers* (2004), to decidedly mixed reactions, but this retreading of the 1969 Henry Hathaway classic featured a barnstormer of a performance from Coen fave Jeff Bridges in the John

The worst remakes...

PLANET OF THE APES
(Tim Burton, 2001)

Burton was always an odd choice for this re-imagining of the 1968 sci-fi classic. Mark Wahlberg seems lost, the vital political subtext has evaporated, the plot makes no sense and, unusually for Burton, it doesn't even look very good either.

THE PINK PANTHER
(Shawn Levy, 2006)

An utterly depressing, mirthless attempt to raise Clouseau from the dead by Steve Martin, a comedy actor capable of so much more. The most astonishing thing about it was that they actually made a sequel in 2009. If anything, it was worse.

HALLOWEEN
(Rob Zombie, 2007)

The great strength of John Carpenter's 1978 classic was the terrifyingly motiveless nature of killing-machine Michael Myers. In this inept retread, Rob Zombie helpfully provides exactly the backstory – childhood abuse, *yawn* – that Carpenter knew was not only unnecessary but would destroy the atmosphere of pure unadulterated terror.

SLEUTH
(Kenneth Branagh, 2007)

Director of the Worst British Film Ever Made (*Peter's Friends*, 1992), Kenneth Branagh returns to terrible form in this revival of the 1972 twisty two-hander. Harold Pinter's adaptation of Anthony Shaffer's original screenplay plays like Pinter-pastiche, Jude Law's performance might best be described as eccentric and Michael Caine, who starred in the original, clearly gives up and switches on the autopilot halfway through.

ARTHUR
(Jason Winer, 2011)

A cursory glance at the 1981 surprise smash-hit would have revealed that it relied almost completely on Dudley Moore's unforced charm and finely calibrated performance. Russell Brand is no Dudley Moore and Helen Mirren, never a comedy actress anyway, is hopelessly miscast in a version of the role

Femme Fatale

2002, Fr, 114 mins, 15 (UK) R (US)

••

cast Rebecca Romijn-Stamos, Antonio Banderas, Peter Coyote, Eriq Ebouaney *scr* Brian De Palma *cin* Thierry Arbogast *m* Ryûichi Sakamoto *dir* Brian De Palma

The irrepressible playfulness of Brian De Palma's paean to *film noir* begins even before the movie itself, with the trailer. In it the image of an icy blonde is reflected in a television screen on which is playing Billy Wilder's classic *noir*, *Double Indemnity* (1944). The images suddenly accelerate and we witness the whole film right through to the credits. "You've just watched Brian De Palma's new film …" a title card reads. "Didn't get it? Try again…"

Explaining the plot is a fool's errand; suffice it to say that it involves the daring heist of a ridiculous piece of clothing-cum-jewellery (worn to the Cannes Film Festival) by a meticulously organized gang which includes icy Laure (Rebecca Romijn-Stamos). She subsequently betrays her pals and high-tails it to the US, only to crop up back in France seven years later, it seems, as Lily, the wife of an American diplomat in Paris. There are doppelgängers, double, triple and quadruple crosses, mistaken identity, premonition, outrageous time-shifting and murder, all seasoned with a dangerous, almost sleazy sexuality, an aesthetic familiar to De Palma devotees from his equally daring, and audience dividing, *Body Double* (1984). Romijn-Stamos is superb as the protean deadly female; sometimes she conjures the classic Hitchcockian blonde, at others she's a thoroughly modern predator, Sharon Stone out of *Basic Instinct* (1992). If there's a weak link it's Antonio Banderas, cast no doubt to add some movie-star lustre, as the paparazzo drawn into her insanely complex web. But no matter, this is not a movie that depends for much on its actors: this is the director's show.

De Palma, always the technical maestro, delivers possibly his most accomplished work here. The sublime opening heist sequence is a wordless fifteen-minute montage set at the (real) Cannes Film Festival that involves a lesbian sex scene/striptease/jewellery theft played out against a frosted toilet cubicle window, a descent by wire à la his own *Mission: Impossible* (1996), night vision and the amusing intervention of a curious cat, all cut to Ravel's *Bolero*. De Palma employs his full array of tools fearlessly. Ultra deep focus, unbroken steadicam shots, simultaneous multiple viewpoints and razor editing are all deployed to dazzling effect.

Icy blonde: Rebecca Romijn-Stamos channels Hitchcock in Brian De Palma's technically brilliant homage to *noir*.

It is, of course, nowhere near realism. This is a kind of *haute cinema*: just as the clothes on the catwalk are unlikely to be entirely practical for use anywhere else, so De Palma's movie doesn't really function as a conventional thriller, but as a deliriously inventive essay on how far he can push the genre and about how far we are willing to come for the ride. It's more than thirty years since Michael Pye and Linda Myles's book christened the directors of Hollywood's second golden age *The Movie Brats*. Of those directors – Spielberg, Scorsese, Lucas, Coppola, Milius – De Palma remains the most unpredictable, capable of brilliance like this, commercial misfires such as *Mission To Mars* (2000) and extreme avant-gardism like *Redacted* (2007). But *Femme Fatale* is as good as he gets. As the trailer cheekily suggests, it's a movie to enjoy again and again and again.

The Fighter

2010, US, 116 mins, 15 (UK) R (US)

••

cast Mark Wahlberg, Christian Bale, Melissa Leo, Jack McGee, Amy Adams *scr* Scott Silver and Paul Tamasy & Eric Johnson *cin* Hoyte Van Hoytema *m* Michael Brook *dir* David O. Russell

The real fight surrounding this splendidly entertaining boxing flick was to get it made at all. Mark Wahlberg (see box, p.68) had first been pitched the idea in 2001 and was enthusiastic enough about playing real-life welterweight champ "Irish" Micky Ward that he had a boxing ring installed in his home and started training. He turned out to have plenty of sparring time, as it would be almost a decade before the movie began shooting. Wahlberg was at one point replaced with rapper Eminem, director Darren Aronofsky left to helm his own fight-movie *The Wrestler* (2008, p.255), Matt Damon arrived and departed, then so did Brad Pitt. To cap it all studio Paramount suddenly took fright at the projected $100 million budget and cancelled the project. When a director did call action it was David O. Russell, who had worked successfully with Wahlberg on *Three Kings* (1999) and the underrated *I ❤ Huckabees* (2004), armed with a relatively tiny budget of $24 million and 37 days to shoot a movie packed with complicated pugilistic action.

Russell cleverly uses the film's low budget to great advantage, delivering a loosely shot "indie"-looking film that effectively disguises the high performance, six-cylinder Hollywood triumph-against-the odds tale that thrums at its heart. Micky is a struggling amateur fighter who works laying asphalt in blue-collar Lowell, Massachusetts, while he's supposedly being trained by his motormouth brother Dicky

CHRISTIAN BALE

b. 30 January 1974, Haverfordwest, UK

Early success in the movie industry is often more of a curse than a blessing. The perilous path from child star to adult actor is lined with failed careers, and in some cases – River Phoenix and Brad Renfro come to mind – more tragic outcomes. Christian Bale had shot to prominence at the tender age of thirteen for his performance in Steven Spielberg's *Empire of the Sun* (1988) but his career in the 1990s yielded mixed results and for a while it looked like he may have been destined for an appointment with some "Where Are They Now?" column. But all that changed in 1999 when director Mary Harron cast him as Patrick Bateman, the unforgettable lead in her darkly funny adaptation of Bret Easton Ellis's satire of 80s excess *American Psycho* (2000). (Or rather she cast him twice, at one point walking off the film when the studio replaced him with Leonardo DiCaprio.) Bale's performance here would be typical of his future approach, harnessing an exceptional psychological intensity to radical physical transformation (he spent months creating Bateman's "Olympian" physique) with impressive effect. His first mature attempt at a conventional blockbuster, dragon-themed fantasy *Reign of Fire* (2002), failed to ignite the box office and his sci-fi effort *Equilibrium* (2003) didn't do much better, though typically he spent weeks learning its manufactured martial art "Gun Kata". He then returned to indie fare, losing more than sixty pounds on a diet consisting of a can of tuna and a single apple a day, for his role as insomniac factory worker Trevor Reznik in intriguing and finally harrowing mystery *The Machinist* (2005), only to have to bulk up again when Christopher Nolan cast him in his wildly successful re-imagining of the caped crusader in *Batman Begins* (2005). His attempt to revive a second dormant franchise with McG's *Terminator Salvation* (2009) was disastrous, more famous for a leaked on-set rant at cinematographer Shane Hurlbut than anything else, though his co-starring role as a crack-addicted former pugilist in *The Fighter* was a return to blazing form. After the Batman trilogy came to a close with *The Dark Knight Rises* (2012), he signed up with Terrence Malick for *The Knight of Cups* and *Lawless*, which were shot back to back in 2011–12 amidst the secrecy typical of the fastidiously mysterious director.

(Christian Bale), a minor ex-champ living on the fumes of his past glory and his crack-pipe. But most of the film's drama happens outside the ring, in the working-class kitchens, bars and bedrooms of this industrial city. Micky's real problem isn't his relative lack of success in his chosen sport but his utterly dysfunctional family: mom (the fantastically harridanish Melissa Yeo) is supposedly his manager but puts him up against opponents that make mincemeat of him, while his dad (Jack McGee) spends most of his time dodging the flying cookware. Only girlfriend Charlene (Amy Adams) sees that Micky's real fight – the one he really has to win – is to separate himself from his screwy family and strike out on his own.

Much critical praise (as well as a best supporting actor Oscar) was directed towards Bale, who is excellent as the mile-a-minute gabbing, self-deluded ex-champ. But it falls to Wahlberg to deliver the much less showy, more complicated (and unfortunately less Oscar-friendly) role of Micky. Introverted, wounded more by his family's inability to come together to support him than by the punishment he endures in the ring, he's the battered soul at the centre of this movie. There's something infinitely attractive and finally touching about his quiet, bruised presence: it's another nice surprise in a career that seems to have been full of them. And if you were ever in any doubt about the Hollywood credentials of this unashamed audience-pleaser it delivers the stand-up-and-cheer ending that even the mighty *Rocky* (1976) denied them: Micky wins.

Sibling rivalry: amateur fighter Micky Ward (Mark Wahlberg) in the ring with ex-champ brother Dicky (Christian Bale) in David O. Russell's loosely shot pugilistic prizewinner.

Fish Tank

2009, UK, 123 mins, 15 (UK) Unrated (US)

ANDREA ARNOLD

b. 5 April 1966, Dartford, UK

Andrea Arnold began her professional life on TV – as a dancer on *Top of the Pops* and presenter of ITV's live Saturday morning children's show *No. 73* (alongside Sandi Toksvig) – but by the beginning of the noughties she had attended the prestigious American Film Institute Conservatory and reinvented herself as a filmmaker. Her debut was *Red Road* (2006), a Glaswegian-set study of surveillance and obsession centred on a CCTV operator. Conceived by Lars von Trier as part of the Advance Party project – a trilogy of films featuring the same characters, initially devised by him and his collaborators, but made by different directors (the second film, *Donkeys* by Morag McKinnon, was released in 2010 with the third remaining unproduced) – it gained critical raves and a Cannes Jury Prize. *Fish Tank* took Arnold directly into British social realist territory with its achingly moving depiction of a young teenage girl's hopes and disappointments on a deprived housing estate. Her next move, in 2011, came as a surprise: an adaptation of *Wuthering Heights*, though her habit of casting non-professional actors continued with her choice of complete newcomer James Howson, who is black, as Heathcliff. She and regular cinematographer Robbie Ryan also gave the film a raw, brutal look completely at odds with the BBC heritage style of adaptations of literary classics, presenting the harsh desolation of the Yorkshire landscape in images so stark one critic wrote that it "looked like it was set a hundred years after a nuclear strike". She remains one of Britain's brightest directorial hopes, though is perhaps so far more famous worldwide for inadvertently introducing a billion Oscar viewers to the phrase "the dog's bollocks" in her acceptance speech for her short film *Wasp* in 2003. Moving out of live television might, it appears, have been a good decision in more ways than one.

cast Katie Jarvis, Michael Fassbender, Kierston Wareing, Rebecca Griffiths, Harry Treadaway
scr Andrea Arnold *cin* Robbie Ryan *dir* Andrea Arnold

With its struggling working-class characters, kitchen sinks and gritty housing estates, Andrea Arnold's second feature might seem to fall neatly into the grand tradition of British social realism, a venerable cinematic movement that has been dominated by those masters of miserabilism Ken Loach and Mike Leigh for four decades now. But Arnold's film brings a new energy to the deliberately depressing tropes, while deftly avoiding the didactic preachiness that often bedevils them. Key to her success is an astonishing, seemingly one-off performance from Katie Jarvis, a young woman from a background almost identical to that of the character she plays.

We meet Mia (Jarvis) as she wanders, charged with a fifteen-year-old's boundless, unfocused energy, around the estate, located on the fringes of London where the city peters out into Essex and the Thames estuary, where she lives with her emotionally abusive mother (Kierston Wareing, who doesn't look much older than Jarvis does), and her younger, tomboyish sister (energetically played by Rebecca Griffiths). Together they occupy their time with booze, bad television and relentless verbal. Mia, expelled from school and, quite understandably, happiest out of the house, spends her time swigging cheap cider when she can afford it and practising her hip-hop dancing in an abandoned flat (in clear evidence that we're not in Hollywoodland, she's not very good). But one day she comes home to find that Connor (Michael Fassbender), a good-looking young security guard with a broad chest and winning smile, has moved in to the already cramped flat and into her mother's bed. Connor takes the family on a drive to the countryside, encourages Mia in her dancing and refrains from telling her to fuck off. Is it surprising then that a dangerous attraction develops between them?

Some critics wondered whether Jarvis's titanium-edged performance was much of an acting feat, or whether she was just playing herself. She was, after all, famously discovered at a railway station having an across-the-platforms slanging

Katie Jarvis as boundlessly energetic Mia, practising her urban moves in Andrea Arnold's naturally lit drama, *Fish Tank*.

match with her boyfriend, and had grown up on the same kind of estates featured in the film. There's clearly a lot of Katie in Mia, but she was seventeen at the time of filming yet manages to channel the riptide of incoherent, overwhelming emotions of a fifteen-year-old. Arnold's precise direction finds in Mia moments of unsentimental pathos and vulnerability, as when she finds that the dancing audition she is excited about is for a strip club, but also, towards the end of the film, a much darker side to her character manifests in a sequence of almost unbearable, nail-biting tension. Fassbender meanwhile manages to shroud Connor's character in some ambiguity. He is no uncomplicated predatory paedophile, as some have suggested, more a manipulative man who uses his looks and easy charm to extract exactly what he wants – materially and emotionally – from vulnerable women, but whose concern and kindness can also be genuine.

Arnold and cinematographer Robbie Ryan shoot for the most part in the traditional *verité* style – largely handheld and using only natural light. But the film is also studded with moments of ragged lyricism: a mangy white horse chained up on a piece of scrubby wasteland who Mia tries to free has distant echoes of the white steeds of fairy tales; a wide horizon shot of a thunderstorm over the estate or sparrows wheeling in an azure sky act as brief but jolting visual contrasts to the physical monotony and emotional poverty of Mia's life. It's sad to say, but the one moment in *Fish Tank* that doesn't reek of authenticity is the tiny note of hope at the end.

CRUEL INTENTIONS
The new cinema of suffering

A semi-naked American backpacker, strapped to a chair in an abandoned Slovakian factory, looks on in terror as his captor reaches for a drill. In the Australian bush a bound woman has her spine deliberately severed by a crazed serial killer. "Now you're just a head on a stick," he leers at her. Sometime in 2006 *New York Magazine* film critic David Eldelstein, having peered through his fingers at scenes such as these (from *Saw* and *Wolf Creek*, respectively), coined the phrase "torture-porn" to describe the gory new trend, in the process offending horror fans, who resented having the genre so denigrated, and providing grist to thousands of alarmed opinion pieces in the world's media.

James Wan's low-budget shocker *Saw* (2004), in which a terminally ill psychotic known as "Jigsaw" designs fiendish traps for his victims, escape from which almost inevitably involves dismemberment in some form or other, is commonly held to be the genesis of the bloody fad. Costing just $1.2 million to make, the film was an unexpected sensation, taking more than $100 million at the box office. Eli Roth's *Hostel* (2006, p.129) followed, as did Rob Zombie's (aka Robert Cummings) *The Devil's Rejects* (2005), the continuing and even bloodier adventures of the Firefly family, a nightmarish brood of motiveless killers to whom he had introduced audiences in *House of 1000 Corpses* (2003). Other notable entries in the gruesome canon included Australian contribution *Wolf Creek* (2005), *The Collector* (2010), *Captivity* (2007) and Tom Six's outrageous *The Human Centipede: First Sequence* (2010), in which a trio of victims find themselves stitched together by a deranged surgeon.

Many appalled critics bewailed what they saw as a new low in horror cinema, while some feminists claimed to detect a newly strident misogyny in the movies. In fact, one of their unusual characteristics was their equal-opportunities sadism: the principal victims in *Hostel* are all male and all seven films in the *Saw* franchise were pretty much gender neutral in terms of the unfortunates Jigsaw strapped into his increasingly ludicrous contraptions.

But by the end of the decade the trend seemed to have exhausted itself. *Hostel Part II* (2007) failed to repeat the box-office success of the first movie, the *Saw* franchise clanked and shrieked to a halt with *Saw VI* (2009), presented, somewhat inevitably, in 3D, while *A Serbian Film* (2010) pushed the sub-genre further than either audiences or censors were willing to tolerate, gaining only a limited release in the UK after the BBFC cut more than four minutes of footage which featured, among other outrages, the rape of a newborn baby. Tom Six's *The Human Centipede II (Full Sequence)* was initially banned outright in 2011 before being released in a heavily censored form. Despite the emergence of the occasional genuinely original horror – found-footage poltergeist flick *Paranormal Activity* (2009) and British director Ben Wheatley's excellent *Kill List* (2011) among them – it left the genre to be dominated by insipid remakes of 1980s slasher franchises such as 2009's *Friday the 13th* and *Nightmare on Elm Street* (2010), which, in their dreary predictability, subjected horror fans to an exquisite little torture of their own.

Funny Games U.S.

2008, US, 111 mins, 18 (UK) R (US)

....

cast Michael Pitt, Brady Corbert, Tim Roth, Naomi Watts *scr* Michael Haneke
cin Darius Khondji *dir* Michael Haneke

Not what they seem: clean-cut duo Paul (Michael Pitt) and Peter (Brady Corbert) confront affluent Ann (Naomi Watts) in her vacation home and it's not a game of golf they're looking for.

Whatever else there is to say about it, there is something magnificently bloody-minded about Michael Haneke's virtually shot-for-shot American remake of his 1997 German-language film of the same title. The visually identical do-over has been tried before of course, most notably with Gus Van Sant's cinematic Xeroxing of *Psycho* (1998). Haneke's motives were not some kind of formal cinematic experiment, though, but highly practical and fearsomely didactic. His original had

been made, he has said, with the intention that it be seen by a wide audience, the kind that went to the violent thrillers and horror movies of which it is in great part a blistering critique. As it bore for American audiences the cinematic Mark of Cain – subtitles – it had been predictably ignored. When the possibility of a US remake came up he agreed to it on condition that he direct and that it would be an identical copy in English. He wasn't going to let them have the excuse of subtitles any more.

The picturesque Austrian locales have been switched for The Hamptons, but otherwise events unfold with the same relentless cold-eyed horror as in the original. Ann (Naomi Watts) and George (Tim Roth) arrive at their vacation home only to be assailed by two well-spoken sociopaths dressed in tennis whites (a nod to another cinematic study of violence, Kubrick's *A Clockwork Orange* and its Droogs?). Referring to each other variously as Peter and Paul, Beavis and Butthead, and Tom and Jerry, they provide inconsistent and conflicting accounts of their motivations and coolly announce to the terrified family that they wish to make a bet: "You bet that you'll be alive tomorrow at 9 o'clock, and we bet that you'll be dead."

The obvious interpretation of this genuinely unsettling, undoubtedly skilfully made film is that it is a rebuke to the audience as being complicit in the violence on screen. At a key moment, while he is forcing a terrorized, blindfolded Ann to search for the the family's slaughtered dog (this is one of the milder moments), one of the tormentors turns to the camera and treats the audience to a complicit smile. This is the first in a series of increasingly strenuous Brechtian devices. Do you like what you are seeing? Enjoying it yet? *More?* Haneke's stated view is that violence can under no circumstances be entertaining, and yet Hollywood demands that we be entertained by it all the time. But there are other elements to the film that the relentless atmosphere of threat and horror often occlude, notably a commentary on race and class: the pair are immediately trusted because they are white and clearly middle-class; Ann and George would hardly have let a pair of black kids in. And the family have managed to isolate themselves from potential help by walling themselves inside an upper-class gated ghetto.

Like pupils forced to stand in the headmaster's office and be subjected to a lecture, critics reacted with a sullen rage. "It was like being told off for an hour and a half in German and now it's like being told off for an hour and a half in English," was one angry response. *Funny Games U.S.* is, like its identical twin, a brilliantly made, unapologetically moral piece of provocation – film as film criticism – but it was delivered to an empty room. Its intended audience was in the screen next door watching *Saw V* instead.

Gomorrah

2008, It, 131 mins, 15 (UK) R (US)

....

cast Salvatore Abruzzese, Toni Servillo, Gianfelice Imparato, Marco Macor, Ciro Petrone *scr* Maurizio Braucci, Ugo Chiti, Gianni Di Gregorio, Roberto Saviano, Massimo Gaudioso and Matteo Garrone (from the book by Roberto Saviano) *cin* Marco Onorato *dir* Matteo Garrone

Over the decades the Hollywood gangster movie has evolved into a genre that has about as much to do with the realities of organized crime as the cowboy flick has with the socio-political conditions of the American West in the mid-nineteenth century. Even at its very best it has become for the most part an assemblage of well-burnished tropes and high-end clichés: meticulously crafted bloodletting set to lush orchestral scores or fastidiously selected pop music. This, then, is a much needed corrective; it's a picture of what a society is really like when terminally infected with organized crime, whose corrosive tentacles wrap themselves round every part of life, choking off hope. There is no highfalutin talk of *omertà*, family or honour here. Just fear, desperation and dead teenagers.

The title is both a reference to the hellish situation of a city (in this case Naples) utterly corrupted and a pun on the name of the organization responsible, the Camorra. Based on a non-fiction book by Roberto Saviano, who is now forced to live under armed guard in case of reprisals, *Gomorrah* is structured as a tapestry of half a dozen interweaving tales: Totò (Salvatore Abruzzese) is a fresh-faced boy desperate to join the Camorra, but unprepared for the dreadful choice it will force him to make; Ciro (Ciro Petrone) and Marco (Marco Macor) are a pair of adolescent yahoos who enthusiastically quote De Palma's *Scarface* (1983) and whose thieving from gun-runners attracts the deadly attention of the local bosses; Don Ciro (Gianfelice Imparato) is a mostly terrified courier, a middle-aged errand boy doling out cash to those the mob deems deserving.

The result is narratively gripping and beautifully acted by a mainly non-professional cast in the tradition of Italian neorealism. But it is the sense of place created by director Matteo Garrone that really impresses. The main action is set in a rotting housing estate in the Naples suburb of Scampia, a concrete ziggurat that could have been designed for crime (and who knows, given the way building contracts are awarded, may well have been), through which his mostly handheld camera darts and weaves. But then occasionally he breaks out into moments of visual surreality. A wide shot shows a pool party taking place on the roof above the sprawling estate. Marco and Ciro fire their guns and grenade launchers, mysteriously clad only in their underpants, on a deserted sandbar. He studiously avoids, though, the glamour of his American counterparts: the dispiritingly frequent shootings are rapid and shocking in their mundanity; there is blood, but it is not dwelt upon or marvelled at, just spilled.

One of the odd things about those classic American gangster movies is how little you ever see what all this utter misery is really about: money. Here it is everywhere, grubby Euros doled out to bad-tempered retired thugs, exchanged in minor drug deals, shoved into pockets and wallets. It is endlessly counted and recounted. There is one moment of muted optimism, in a film that cries out for it, when a single character walks out on the corruption. But you don't hold out much hope for him. His boss (Toni Servillo), a local politician and the nearest thing here to the urbane thugs of a Coppola movie, has been illegally flooding dumping sites with carcinogenic waste. In Gomorrah the very earth you walk on is poisoned.

Naked guns: Ciro (Ciro Petrone) and Marco (Marco Macor) shoot up the Neapolitan riverbank in *Gomorrah*, a bleak tale of organized crime.

Gone Baby Gone

2008, US, 114 mins, 15 (UK) R (US)

....

cast Casey Affleck, Michelle Monaghan, Morgan Freeman, Ed Harris, Titus Welliver, Amy Ryan *scr* Ben Affleck & Aaron Stockard (from the novel by Dennis Lehane) *cin* John Toll *m* Harry Gregson-Williams *dir* Ben Affleck

Gone Baby Gone, Ben Affleck's hugely impressive feature-length directorial debut, begins with a montage of images of working-class Boston. "I lived on this block my whole life, most of these people have," a man's voice, soft, resigned, almost regretful, says as images of hardened faces and battered bodies float by. "When your job is to find people who are missing, it helps to know where they started. I find the people who started in the cracks and then fell through." Then the tone of the montage shifts. We see flyers with a child's face on them. A four-year-old girl has vanished without a trace and the grim circus that surrounds such a catastrophe, the flashing cameras, forest of microphones and stricken faces, has rolled into town.

It's fair to say that things will not get any more cheerful. The voice is that of Patrick Kenzie (Casey Affleck), who works alongside his partner both professional and personal, Angie Gennaro (Michelle Monaghan), as a private detective. They are asked by the little girl's aunt and uncle – her mother (an excellent Amy Ryan), a foul-mouthed drunk, feckless and a coke-head to boot, seems singularly unhelpful – to help the police find her. At first they demur. Their expertise is in bail-jumpers and petty thieves. What they uncover is a cast of corrupt cops, psychotic drug dealers and paedophiles all with motives as thick as their accents. And at the heart of this stew is a genuinely wrenching moral dilemma, one with no obviously right answer: the very definition of a tragedy.

Affleck captures the texture of Dorchester Heights, the blue-collar area of Boston where he and Matt Damon set their breakthrough movie *Good Will Hunting* (1998), its mean streets, grimy bars and flimsy housing, as well as the half-wrecked lives of its more desperate inhabitants, with a keen director's eye. And he conjures a sombre, almost despairing atmosphere around this gripping, constantly surprising story, adapted from fellow Bostonian and *Mystic River* author Dennis Lehane's novel. Actor-wise, of course, there's not a first-time helmer alive who wouldn't give thanks to the patron saint of casting for the good fortune of having both Ed Harris and Morgan Freeman in their debut film (both reliably excellent as policemen with secrets), but perhaps surprisingly in company as distinguished as this, the film's strongest performance, and its dramatic core, comes from Casey Affleck. As Patrick, a private detective with a code of honour, he's a decent Catholic, a believer

A thoughtful Patrick Kenzie (Casey Affleck) ponders a murky moral universe against a Boston skyline.

CASEY AFFLECK

b. 12 August 1975, Falmouth, MA, US

For more than a few years it must have seemed to Casey Affleck that he would never escape the shadow of his older brother. But by the end of the 2000s, as Ben reinvented himself as a talented director, it was becoming clear that it was Casey who was the more interesting and versatile actor, regularly delivering the kind of complex and subtle performance that had for the most part eluded his more starry sibling. Until the mid-2000s his roles were often thespian table scraps from either big brother or his best mate Matt Damon: he had a small but highly enjoyable role in the pair's breakthrough movie *Good Will Hunting* (1998) as a youthful onanist; he was a Mormon getaway driver alongside Scott Caan in *Ocean's Eleven* (2002) and its sequels; and he starred alongside Damon again in Gus Van Sant's mysterious, elliptical and for non-Van Sant initiates, stupefyingly dull *Gerry* (2003), a film about two young men who get lost in the desert. His real breakthrough came with the Western *The Assassination of Jesse James by the Coward Robert Ford* (2007), in which he played Ford, delivering a fearlessly unappealing performance as the craven underling and eventual killer of Brad Pitt's eponymous outlaw. It was a part for which, as director Andrew Dominik remarked, a lifetime of living with a movie-star brother had perfectly prepared him. He was equally impressive in a very different role as the conscience-stricken private detective in Ben's directorial debut *Gone Baby Gone*. His most controversial role to date has been as Lou Ford, a small-town sheriff and psychotic sadist in Michael Winterbottom's *The Killer Inside Me* (2010), a movie that prompted walk-outs with its graphic depictions of misogynistic violence. Appearing in action hack Brett Ratner's *Tower Heist* (2011), though, was a retrograde move. A high concept star-hash intended at least partially as yet another attempt at a career resurrection for Eddie Murphy, it was, frankly, the kind of cynically conceived Hollywood fluff in which, a few years ago, you might easily have found his brother.

in good and evil, sin and redemption, and a man unprepared for a world in which such neat categories don't hold, where very bad things can be done for the most unexpected of reasons. It's a restrained, uncompromising and finally anguished performance.

Ben Affleck's career as an actor had frankly been faltering before he turned to directing. He had always looked mildly uncomfortable in the action star or matinee idol straitjacket into which Hollywood seemed determined to force him (see 2001's *Pearl Harbor* and 2003's catastrophic debacle *Gigli* for ample evidence). With this, and the similarly well-wrought, morally sophisticated heist movie *The Town* (2010), he proves himself not only a talented champion of a somewhat neglected genre, the intelligent adult crime thriller, but also an astute judge of material. Has he been on the wrong side of the camera all along?

Good Bye Lenin!

2003, Ger, 121 mins, 15 (UK) R (US)

....

cast Daniel Brühl, Katrin Saß, Maria Simon, Florian Lukas, Chulpan Khamatova
scr Bernd Lichtenberg & Wolfgang Becker *cin* Martin Kukula *m* Yann Tiersen
dir Wolfgang Becker

No less a personage than Vladimir Putin once said of Soviet Communism that you'd have to have no heart to miss it, and no brain to want it back. Wolfgang Becker's sprightly take on the Rip Van Winkle story addresses this very paradox: nostalgia for something you're largely relieved has gone forever. Set in East Germany just before the fall of the Berlin Wall, it has Christiane Kerner (Katrin Saß), a middle-aged supporter of the ruling Communist Party, spending much of her time dictating sharply worded missives to the commissariat regarding, among other matters of socialist sartorial concern, the inadequacy of women's underwear. When her son Alex (an instantly likeable Daniel Brühl) is beaten up in a demonstration the shock sends her into a months-long coma, during which the Wall falls. When she wakes up her doctors inform Alex that the slightest shock might kill her; the implosion of Communism obviously falls into this category, and so Alex, with the reluctant help of his sister (Maria Simon) and new nurse girlfriend Lara (Chulpan Khamatova), retrofits their flat back to its 1950s Communist look and strives to hide the new political realities from his mother.

This involves all kinds of entertaining subterfuge. Old pickle jars with pre-reunification labels are sourced and refilled. Alex and his sister return to wearing the dire duds of the GDR and engage the services of friends and neighbours to re-enact life as it was, which they do with varying levels of competence and enthusiasm. When a vast new Coca-Cola sign becomes visible from her window, Alex improvises a TV news broadcast with wannabe film-director workmate Denis (Florian Lukas), which informs his puzzled mother that the West has finally admitted that East German scientists invented Coke in the 1950s. And when mum eventually gets to the window, only to see the streets full of West German cars, he reverse-engineers the entire fall of Communism, informing her that East Germany is being overrun by refugees from the West escaping the free-market rat race.

Of course it is as much for his own sake as his mother's that Alex is trying to freeze time: not only can he see his childhood, like the GDR, receding into history, but the possibility of his mother's impending death is inherently associated with these geopolitical ructions. But as well as being a deftly played comedy, *Good*

Seeing is believing: the family of Christiane Kerner (Katrin Saß), crammed into a Trabant, conspire to keep the red flag flying despite the collapse of Communism.

Bye Lenin! might, politically speaking, be a more complex, nuanced film than the simple nostalgia-fest that some critics took it for. The benefits of capitalism are not immediately apparent from Alex's point of view. His sister drops out of university to get a job in that triumph of Western cuisine, Burger King. He loses his job when his admittedly ramshackle TV repair shop closes, but is subsequently forced into corporate-branded overalls to hawk mostly unwanted satellite dishes that rarely work. In one of Alex's more striking narrations he admits that in recreating Communism for the benefit of his mother, he is creating a kind of socialism that he could live with, a German Democratic Republic he would have wanted.

It may be difficult to rationally justify such affection for a regime that oppressed and murdered its citizens (see one of Germany's other key films of the millennium, *The Lives of Others*, 2007, p.161, for a contrasting view). But then *Good Bye Lenin!* is a funny, bittersweet movie that thinks not with its brain, as Putin would put it, but with its heart.

DOWN TO EARTH

The strange demise of the Hollywood star...

"More stars than there are in the Heavens" used to be MGM's slogan during the 1940s and 50s. Back then the dazzling actors and actresses that lit up the screens and fuelled the world's gossip rags were the movies' main draw. And even after the studio system collapsed in the 1960s and 70s, movie stars retained and expanded both their wealth and power, transforming themselves into freelancers who soon teamed up with newly important superagencies such as Creative Artists Agency and William Morris. The agents would then package them together with screenplays and directors, offering bundled deals to the studios, which in some cases acted as not much more than providers of venture capital. As *Battleship* director Peter Berg put it in 2012 when asked about his casting unknown Taylor Kitsch in his gazillion-dollar maritime spectacular: "It used to be they'd give you a list with eight actors on. And the actors fucked you. They either said no or they asked for ridiculous amounts. And because everybody was fighting for the same eight actors they got what they wanted. But it was like the housing bubble, and it burst." In the 2000s Hollywood's stars saw their power (and pay-packets) dramatically reduced as the studios staged a comeback: and their weapon was the franchise.

Hollywood-watchers might have detected straws in the wind with the debacle over *Spider-Man 2* (2004). Sam Raimi's first entry in the series, with Tobey Maguire donning the spider-suit, had been an outrageous success, generating nearly $1 billion in box-office receipts. But when the inevitable sequel was announced a complicated row involving Maguire led to Sony Pictures publicly approaching Jake Gyllenhaal about taking on the role. Sony's gamble, which must have set alarm bells ringing in agents' offices across LA, was that audiences didn't much care who wore the Spidey Tights; they went to see Spider-Man, not Tobey Maguire. In the end Maguire and Sony came to an agreement, but the writing was on the wall: the stars' power, for the better part of a century unchallenged by the Hollywood studios, was under attack.

But the Maguire spat was a mere dress rehearsal for the sudden dethronement of Hollywood's most visible star, Tom Cruise. The poster-boy in the 80s and 90s for the new agent-driven star system, Cruise ruthlessly deployed agents, driving his fee per movie to near the $30 million mark *plus* a share of every dollar spent at the box office even before studio costs had been made back. But after his infamous sofa-jumping performance on *Oprah* together with some ill-advised comments on the proper treatment of postpartum depression, Sumner Redstone, CEO of Paramount's parent company Viacom, with whom Cruise had a longstanding production deal, decided enough was enough, firing him. The increasing public perception that the *Top Gun* (1986) star had a screw loose may have played a part, but no doubt the famously hard-nosed exec was also becoming tired with the increasing cost of maintaining expensive actors at a time when Hollywood faced declining revenues.

Things haven't been much better for his contemporaries. Along with Cruise, Tom Hanks and Will Smith were in the 90s regarded as sure-fire openers: names above the marquee that all but guaranteed financial success. But in the noughties all have had their flops, Hanks with Steven Spielberg's *The Terminal* (2004) and more recently *Larry Crowne* (2011), while Will Smith's *I Am Legend* (2007) and *Seven Pounds* (2009) were both lacklustre performers at the box office. And if the older generation are having a hard time of it, the newer generation is failing to produce any stars at all. Not only are large movie franchises now often launched without known actors in the leading roles, these youngsters are not guaranteed stellar status even if the movie is a huge hit. The cast of Peter Jackson's *Lord of the Rings* movies have failed to capitalize on the series' incredible success (Orlando Bloom, key player in both that and *Pirates of the Caribbean*, p.193, has all but vanished). Christian Bale, the anchor of the millennium's most feted comic-book franchise in Christopher Nolan's Batman films, has been unable to bring a fanbase with him to other projects, even once popular franchises such as *Terminator Salvation* (2009). (Contrast the career of Harrison Ford, who after turning up in 1977 as an unknown as Han Solo was soon capable of opening movies and subsequently produced two decades' worth of almost consistent box-office hits.) Meanwhile the public's thirst for celebrity Hollywood gossip and intrigue is nowadays increasingly sated by an endless stream of reality TV casts, nolebrities manufactured by media companies, wrung dry, and then discarded in favour of a new crop with dizzying rapidity. Certainly Hollywood still has its stars, but their light shines less brightly and their future is more uncertain than it was just a few short years ago.

Gran Torino

2009, US/Ger, 116 mins, 15 (UK) R (US)

. . . .

cast Clint Eastwood, Bee Vang, Ahney Her, Christopher Carley *scr* Nick Schenk (story by Dave Johannson & Nick Schenk) *cin* Tom Stern *m* Kyle Eastwood, Michael Stevens *dir* Clint Eastwood

In 1954 a fresh-faced, exceptionally tall and, according to most people who had seen him audition, utterly unpromising young actor delivered his first lines in a feature film. The movie was *Revenge of the Creature*, cashing in on *The Creature from the Black Lagoon*. It was not an auspicious start. Fifty-four years later, the same actor, now with a face that looked like it was hewn from granite and a gravelly rasp of a voice to match, delivered his last – and one of the greatest acting careers in Hollywood history drew to a close.

Clint Eastwood had announced that *Gran Torino* would "likely" be his final appearance in front of the cameras, so it's reasonable to ask with what kind of film he wanted to conclude his acting career. An almost perfectly pitched cinematic grace note is the answer. If *Unforgiven* (1992) was his mature response to the Spaghetti Westerns that provided his refuge from weekly television in the 1960s, then *Gran Torino* does the same job with the 70s cop flicks that made him a bona fide movie star. It's no surprise that the lead character was at one point rumoured to have the surname Callahan. The spirit of *Dirty Harry* (1971) haunts every frame.

But he's not Harry, he's Walt, a retired, recently widowed autoworker and Korean War vet whose grasping family have moved away and who finds his old neighbourhood changing in ways he doesn't like, particularly the predominance of Asian families who now fill the houses left by unemployed Detroit car workers. An unashamed racist and foul-mouthed to boot, he sits on his porch drinking beer and expressing his disapproval of the passing world with a low guttural growl. He's as out of time as the eponymous 70s car, his pride and joy, that sits gleaming in his driveway. But after Thao (Bee Vang), the shy son of the family next door, is forced by local thugs to try to steal the car, and his family then tormented, it turns out that Harry – sorry, Walt – hates bullies more than he hates Asians and the film takes a detour first into vendetta territory, but then into something more surprising, tragic and ultimately moving.

In a sense *Gran Torino* is a movie that manages to have its cake and eat it: giving us the autumnal pleasures of an older, mellower Eastwood finally making a kind of peace with the world, but also reminding us of the younger, laconic, heat-packing vigilante. So while we marvel at the subtleties of his acting in the quieter scenes, we cheer as he climbs out of a battered truck and informs a bunch of gangbangers in the process of attacking a young Asian woman: "Ever notice once in a while you come across someone you shouldn't have fucked with?" You can almost hear the Lalo Schifrin score in the background, and isn't that gun slung from his waist a Magnum? It's testament to debut screenwriter Nick Schenk's script, and Eastwood the director (as always, his directorial style is wonderfully loose and unfussy) that he manages to amalgamate these contrasting tones into something unique and, in its closing moments, unmistakeably final. And it would take a man tougher than either Harry Callahan or Walt Kowalski not to feel a lump coming to the throat as, over the titles, the old timer rasps a few notes of the beautifully written title track: literally his swan song.

Nearly forty years on, in a much changed America, marginalized Walt (Clint Eastwood) channels the self-righteous indignation of Harry Callahan in (probably) his last starring role.

Grizzly Man

2006, US, 104 mins, 15 (UK) R (US)

cin Peter Zeitlinger *m* Richard Thompson *dir* Werner Herzog

Timothy Treadwell was by all accounts an extraordinary man, albeit one labouring under what would turn out to be a fatal delusion. Between 1990 and 2003 he spent his summers in Katmai National Park, Alaska, observing, recording and, in his

opinion, protecting the local bear population from poachers and hunters. For his last six expeditions he took a video camera and the often astonishingly intimate footage and still photographs he took formed the material for presentations he would give for free in schools. He was, however, the bane of the National Park Service, refusing to obey their rules about remaining 100 yards from the animals, for their protection as much as his, and slowly began to regard the bears as his own, giving them names and frantically warding off entirely legal, licensed hunters (though a small number of individual animals were legitimately hunted, the bear population was entirely stable and safe). Then what many felt was inevitable happened: towards the end of his thirteenth season he encountered a bear whose appetite overcame his better nature and Treadwell and his girlfriend became ursine appetizers.

The story itself is obviously manna for any documentary filmmaker – but we should be immensely thankful that it fell to Werner Herzog to explore the strange story of Treadwell's life and death, since he does it with typical sensitivity, humanity and insight, resisting the urge to patronize or make fun of a character who is at least on some level completely nuts. Though he is as fascinated with nature as Treadwell was, Herzog's own attitudes to it are diametrically opposed to the romanticized and anthropomorphized idealism of his subject. Herzog, after all, remarked during the shooting of *Fitzcarraldo* (1982) that in the jungle the birds do not sing, "they scream in pain". The common denominator of the universe, he informs us in this movie, is "hostility, chaos and murder". Treadwell meanwhile eulogizes a dead bee.

Herzog skirts over some of Treadwell's real-life dissimulation – he claimed to be alone in the wilderness but in fact frequently took female companions, he posed as a British-born Australian-reared orphan and concocted a bizarre accent to match, when in fact he was born in Long

Treadwell's intimate footage contrasts fantastic Mr Fox with ultimately not so fantastic Mr Grizzly.

WERNER HERZOG

b. 5 September 1942, Munich, Germany

Even though he was born in the middle of World War II and made his first film half a century ago, Werner Herzog remains one of the most consistently fascinating contemporary directors, as well as one of the most prolific. A pioneer of the German New Wave alongside Rainer Werner Fassbinder, he vanished from wider view a little in the 1990s, though remained as productive as ever in Germany. But with the turn of the millennium he staged an international renaissance predominantly fuelled by his compelling documentaries, which show a fascination for extreme characters and situations seasoned with a profound and appealing humanism. He flew over Guyana's rainforest in an airship in *The White Diamond* (2004); *Grizzly Man* (2006) told the strange, tragic tale of bear-attack victim Timothy Treadwell; in *Encounters at the End of the World* (2009) he is as interested in the lives of the staff of McMurdo station as he is in the desolate Antarctic landscapes; and in *Into the Abyss* (2012) he sympathetically investigated the subject of the death penalty in America, skilfully avoiding crass polemic and demonstrating his characteristic humanity and curiosity. His "pure" fiction films, though fewer in number, have remained as quixotic as ever: *Invincible* (2002), based on a true story about a Jewish strongman in pre-war Germany, had Tim Roth as a Nazi occultist, while *The Bad Lieutenant: Port of Call – New Orleans* (2010, p.26) was an irresistible symphony of dark surrealism. Most intriguingly, in his continued search for what he calls "ecstatic truth", he has continued to probe the boundaries between documentary and fiction (a process he might have covertly started with his masterpiece *Fitzcarraldo* in 1982). In *Rescue Dawn* (2007) he takes a story he has already told in documentary form (*Little Dieter Needs to Fly*, 1998) and presents a fictionalized account of the same events, while in *The Wild Blue Yonder* (2007) he muses on the state of planet Earth via documentary footage and Brad Dourif as a stranded extraterrestrial. Nearing seventy, whether working in documentary or fiction or some unique hybrid, he remains possibly the single most versatile, surprising and inspiring director working anywhere in the world.

Island, was a former high-school diving champ and failed actor who turned to drink and drugs and found himself in the wilderness after a near-fatal heroin overdose. His obsession with the bears can also be seen as a symptom of a darker, almost pathological misanthropy, equally alien to Herzog. But then this is exactly the kind of obsessive, driven, near lunatic that has always fascinated the director both in fiction and in his documentaries. There is a moment in *Grizzly Man* where Treadwell plays with seemingly unafraid Alaskan foxes that is eerily reminiscent of footage of Herzog's original muse "dancing" with a butterfly in *My Best Fiend* (1999). Does the ghost of that other blond, temperamental misanthropist Klaus Kinski haunt this beautiful, fascinating film?

Grizzly Man is a mesmerizing, unforgettable portrait of a man whose devotion to nature would be his undoing. Perhaps the most economical illustration of the divergent views of the natural world this film explores can be found in the bears' names. Treadwell gave them saccharine monikers: Satin, Tabitha, Mister Chocolate. The one in which his still-ticking watch was found, attached to its owner's arm, had previously been tagged by the Alaskan Park Service. Their name for him? Bear 141.

Hanna

2011, US/UK/Ger, 111 mins, 12A (UK) PG-13 (US)

....

cast Saoirse Ronan, Cate Blanchett, Tom Hollander, Eric Bana, Jason Flemyng, Olivia Williams, Jessica Barden *scr* Seth Lochead and David Farr *cin* Alwin H. Kuchler *m* The Chemical Brothers *dir* Joe Wright

Director Joe Wright's childhood might best be described as schizophrenic. On the one hand he was born and raised in one of the tougher parts of North London, spending most of his days dodging school and avoiding beatings from the local skinheads. But his home life was very different. His parents ran a famous puppet theatre and the family lived above the shop; he grew up, then, surrounded by a sense of magic, imagination and wonder. He has said that his career as a director has been an attempt to fuse these two worlds, the gritty, frightening real world and the enchantment to which he escaped. With *Hanna*, this chasm has been well and truly bridged: it's *The Bourne Identity* re-imagined by the Brothers Grimm.

We meet sixteen-year-old Hanna (a luminous, otherworldly Saoirse Ronan) in the icy wastes of the Arctic Circle stalking and efficiently dispatching an elk. It turns out to be not her only unusual skill. Living alone with her father (Eric Bana),

Cool as ice: Hanna (Saoirse Ronan) shows off just one of the skills learned during an unorthodox upbringing.

an ex-CIA asset, in a cottage that looks like it might have been designed to be built out of gingerbread, she speaks a multitude of languages, excels in combat both armed and unarmed and spends her evenings learning about the world from the encyclopedia that her father reads to her. But one day, to her and the audience's surprise, her father produces an electronic box: it is a transponder and when the switch is flicked whoever is *out there*, whoever they are hiding from, will know that they are alive and where they are. Later he returns from hunting. A light flashes on the transponder, and the chase is on.

As with all good fairy tales there is a wolf lurking in the woods, in this case CIA agent Marissa (a fantastically icy Cate Blanchett, a sequence in which we see her meticulously polishing her bloody teeth establishing her lupine credentials). Determined to terminate Hanna and her father, she employs the services of peroxide blond, shell-suit-wearing sadist Isaacs (Tom Hollander delivering a gleefully batty performance) and his skinhead goons.

There doesn't seem to be a genre that this constantly inventive film doesn't at some point touch: a pacy, effective euro-thriller, at one level it is also both a strange coming of age story *and* a fish-out-of-water tale. Hanna is a kind of holy fool: able to break an arm with a single blow, she has never seen the world outside her log-cabin home, or for that matter met another human being other than her father. The buzzing neon strip-lights and blaring television of a small Moroccan hotel room provoke a full-on anxiety attack. When she meets Sophie (the wonderfully sassy Jessica Barden) and her ditzy vacationing parents (Jason Flemyng and Olivia Williams), the possibilities of friendship and even love open up, though her unusual upbringing presents its own problems: a sweetly written first kiss ends with the teenage boy on the ground in an excruciating arm-lock. "Should I let him go?" Hanna asks the surprised Sophie.

Wright, who has previously favoured historical dramas, proves himself a skilled action director: a hand-to-hand fight in a German subway station shot in one long Steadicam take is as good as anything in the modern action canon, as is a meticulously choreographed chase/fight-sequence involving Isaacs' thugs in a shipping container yard. Skinheads beaten up by a little girl? It seems that Joe Wright's childhood informs his films in more ways than one…

Harry Potter and the Prisoner of Azkaban

2004, UK/US, 141 mins, PG (UK)
PG (US)

●●●

cast Daniel Radcliffe, Rupert Grint, Emma Watson, Tom Felton, Alan Rickman, Maggie Smith, Robbie Coltrane, Michael Gambon *scr* Steve Kloves (from the novel by J.K. Rowling) *cin* Michael Seresin *m* John Williams *dir* Alfonso Cuarón

The third in the blockbuster series, *Harry Potter and the Prisoner of Azkaban* is, by most fans' estimation, the most perfectly realized of the adaptations, capturing the blend of minutely observed detail and epic drama that devotees had devoured obsessively in J.K. Rowling's novels. After the relative disappointments of Chris Columbus's first two instalments (the *Home Alone* director was an odd choice, his directorial work, mainly in comedy, having shown not much more than competence), Warner Bros chose Mexican director Alfonso Cuarón for the third outing, presumably having seen his ability to conjure a believable sense of enchantment in *A Little Princess* (1996), as well as his facility for working with young people in *Y Tu Mamá También* (2002). Cuarón sheds the somewhat synthetic, theme-park atmosphere that had dogged the opening films, bringing a romanticism, playfulness and rich visual imagination that blends whimsy, action and menace to perfection.

The prisoner in question is Sirius Black (played by Gary Oldman, reaching the front of the long queue of British character actors who would populate the series), arch-enemy Voldemort's henchman, who has escaped from the titular gaol, and as the implacable

ALFONSO CUARÓN

b. 28 November 1961, Mexico City, Mexico

A leading light of the Mexican New Wave of directors (see box on p.190), Alfonso Cuarón made his feature debut with *Sólo con tu Pareja* (1991), a black comedy about a suicidal businessman wrongly diagnosed with Aids. But he got his break in the US with a brace of contrasting adaptations of literary classics: a charming, traditional version of *A Little Princess* in 1996, and his under-appreciated modern-day take on Dickens' *Great Expectations* with Ethan Hawke and Gwyneth Paltrow in 1998. *Y tu Mamá También* (2002), a raucous, unapologetically sexy road-trip movie with Diego Luna and Gael García Bernal, was an arthouse hit and, with its focus on young people and the trials of adolescence, was probably key in getting him his first genuine blockbuster, *Harry Potter and the Prisoner of Azkaban*. His dystopian sci-fi film *Children of Men* (2006) was very different in its tone, though in a sense still concerned with children, or rather their absence. Based on a novel by P.D. James and set in a childless Britain of 2027 which has descended into anarchy, it follows a group of renegades as they escort the world's single pregnant woman to a safe delivery. Grim, gritty and exciting, it nevertheless maintained the humanism at the centre of Cuarón's work, establishing Theo Faron (Clive Owen) as a realistically terrified protagonist rather than a conventionally unperturbed Hollywood action hero. His next film, *Gravity*, is another sci-fi outing but, cementing Cuarón's continued thematic unpredictability, of apparently a very different type. As co-star (with Sandra Bullock) Clooney tantalizingly puts it, "a satellite blows up and space junk causes damage. We go out in space suits, and she and I are tethered together... It is a very odd film, really. Two people in space. It's more like 2001 than an action film." It is tentatively scheduled for release in late 2012.

enemy of Harry (he may have been involved in the killing of his parents) pursues him to Hogwarts in order to continue the Potter family massacre. Coming to Harry's aid is new Defence Against the Dark Arts teacher Professor Lupin (David Thewlis), who may have a sinister secret of his own (the clue's in the name, kids!).

Though the films would follow the books in becoming progressively darker, Cuarón leavens the increasing seriousness of purpose and sense of peril of this

Mission Improbable: Hermione (Emma Watson), Harry (Daniel Radcliffe) and Ron (Rupert Grint) negotiating their way through the wild and craggy setting of Hogwarts' grounds in the best of the *Harry Potter* series.

transitional episode with richly observed character moments – an entertaining exeat to Hogsmead, an enchanted local village, and a spectacular flight on the back of a Hippogriff, a dignified bird/horse hybrid who demands that he be bowed to before being mounted (ILM excelling themselves here) are standout – as well as delivering the propulsive plotting that underpins the franchise, here made even twistier by a novel time travel element. Cuarón pushes the series' production values to greater heights, opening the movie up and exploiting the spectacular Scottish locations to make Hogwarts feel distinctly more real. (And he has the good sense to keep the inevitable Quidditch match mercifully brief.)

If, in retrospect, Columbus's direction of the previous movies was undistinguished, what can't be doubted is that the original casting, his enduring gift to the series, was absolutely spot on. All three principals develop their characters in pleasing ways. Daniel Radliffe's Harry gains more steel, in the opening sequence finally getting his own back on his ghastly step-parents (the manner of his revenge owes more than a little to Roald Dahl's *Charlie and the Chocolate Factory*), and having to face down genuinely scary wraith-like, soul-sucking Dementors. Rupert Grint's developing comic timing was by now becoming one of the series' small joys, while Emma Watson's Hermione grows as a character in her own right, even managing to land a effective left hook on Hogwarts' resident bully Malfoy (Tom Felton).

Cuarón would not direct another Potter movie, with British directors Mike Newell and especially David Yates effectively midwifing the remaining instalments. But his sense of romance and magic, as well as his painterly eye, would be missed. Of all the Potter films, *Azkaban* is the only one that can be enjoyed as a work of art on its own terms.

WORLD HOTSPOTS #2: ASIA

Eastern promises...

Asia is a vast continent, with the glitz and glamour of Bollywood seeming a million miles away from the acerbic political protests of Kurdish and Palestinian filmmakers and the trenchant social realism of emerging filmmaking nations like the Philippines, Vietnam and Singapore. As the 21st century dawned, the formulaic musicals that had enabled India to develop the world's biggest film industry found a new international audience beyond the traditional diaspora. And though Amitabh Bachchan, Shah Rukh Khan and Aishwariya Rai could still rival any Hollywood star in the celebrity stakes, 83 percent of Indian movies made a loss, while scandals involving gangsters and religious zealots tarnished the image of the dream factory.

For many Asians, movies are much more than mere entertainment. They are expressions of identity and statements of intent that are often produced in spite of strict censorship and the risk of sanction. In 2010, the Iranian director Jafar Panahi was jailed for six years and banned from working for another twenty for supposedly producing anti-government propaganda. Yet, he defiantly shot the documentary *This Is Not a Film* (2012) in the subversive spirit that had characterized much Iranian filmmaking since the early 1990s.

Even leading lights Mohsen Makhmalbaf and Abbas Kiarostami risked official ire by experimenting with both content and form in questioning the theocratic patriarchy of the Islamic Republic in films like *Kandahar* (2001) and *Ten* (2002), while Makhmalbaf's wife Marzieh and daughter Samira promoted the feminist cause in *The Day I Became a Woman* (2000) and *At Five in the Afternoon* (2004). Indeed, not even the failure of the "green wave" following the disputed 2009 presidential election could curtail the Iranian cinema of moral anxiety, and *A Separation* (2011), Asghar Farhadi's powerful treatise on faith, gender and justice, won the Oscar for best foreign film. Moreover, millions watched on illegal satellites and web feeds as the director defied a regime that had denounced his unflinching drama by offering the award "to the people of my country, the people who respect all cultures and civilizations and despise hostility and resentment".

The Chinese censor has also been busy since the emergence of Sixth Generation graduates from the Beijing Film Academy, who abandoned the lush lyricism of Chen Kaige and Zhang Yimou exemplified by Zhang's *Hero* (2004, p.123) to expose the effects of the economic boom on the urban and rural poor in such stark and uncompromising dramas as Jia Zhangke's *Platform* (2002), which followed a theatre troupe as it adapted to political change, and Li Ying's mining-themed *Blind Shaft* (2003). But despite the arthouse acclaim for Hong Kong's Wong Kar-wai and Taiwan's Ang Lee, the success stories of Southeast Asia were the anime fantasies fashioned by Hayao Miyazaki at Studio Ghibli (which cut a groundbreaking distribution deal with Disney), such as 2003's *Spirited Away* (p.218), and the horror flicks produced in Japan and South Korea by new generations of indie mavericks.

Hideo Nakata started the J-horror trend with atmospheric ghost stories such as *Ring* (2000) and *Dark Water* (2003, p.62), both of which were remade in Hollywood. But sombrely comic splatterfests like Takashi Miike's *Ichi the Killer* (2003, p.136) and Sion Sono's *Noriko's Dinner Table* (2006) and such Korean horror items as Kim Ji-woon's creepy psychological chiller *A Tale of Two Sisters* (2004) and Bong Joon-ho's monster movie *The Host* (2006) had to be content with becoming cult favourites. The latter pair did contribute to the "hallyu" or "Korean Wave", however, which embraced such bleakly baroque Park Chan-wook sagas as *Oldboy* (2004, p.185), which formed the second part of his acclaimed "vengeance trilogy", and Kim Ki-duk's contemplative emotional odyssey *Spring, Summer, Fall, Winter... and Spring* (2004), as well as the humanist realist studies of Lee Chang-dong (*Poetry*, 2011) and the witty manners comedies of Hong Sang-soo such as *Hahaha* (2010).

By contrast, the Thai New Wave was built on the offbeat authenticity of Nonzee Nimibutr's erotic period drama *Jan Dara* (2001) and the supernatural surrealism of *The Eye* (2002), which was produced by émigré Hong Kong twins Danny and Oxide Pang and spawned two sequels and a US remake. However, it was the poetic, hypnotic and downright peculiar meditations on nature, sexuality and the unconscious produced by Apichatpong Weerasethakul that eventually came to the fore, with *Uncle Boonmee Who Can Recall His Past Lives* (2010) winning the Palme d'Or at Cannes and confirming that there was much more to Asian film than chop-socky, sword-wielding samurai and masala dance numbers.

Hero

2004, HK/Chi/US, 99 mins, 12 (UK) PG-13 (US)

•••

cast Jet Li, Tony Leung, Maggie Cheung, Chen Daoming *scr* Li Feng and Wang Bin and Zhang Yimou *cin* Christopher Doyle *m* Tan Dun *dir* Zhang Yimou

In a rain-drenched outdoor chess arena two warriors fight to the sound of an old man plucking a Chinese harp, their bodies describing impossible arcs in the air. Among the yellow treetops of a vast autumnal forest a pair of female fighters fly, their swords slicing pieces off their billowing red silk dresses, slivers of scarlet which flutter to the ground among the falling leaves. Above the surface of a pellucid lake a faux battle is enacted and a pair of figures swoop and dive, their swords making tiny ripples on the glassy surface. With scenes like these it should be no surprise that *Hero* was at the time the most expensive Chinese film ever made. And the money was well spent. It is a film of unsurpassed beauty, one ravishing image after another becoming almost overwhelming in their intensity.

Mainstream Western audiences had been introduced to *wuxia* by Ang Lee's international hit *Crouching Tiger, Hidden Dragon* in 2001, which typified the genre with its tale of chivalry, honour and martial arts. But Fifth Generation filmmaker (a school of Chinese directors that emerged in the 1980s, defined by their exposure to Western movies and new filmmaking technologies) Zhang Yimou's first foray into the genre feels more authentic and is certainly more magnificent to look at.

That *Hero* is best taken as a purely visual experience becomes clear when the somewhat anaemic plot is given more than a cursory glance. Inspired perhaps by Akira Kurosawa's *Rashomon* (1950), with its telling of a story from three different perspectives, it has a warrior, referred to simply as "Nameless" (Jet Li), travelling to the palace of the king (Chen Daoming) to tell of how he has assassinated three of the monarch's most feared enemies. But each story is inconsistent with the others, and the king's saviour may not be all he seems.

It was the story, though – little discussed by Western critics at the time – that caused something of a controversy over Zhang's film in the East. Many there detected in it a strong thread of authoritarian thought in which the individual must be sacrificed for the greater good – as the final credits explain, Nameless is executed in the service of uniting the country under one Emperor. It is perhaps no coincidence that the Chinese government found itself able to provide the thousands of soldiers that made the vast battle scenes possible, though of course the same kind of script vetting takes place on any number of Hollywood

military-themed films. So during the feast of astonishing colour and light provided by cinematographer Christopher Doyle – a drop of water is batted between swords like a tennis ball, the air turning black with flying arrows – it might be worth remembering that propaganda can be ravishingly beautiful too. But with that in mind it's no exaggeration to say that the 21st century has not produced a more breathtaking film. The 20th would have a hard time finding much to put against it.

Lady in Red: Maggie Cheung ready for battle amidst the autumnal forest in one of *Hero*'s most breathtaking scenes; the film is a magnificent visual experience.

Hidden (Caché)

2006, Fr/Aus/Ger/It, 118 mins, 15 (UK) R (US)

....

cast Daniel Auteuil, Juliette Binoche, Maurice Bénichou, Walid Afkir, Lester Makedonsky *scr* Michael Haneke *cin* Christian Berger *dir* Michael Haneke

Michael Haneke's brilliant, unsettling drama begins with what seems to be a still photograph of a house on a quiet French street: it lingers on screen for what seems like an age and so when someone does walk through the frame it comes as an almost visceral shock. When suddenly the image rewinds it emerges that we have been watching a video recording of the home of successful TV intellectual Georges Laurent (Daniel Auteuil), his publisher wife Anne (Juliette Binoche) and their twelve-year-old son Pierrot (Lester Makedonsky). The mysterious tape has been sent anonymously to Georges, who, as we fast forward, pause and rewind with him, concludes that it must be a bad joke or the work of a crank fan. But then another tape arrives, this time showing the apartment from a different angle, accompanied by a childish crayon drawing of a boy with a bloody face. And then comes a video of Georges's childhood home. Slowly his feelings of comfortable privilege begin to fray, and he remembers events of forty years ago involving a young Algerian boy who once lived with the family.

The metaphor of watching is of course a particularly potent one in cinema: think of the use Hitchcock made of it in *Rear Window* (1954) or Michael Powell in *Peeping Tom* (1960). Here it is the profoundly disconcerting experience of *being* watched that Haneke explores in typically chilly style. The Laurents' lifestyle is a model of bourgeois respectability: books line the walls of their stylish apartment, dinner parties revolve around discussions of literature and friends' movie screenplays. But is all this agreeable civility built on rotten foundations? Whatever the motive of the tape-maker might be, the result of this "watching" is to force Georges to confront his past, and to make his sense of middle-class entitlement seem very fragile indeed.

Hidden works first of all as a brilliantly subtle study of one man's psychological unravelling. Auteuil underplays beautifully the comfortable family man unwilling or unable to face his past, though special mention must go to veteran Algerian-French actor Maurice Bénichou, whose quiet, dignified performance as Majid, the Algerian boy grown up, makes the film's single moment of violence all the more devastating. But the film also functions as a political commentary, specifically about the Paris Massacre of 1961 in which up to 200 Algerians were murdered, the majority by the police, many being drowned in the Seine. It was a shameful event which the French government has still properly to address and which, Haneke seems to be saying, civilized French society has conveniently buried in its subconscious.

Critics who left their seats too early complained that *Hidden* seems to end on a bathetic note with not much resolved. In fact the whole film may have been working up to one carefully camouflaged vertigo-inducing moment of cinema. The film ends with another fixed-angle shot, just as it began, although this one shows a busy school entrance. Something small, easily missed, happens in the midst of the crowd that leaves the viewer shell-shocked: conclusions about what has just been seen tumble away and unnerving new possibilities are revealed; fresh mysteries constitute themselves. You have to look carefully, though – it is, of course, exquisitely well hidden.

As secrets from the past threaten to wreck his comfortable, middle-class Parisian existence, Georges (Daniel Auteuil, with Juliette Binoche as Anne) explodes at a passing cyclist (Diouc Koma).

A History of Violence

2005, US/Ger, 96 mins, 18 (UK) R (US)

....

cast Viggo Mortensen, Maria Bello, Ed Harris, William Hurt *scr* Josh Olson
(from the graphic novel by John Wagner & Vince Locke) *cin* Peter Suschitzky
m Howard Shore *dir* David Cronenberg

Until relatively recently the films of Canadian director David Cronenberg have
been the definition of an "acquired taste". *Shivers* (1975) gave us sex-crazed
zombies, *Scanners* (1980) delivered detonating human heads, *Videodrome* (1982) had
fleshy VCR slots erupting on its victims. But in the 21st century he has gradually
moved towards a new accessibility with films such as the flawed but underrated
London-set thriller *Eastern Promises* (2007), Freud and Jung biopic *A Dangerous
Method* (2011) and this small-town drama based on a cult graphic novel. His great
achievement with both those and *A History of Violence* has been to pursue his
perennial concerns – questions of identity and mutation, disease and contagion
– while fashioning movies that don't necessarily have nauseated mainstream
audiences revisiting their lunch.

Tom Stall (Viggo Mortensen) is the mild-mannered owner of a diner whose
peaceful life is shattered when a pair of thugs attempt to rob his business. Acting
apparently entirely out of character he pulls a gun and shoots the criminals with
shocking efficiency. But this single act of (seemingly entirely justified) violence
has all kinds of unexpected effects both for him and his family. He becomes a
reluctant local celebrity, feted for an act that is, he says, repugnant to him. His son,
bullied at school, over-retaliates and breaks the nose of his tormentor; it's almost
as if the violence revealed in his father is somehow infectious. Things take a turn
for the mysterious when black-suited one-eyed stranger Carl Fogarty (Ed Harris)
turns up, insisting that he is not in fact "Tom Stall" at all, but a violent mobster
called Joey – and that his presence is required back in Philly…

Just as with Seth Brundle's insectoid identity crisis in *The Fly* (1986), one of the
elements that obviously attracted Cronenberg to this material is the persistent
question of who is the "real" Tom Stall? The doting family man, pillar of the
community and attentive husband whose sexual fantasies extend only so far as
liking his wife to play cheerleader? Or the cold-blooded killer who dispenses death
with casual confidence? And, more disturbingly, does *he* really know who he is?
Just as disconcerting is the suggestion that his wife Edie (Maria Bello) feels a dark
attraction towards this newly dangerous side to her husband: a fact attested by the

Small-town criminal: Tom Stall (Viggo Mortensen) is pretty handy with a gun for your average mild-mannered café owner and family man.

sudden ferocity that characterizes their previously tender lovemaking. Quite apart from the psychological and philosophical conundrums, some critics have found in the film a political parable in which the peace of American suburban life is bought at the cost of violence safely committed, out of sight, in other parts of the world.

Cronenberg's movie ends with the family at least physically united, looking uneasily at each other over the dinner table, wondering perhaps if any of them truly knows the others. It's an aptly ambivalent final image for a deceptively simple story: one that, like the best of the director's early work, raises a host of interesting questions and offers no easy answers.

Hostel

2006, US, 93 mins, 18 (UK) R (US)

....

cast Jay Hernandez, Derek Richardson, Eythor Gudjonsson *scr* Eli Roth
cin Milan Chadima *m* Nathan Barr *dir* Eli Roth

When it was released in 2005 Eli Roth's sophomore film *Hostel* (he'd arrived with
a fanfare of goo and gore in "melt" movie *Cabin Fever* in 2002) was seen by many
critics as just another example of the "torture porn" that was then beginning
to infest the world's multiplexes (see box on p.101). But while it boasts the drills,
claw hammers and ball-gags typical of the genre's rococo sadism, *Hostel* has a
surprisingly satirical edge. Most horror films are in some way about a fear of the
foreign, of what doesn't belong. In an interesting reversal *Hostel* is about a fear
of *being* foreign. This is a horror movie that plays, at least in part, on American
anxieties about being hated abroad: fears thrown into sharp relief in the mid-
noughties by the country's unpopular (in much of Europe at least) foreign policy
during the Iraq war as well as the controversial Bush presidency.

 Hostel begins with a pretty unappealing pair of American frat-boy backpackers
Paxton (Jay Hernandez) and Josh (Derek Richardson) and their Icelandic pal Oli
(Eythor Gudjonsson) looking for adventure – read sex and spliff – in Amsterdam.
After having patronized a neon-lit brothel, a Russian guy tells them of the many
erotic prospects in Bratislava. "There's no guys there because of the war," he
explains. Subsequently they find themselves drugged and tied to chairs in an
abandoned factory, the victims of Elite Hunting, a company that provides captives
for plutocratic sadists to torture to death. (In a mordantly witty touch it turns out
that American frat-boys attract the highest prices, with Japanese schoolgirls just a
sliver cheaper.)

 Of course this fate, depicted in excruciating detail for half an hour or so, might
be seen as the traditional punishment that the conservative horror genre metes
out to teens of either gender who engage in sexual activity. But is there a feminist
element at play? Not only are all the victims male, unusual for a horror flick, but
it's impossible not to see the echoes of the Amsterdam brothel in the factory filled
with rooms in which rich perverts take their pleasure from annihilating other
human beings: treat women like meat and you might wind up being so treated is
the Sunday school moral. The one unexpressed fear that these young alpha males
might be expected to manifest, that of *Deliverance*-style sexual abuse, goes almost
entirely unexplored. (Roth can hardly claim that good taste prevents him from

exploiting this particular anxiety: presumably it is simply a step too far for the typical young male audience.)

Much of this original, sometimes provocative work is undone in a third act that could have come from a Hollywood producers' story conference. Paxton reasserts his masculinity by escaping and exacting revenge upon his torturers as well as attempting to save a fellow female victim. It's a disappointingly quotidian turn of events from a writer/director with a fertile, if unpleasant imagination. Though *Hostel Part II* (2007) was a relative flop, this didn't result in Roth's abandonment of the *Hostel* "brand". In 2011 he announced plans for a *Hostel*-themed maze at Universal Studios Hollywood, which, according to a press release: "Will re-imagine the film's dehumanizing torture chambers and send guests on a spiraling journey through the corrupt halls of Elite Hunting's torture factory!" No doubt a fun day out for all the family.

Holiday from hell: blood-drenched frat-boy Paxton (Jay Hernandez) discovering another side to European accommodation in Eli Roth's gore-fest.

The Hunger Games

2012, US, 142 mins, 12A (UK) PG-13 (US)

••

cast Jennifer Lawrence, Josh Hutcherson, Liam Hemsworth, Stanley Tucci, Woody Harrelson, Donald Sutherland, Wes Bentley *scr* Gary Ross and Suzanne Collins and Billy Ray (from the novel by Suzanne Collins) *cin* Tom Stern *m* James Newton Howard *dir* Gary Ross

Oh it's not easy being a teenager! The spots, the angst, the constant war of attrition between gravity and your trousers, if you happen to be male. And then there's the being selected to represent your district in a fight to the death in a dystopian game show that, for reasons never adequately explained, guarantees peace in a war-blasted future society. *The Hunger Games* boasts a set-up that perfectly captures and exploits the sense of persistent low-level martyrdom that accompanies the condition of adolescence. You can hear the anguished cries of "*Muuuum… it's not fair…*" from decades away.

It must be admitted that it's hardly the most original of concepts. There are significant borrowings from the likes of *Battle Royale* (2001), *The Running Man* (1988) and its French forebear *Le Prix du Danger* (1983), though unlike in the last two, or the similarly themed *Series 7: The Contenders* (2001) for that matter, not much of a satirical nature is made of the reality TV aspect. But no matter, Gary Ross's direction (he helmed solid Hollywood fare such as *Pleasantville* in 1998 and *Seabiscuit* in 2003) is robust and straightforward, though some older patrons were mildly nauseated by his consistent use of youth-friendly jittery-cam, and he gets the pacing absolutely spot on – the movie feels taut and exciting even with a near two-and-a-half-hour running time. He's sharp enough to keep a fair proportion of the action in the gleaming metropolis (the Capitol), where everyone wears fright wigs and looks like they've been dressed by Jean-Paul Gaultier after a long night on the absinthe, establishing characters that we subsequently actually care about before relocating the action to the forest arena, where the borrowings are more from survivalist flicks such as *Deliverance* (1972) and *First Blood* (1982). The violence is present and frightening but brief and not dwelt upon (a few seconds' worth of cuts were required for the film to achieve a 12A rating).

But the success of the movie hangs on relative newcomer Jennifer Lawrence's performance as Katniss (cast apparently as a result of her impressive performance in 2010's *Winter's Bone*), and she doesn't disappoint. She's a fiercely convincing, resourceful female hero, just a little reminiscent of Sigourney Weaver in *Alien*

Survival of the fittest: teen-friendly heroine Katniss (Jennifer Lawrence) draws a bead in *The Hunger Games*.

(1979), and a breath of fresh air to summer blockbusters that generally relegate girls to stricken arm-candy status. Josh Hutcherson is cute and noble in an ever so slightly doughy way, though the screenplay struggles a little to find much to do with him (placing him in peril and setting him up for a rescue would no doubt be unpalatable to the movie's reasonably large male audience, so he spends much of the time nursing a bum leg in a cave, though perhaps Collins et al will find more for him to do in the sequels). Meanwhile a top-notch supporting cast bolsters the youthful leads: former Hunger Games winner Woody Harrelson is at first boozily dismissive but later supportive as the District 12 kids' mentor, while Stanley Tucci is perfectly chosen as the oleaginous game show host Caesar Flickerman. Donald Sutherland makes a brief appearance as the Capitol's sinister, silver-haired leader. *The Hunger Games* is superior, refreshingly uncynical entertainment for teenagers, and it left its target audience positively salivating for the next two courses.

BREAKING THE CELLULOID CEILING...

Ten women directors who scored hits in the millennium

One of the more depressing facts about Hollywood in the 2000s is that not only are women directors no better represented than they were in the 80s or 90s but things might actually be getting worse, with a scant five percent of Hollywood movies made by women in 2011 down from seven percent in 1998. The reasons might be many and varied, but any lack of a wide range of distinctive cinematic voices is certainly not among them.

KATHRYN BIGELOW (b. 1951)

Bigelow's *The Hurt Locker* (2010, p.134) was the first film directed by a woman to win a best director Oscar and one of only four ever nominated. It was the culmination of a career that gives the lie to the prejudice that women can only direct rom-coms and period dramas. From sexy vampire flick *Near Dark* (1988) through stylish actioner *Point Break* (1991) and sci-fi thriller *Strange Days* (1996) she remains one of Hollywood's most versatile helmers.

NORA EPHRON (b. 1941)

Though dismissed by some feminists as a purveyor of celluloid fluff, the *Sleepless in Seattle* (1993) writer/director has been a consistent directorial presence throughout the 80s, 90s and 00s, delivering lightweight, audience-pleasing fare such as *You've Got Mail* (1999), *Bewitched* (2005) and kitchen-set drama *Julie and Julia* (2009).

CATHERINE HARDWICKE (b. 1955)

After serving a long apprenticeship as one of Hollywood's top production designers, working on *Three Kings* (2000) and *Vanilla Sky* (2002) among others, Hardwicke moved into directing in the 2000s, specializing in intelligent teen fare. *Thirteen* (2003) was a sassy coming-of-age movie while *Lords of Dogtown* (2005), starring Heath Ledger, charted the rise of skateboarding in California. She successfully baptised the *Twilight* franchise (2008, p.242) but declined to direct a sequel, moving on to an updating of *Red Riding Hood* in 2011.

MARY HARRON (b. 1953)

Canadian-born Harron made her debut in 1996 with a biopic of radical feminist Valerie Solanas, *I Shot Andy Warhol*, before successfully adapting Brett Easton Ellis's *American Psycho* (2000), turning a novel felt by many to be unfilmable into a blackly funny satire. *The Notorious Bettie Page* (2006) continued Harron's interest in gender politics, reinterpreting the titular 1950s pin-up queen as an early feminist icon.

KASI LEMMONS (b. 1961)

A busy actress noted for her performances in hit 90s movies such as *The Silence of the Lambs* (1991) and *Candyman* (1993), African-American Lemmons moved behind the camera in 1998 with the well-received Samuel L. Jackson starrer *Eve's Bayou*, following it up with the less successful supernatural thriller *The Caveman's Valentine* (2001), before returning to form with a biopic of activist and radio talk show host Ralph "Petey" Green, *Talk To Me* (2007), with Don Cheadle in the lead role.

PHYLLIDA LLOYD (b. 1957)

A major figure in British theatre, having directed to great acclaim at the RSC and the National Theatre, Lloyd made her feature debut with ABBA musical *Mamma Mia!* (2008) which, though savaged by many critics, nevertheless made over $600 million at the world box office, which no doubt helped take the sting out. Her biopic of Margaret Thatcher, *The Iron Lady* (2012), had some bemoaning its lack of politics, but it won Meryl Streep both a BAFTA and Oscar for her uncanny portrayal of the ailing PM.

NANCY MEYERS (b. 1949)

In the 1980s Meyers co-wrote comedy smash *Private Benjamin* (1980) before graduating to directing with *Irreconcilable Differences* in 1984. By the 2000s she was an established directorial presence and a safe pair of studio hands for the likes of Mel Gibson vehicle *What Women Want* (2001), autumn/autumn romance *Something's Gotta Give* (2004) with Jack Nicholson and Diane Keaton, and star-heavy dramedy *It's Complicated* in 2010.

LYNNE RAMSAY (b. 1969)

Ramsay's arresting 1999 debut *Ratcatcher* was a gritty and strangely lyrical coming-of-age drama set in her hometown of Glasgow, which immediately established her as a bright new talent. Her next, *Morvern Callar* (2002), featured a captivating turn from Samantha Morton as a woman trying to pass off her dead boyfriend's novel as her own. Her *The Lovely Bones* project fell apart and it was a full eight years until her next released film, impressive, harrowing *We Need to Talk About Kevin* (2011, p.253).

LONE SCHERFIG (b. 1959)

A co-founder of Dogme 95 along with Lars von Trier and involved in the conception of Andrea Arnold's debut *Red Road* (2006), Copenhagen-born Scherfig worked in TV before her Danish debut, the sweetly romantic drama *Italian for Beginners* (2002). Her first English-language film, a hit adaptation of Lynn Barber's 60s memoir *An Education* (2009), starring Carey Mulligan, was nominated for three Oscars including best picture.

JENNIFER YUH (b. 1972)

The burgeoning field of digital animation has featured mostly male directors, exemplified by the likes of Pixar's Andrew Stanton and John Lasseter. But Jennifer Yuh (along with *Shrek*'s co-director Vicky Jenson) proved that this boys' club might well benefit from a female presence. Her unexpectedly witty *Kung Fu Panda 2* (2011) banked nearly $700 million, thus becoming the most successful film ever directed by a woman.

The Hurt Locker

2009, US, 131 mins, 15 (UK) R (US)

···

cast Jeremy Renner, Anthony Mackie, Brian Geraghty, Ralph Fiennes, Guy Pearce *scr* Mark Boal *cin* Barry Ackroyd *m* Marco Beltrami, Buck Sanders *dir* Kathryn Bigelow

For the most part bomb disposal in the movies devolves into a symphony of tense tropes: clocks tick, sweat drips as our hero ponders whether to cut the red wire or the blue wire (do bomb-makers really conveniently colour-code their components?). But with *The Hurt Locker* Kathryn Bigelow, a director who has made the study of men in action her speciality since *Point Break* in 1991, stays away from such hackneyed flummery and focuses as much on the people as the job. Frankly, in her tautly made, exhausting film it's the human beings that are as likely to explode as the ordinance.

   The Hurt Locker opens in Iraq with Bravo Company, a three-man EOD (Explosive Ordinance Disposal) Unit, in the midst of attempting to disarm an IED (Improvised Explosive Device – if the first casualty of war is truth, its first victor appears to be the acronym) that detonates, killing the company commander. Replacing him is Sgt. William James (Jeremy Renner in a star-making role), an entirely different character to their fallen comrade; his unconventional methods and laissez-faire attitude both to protocol and seemingly to the unnecessary danger in which he puts the unit alarm his colleagues, particularly Sgt. J.T. Sanborn (Anthony Mackie). As the unit's remaining 38 days in theatre count down, tensions mount and Sanborn and James go head to head, with Sanborn convinced that James's recklessness will get them all killed.

   Bigelow, shooting in Jordan just miles from the Iraqi border, ratchets up the tension, using an appropriately jittery, handheld style that for once complements the action rather than distracts from it, but is as interested in the psychology of men who are brave enough to place themselves within arm's length of these deadly devices as she is in the action itself. She's aided by screenwriter Mark Boal, who co-wrote one of the decade's other significant Iraq War films (*In the Valley of Elah*, 2007) and had spent a fortnight embedded with an American bomb disposal squad in 2004, bringing a highly effective blend of researched realism and skilful Hollywood craftsmanship. The disposal sequences brilliantly play off against each other the two sources of danger that the specialists face: the obvious possibility of the device detonating, but also the vulnerability of the unit to attack while they work on making it safe (a situation complicated further by the fact that the bombs are sometimes designed to be triggered by someone in the crowd watching the soldiers). It makes for some fantastically nail-biting sequences.

But if the film's detail is authentic, Boal has the commercial sense to place at its dramatic heart a well-burnished and effective Hollywood set-up. A reckless, "live for the moment" (white) loose cannon coupled with a careful, "do-it-by-the-rules" (black) partner, only for sparks to fly, will be familiar to anyone who's seen Richard Donner's *Lethal Weapon* films. But this is a minor quibble; *The Hurt Locker* is suspenseful and thought-provoking and deserves to rank alongside the likes of *Platoon* (1986) in its visceral re-creation of the realities of modern warfare, and of the price it exacts from the soldiers who fight it.

Staff Sergeant William James (Jeremy Renner) gets the hell out of a not-so-controlled explosion in the gripping Iraq War film *The Hurt Locker*.

Ichi the Killer

2003, Jpn, 125 mins, 18 (UK) R (US)

....

cast Tadanobu Asano, Nao Ohmori, Shin'ya Tsukamoto *scr* Sakichi Satô (from the manga by Hideo Yamamoto) *cin* Hideo Yamamoto *m* Seiichi Yamamoto *dir* Takashi Miike

After making well over fifty movies in twenty-odd years it turns out Japanese director Takashi Miike still has it in him to shock audiences. He had already turned a fair number of stomachs in the 21st century with the final act of his excellent *Audition* (2001), in which a paralysed businessman is tortured with needles and a wire-saw, but with *Ichi the Killer*, his universally controversial yakuza slasher, he wastes no time getting to the point. Within the first five minutes we've witnessed a brutal rape, a man has been reduced to a slurry of offal that drips in clotted clumps from the ceiling and the title of the film has coalesced out of dripping human semen. Whatever else you say, you can't claim not to have been warned.

The plot has yakuza enforcer Kakihara (an impressively pierced and scarred Tadanobu Asano, who can apparently blow cigarette smoke through his perforated cheeks) searching for his kidnapped boss (and sadomasochistic lover) only to run into seemingly mild-mannered Ichi (Nao Ohmori). Ichi, it turns out, moonlights as a kind of sado-superhero, having razor sharp blades concealed in his clothing with which he carves off various bits of people while bawling like a baby and sporting a generously proportioned erection. These two are obviously made for each other, and engage in a kind of bloody courtship acted out against the cramped, filthy and often blood-spattered streets and apartments of the city.

Ichi soon became notorious for its utterly relentless sadomasochistic violence – a reputation encouraged by its distributors, some of whom apparently added a disclaimer reading "all events and characters in the film are entirely sick, any resemblance to persons living or dead is a sad coincidence" and enthusiastically handed sick bags out at international film festival screenings (on one occasion apparently they came in useful). For a UK release the BBFC were compelled to hack over three minutes out of it, mostly of violent rape sequences. But in fact the bloodletting in *Ichi* is so utterly outrageous – a yakuza is strung up on dozens of meat hooks, his tongue, cheeks and genitals sliced with a fish-gutting knife before he has a pan of boiling oil poured over his body, bodies are bifurcated vertically,

Yakuza enforcer Kakihara surveys Ichi's bloody handiwork in Takashi Miike's absurdist gore-fest.

sliced-off faces slide down walls – that it soon becomes akin to a kind of blood-caked absurdist comedy, or *The Three Stooges* performed in an abattoir. (Perhaps a better Western comparison might be the "gorenography" films of cult 60s director Herschell Gordon Lewis, where the sheer quantity and surreal creativity of the slaughter renders it less rather than more shocking.)

But for some Western eyes the inclusion of lovingly shot brutal rape sequences (moments of which survived the BBFC's scissors) are an insurmountable sticking point. It might be a matter of cultural sensitivities (and in the inclusion or indeed celebration of sexual sadism *Ichi* may get closer to the real tone and spirit of some manga than any other film released in the West) but the fact is that Miike makes no distinction between this and any other kind of violence. If this is an impossible idea for you to stomach, then it's fair to say that *Ichi* will genuinely be among the most offensive movies imaginable. But if you can allow the Tarantinoesque dictum – that whatever this is, it has absolutely nothing to do with reality – then it becomes a crazy, visceral, indubitably exciting, thrillingly ludicrous experience. However you may finally judge it, it certainly found at least one devoted fan. Eli Roth gave Miike a cameo in his own, insipid by comparison, blood circus *Hostel* (2006, p.129). That's him looking mildly disappointed coming out of a torture chamber. After his money back, no doubt.

The Illusionist

2010, UK/Fr, 80 mins, PG (UK) PG (US)

....

cast Jean-Claude Donda, Eilidh Rankin, Duncan MacNeil *scr* Sylvain Chomet (from an unfilmed screenplay by Jacques Tati) *m* Sylvain Chomet *dir* Sylvain Chomet

French animator Sylvain Chomet's follow-up to the Oscar-nominated *Belleville Rendez-vous* (2003) is a unique attempt to fuse the comedy of French master Jacques Tati, whose style of clowning, mostly silent, splendidly lugubrious, is instantly recognizable, with traditional two-dimensional and largely hand-drawn animation. Based upon an unfilmed screenplay by Tati himself, like the work of its inspiration it is almost silent, relying for its gentle humour and perfectly judged pathos on the odd mangled Gallic syllable (provided by Jean-Claude Donda) and Chomet's beautiful, washed-out animation.

Set in the late 1950s, it begins in Paris where our hero, Conjurer Tatischeff (the use of Jacques Tati's full surname nodding to the screenplay's semi-autobiographical elements) is struggling to impress thinning crowds with his traditional act which includes the nightly pulling of an increasingly bad-tempered rabbit from a top hat. Travelling to London in search of better audiences he is further disappointed to be relegated to fourth fiddle behind more fashionable rock'n'roll bands, in this case Beatles-alikes "Billy Boy And The Britoons". Through various misadventures, and an exquisitely atmospheric steam-train journey, he finds himself in the highlands of Scotland where his talents are more appreciated (even if his act gets second billing to the turning on and off of a lightbulb, electricity having just been installed). It's here that he meets a young girl, Alice, who takes his sleight of hand to be real magic. Together they travel to Edinburgh where they reside in a tatty (ahem) boarding house packed with equally ragged music hall acts. Meanwhile he showers Alice with gifts, almost bankrupting himself in the process and necessitating various amusing attempts at supplementary employment, while she continues to believe in his magical abilities.

The Illusionist is a charming, subtly moving film: a lamentation for both a life and a style of entertainment slipping inexorably over the horizon. It's imbued with the gentle comedy of bewilderment in which Tati specialized (a sequence in which Tatischeff thinks that the girl has cooked his rabbit and served it up to him *Fatal Attraction*-style is a genuine hoot) but also with a deftly sketched sense of time and place. Rainy Edinburgh has never looked so attractively bleak, its streets, pubs and shops rendered in muted greys and greens.

A controversy erupted on the film's release with surviving relatives of Tati revealing that the original screenplay, penned in the 1950s, had been conceived as an expression of regret to an illegitimate daughter whom he had abandoned along with her mother early in his career. In a long letter to American film critic Roger Ebert, her son castigates the film and its director for failing to acknowledge this: "The sabotaging of Tati's original *l'Illusionniste* script without recognizing his troubled intentions so that it resembles little more than a grotesque eclectic nostalgic homage to its author … shows nothing but a total lack of compassion towards both the artist and the child it was meant to address." The pain is palpable, the anger may be justified. But then, watching this delightful little film, maybe there is more to it. Chomet only became aware of the screenplay's history late in its making, yet its rueful sadness seems to derive from more than the fading world of music hall and an old man's faltering career, while the illusionist's platonic yet intense relationship with the girl is too strange, heartfelt and ambiguous. Tati's mourning and regret seem to have sneaked in when no one was looking, appearing in the finished film as if from nowhere, like a rabbit pulled from an empty hat.

Où est le lapin? At their down-at-heel Edinburgh boarding house Alice and Tatischeff tuck into some stew, while the rabbit. polishes off the sausages.

Inception

2010, US/UK, 148 mins, 12A (UK) PG-13 (US)

cast Leonardo DiCaprio, Joseph Gordon-Levitt, Ellen Page, Dileep Rao, Ken Watanabe, Cillian Murphy, Tom Hardy, Marion Cotillard *scr* Christopher Nolan *cin* Wally Pfister *m* Hans Zimmer *dir* Christopher Nolan

Whatever you thought of Christopher Nolan's insanely complicated dream-drama, and it dazzled many and irritated more than a few, it all but proved what many had been saying for years: that Hollywood consistently underestimates the intelligence and adventurousness of movie audiences. After all here was a $160 million idea-driven movie with nary a superhero or giant fighting robot in sight.

The idea of entering other people's dreams is hardly new to cinema: it turns up in 1984's *Dreamscape*, and of course in various forms in the *Nightmare on Elm Street* franchise to name but two. But Nolan gives the trope a unique twist by bolting it to a kind of corporate thriller while throwing in elements of the classic heist movie and drenching the whole with a sleek post-*Matrix* visual style.

Leonardo DiCaprio is Dom Cobb, a dream "extractor" – an industrial thief-for-hire with a unique m.o. – he lifts ideas from his unsuspecting victims' subconscious. But then he is hired by businessman Saito (Ken Watanabe) to perform the reverse (and hitherto untried) process, to try to *implant* in businessman Fischer's (Cillian Murphy) mind the notion of splitting up his newly inherited conglomerate, an idea that Fischer must believe is his own. Cobb assembles his team and begins work, but his own demons in the shape of dead wife Mal (Marion

Dream weaver: Joseph Gordon-Levitt is the last man standing amidst snoozing subjects in Christopher Nolan's intricate and visually staggering sci-fi crime movie *Inception*.

CHRISTOPHER NOLAN

b. 30 July 1970, London, UK

In the space of just over a decade Christopher Nolan has risen from being the student director of a $6000 festival favourite, *Following* (1998), to the unique position of being able to command vast budgets for both personal projects and idiosyncratic takes on key studio properties. But although his budgets and ability to attract A-list stars may have grown exponentially, his films have maintained a common set of themes established in his early work, particularly *Memento* (2000), which starred Guy Pearce as a man suffering crippling short-term memory loss, and *Insomnia* (2002, a remake of the 1997 Norwegian film of the same title), a gripping psychological crime drama starring Al Pacino in which the lead character's sleeplessness may have its roots in some unspecified guilt. Both films featured central characters whose psychological state is profoundly compromised; given this preoccupation with fragmented identity, it was no surprise he was attracted to the duality of the superhero. He managed to persuade Warner Bros to allow him to revive their stalled Batman franchise, which he did to great box-office success with *Batman Begins* (2005), augmenting the vigilante fantasy with a technological realism that appealed to the target market of adolescent males of all ages. His second Batman movie, *The Dark Knight* (2008, p.58), took the comic-book genre to new heights, while *Inception* (2010) played again with notions of reality and identity, but frustrated some who accused its "dream-within-a-dream" structure of complexity for its own sake. To at least some of his original admirers' disappointment he shows no signs of moving away from blockbuster fantasy with a third Batman movie, *The Dark Knight Rises*, for release in summer 2012 and Zack Snyder's Superman reboot, *Man of Steel*, in which he is creatively involved, scheduled for the following year.

Cotillard), whom he has metaphorically hidden in his subliminal basement, threaten to derail the project…

At times Nolan and his regular production designer Guy Hendrix Dyas's creations are truly awe-inspiring. A vast, crumbling dream-city, its buildings crashing into the sea, at the centre of which are perfect recreations of Cobb and Mal's former homes, is surreal and breathtaking. But then their combined imaginations can become inexplicably enfeebled. Dream sequences are set in upscale hotels, anonymous modern office buildings and, in the final action sequence, a snowy militarized mountainscape more than a little reminiscent of *The Eiger Sanction* (1975). Are these the dreams not in fact of Cobb but of a contemporary movie director who spends much of his time in swanky hotel suites and production meetings?

DiCaprio is more than serviceable as the unusual corporate raider whose need to make peace with his past begins to cloud his judgement, placing his gang in increasing danger, though his expository dialogue occasionally overwhelms – it feels like he starts explaining exactly what's going on at the beginning of the movie and is still talking over the end credits; this was an inevitable risk, given Nolan's absurdly intricate central idea, and one the screenplay fails to address. (When Ariadne at one point asks exactly *whose* subconscious they're plunging into this time, it gets one of this otherwise serious-minded movie's only genuine laughs.)

Studio Warner Bros regarded *Inception* as a big risk, the rumour being that it came as part of a deal that bound Nolan to make the third instalment of their hit Batman franchise. But hearteningly, with a final box-office take of well over $800 million, it proved that when it comes to bold, original, big-budget movies, if the idea is good and original, then audiences will go.

Inglourious Basterds

2009, US/Ger, 153 mins, 18 (UK) R (US)

....

cast Brad Pitt, Christoph Waltz, Diane Kruger, Mélanie Laurent, Michael Fassbender, Eli Roth, Daniel Brühl *scr* Quentin Tarantino *cin* Robert Richardson *dir* Quentin Tarantino

If a single filmmaker is synonymous with American film in the 1990s it is Quentin Tarantino, whose trailblazing 1993 debut *Reservoir Dogs* and triumphant follow-up *Pulp Fiction* (1994) established him simultaneously as both the decade's wunderkind and its *enfant terrible*. In the 2000s his touch became less certain. *Kill Bill* (2003 and 2004) was an uneven piece of chop-socky pastiche, inexplicably stretched over two movies, that despite its length didn't show much in the way of stylistic development, while his and Robert Rodriguez's tribute to 1970s trash cinema, *Grindhouse* (2007), a double feature with trailers by other directors, was a misconceived mess. But with *Inglourious Basterds* he delivers a film that is simultaneously gripping, frustrating, shamelessly funny, undeniably tasteless and finally exhilarating.

At the centre of this sprawling, unapologetically unruly WWII movie is the astonishing Christoph Waltz as SS officer Col. Hans Landa, aka "The Jew Hunter". Ingratiating, playful, mesmerizing and terrifying, Waltz's monstrous creation is the picture of evil (and at least as succulently entertaining as Anthony Hopkins' Hannibal Lecter). In an extended opening that nods to *The Good, The Bad and the Ugly* (1967), he arrives at a small French farmhouse in order to interrogate a French farmer, in three languages with and without subtitles: the camera drifts down below the floorboards to reveal a stricken Jewish family whom the farmer is hiding. The one survivor of what becomes a massacre is Shosanna (the luminous Mélanie Laurent), whom we meet four years later as the owner of a cinema in occupied Paris and the object of the unwanted attentions of a fresh-faced young German war hero (*Good Bye Lenin!*'s Daniel Brühl), a man who has attracted propaganda minister Josef Goebbels' eye and thus become the star of a relentlessly violent Nazi propaganda film. Meanwhile Lt. Aldo Raine (Brad Pitt, complete with a hillbilly accent as thick as molasses) is head of the titular Basterds, a Jewish Allied unit dedicated to killing Nazis and, on Raine's unorthodox orders, taking their scalps. When Goebbels decides to premiere his new masterpiece in Shosanna's cinema with the Führer in attendance, both the Basterds and Shosanna spot an opportunity to eliminate the Nazi leadership and end the war in one fell swoop.

A movie about movies not history: the beautiful Shosanna Dreyfus (Mélanie Laurent) presides over her cinema, scene of *Inglourious Basterds'* bloody denouement.

Inglourious Basterds is full of the euphoric, film-for-film's-sake sequences that are Tarantino's trademark. In one astonishing shot we see Shosanna, curled in a circular window, the startling scarlet of her dress perfectly matching the swastika banners fluttering outside, while David Bowie croons on the soundtrack. It's an example of the artful tastelessness that epitomizes this movie: it's almost impossible not to grin at Tarantino's sheer audacity (though one of the film's less forgivable lapses is its seeming inability to distinguish between members of the SS and ordinary German soldiers). But as with most of the director's work, it's not without flaws: it's overlong and unevenly paced – a sequence in a beer cellar with Michael Fassbender as a film critic turned undercover agent is entertaining for ten minutes before wearing out its welcome and then continuing for as long again. And then of course there is the small matter of the assault on good taste that this revisionist war movie, with its irreverent, exuberant tone, not only commits but relies on. Tarantino had already replied to those who criticized the extreme violence in *Kill Bill* with, "you know, these movies don't happen on planet earth". The problem for many critics was that World War II most certainly did, and in the scale of things relatively recently. But for those who can ignore its many provocations and insensitivities, who can see it as a movie about movies rather than about wars, *Basterds* was the film that put Tarantino back on glourious form.

GRAND THEFT MOVIE!

Is piracy destroying the film industry?

Stolen any good movies lately? Of course not. You're not that kind of person. But the chances are you know someone who has. According to the UK Federation Against Copyright Theft (FACT), in 2011 one in four people obtained or watched pirated films or television programmes – that's around 379 million illegal copies. In the last decade or so movie piracy has, according to the industry anyway, become a serious threat to its revenues and even its future existence.

So how are movies pirated and how much is it hurting the studios? The pirating process consists of three distinct activities: acquiring copies of the film, manufacturing (in the case of pirated DVDs) and distribution. In the case of already released films these are simply copied to blank DVDs in the same way that an 80s schoolboy would copy videotapes with two VHS recorders wired together, but on a much bigger scale. These DVDs are then distributed by criminal networks, with the shifty-looking fellow in a long coat who approaches you in the pub with a dodgy copy of *Avatar* just the bottom of a vast criminal enterprise. Unreleased films find their way into criminal hands in a number of different ways. Sometimes early copies of films on DVD (called screeners), released to legitimate journalists or awards panels, are subsequently sold to pirating outfits. Copies of films can be made by individuals at previews with small digital camcorders in cinema auditoriums (according to the Motion Picture Association of America, a full ninety percent of pirated films are copied in this way) or acquired from cinema projectionists with less than scrupulous morals. In some cases the theft can occur before the film is even finished. An early cut of *X-Men Origins: Wolverine* (2009), complete with special-effects holding shots still in place and a temporary soundtrack, leaked onto the internet from an Australian visual effects company, causing much alarm at studio 20th Century Fox and one American entertainment journalist to lose his job after admitting to having watched it.

DVD copies are then manufactured by criminal gangs on an industrial scale. In 2011 a group of men was jailed for up to seven years after police raided the UK's largest illegal DVD factory, consisting of more than 440 DVD burners capable of producing 250,000 discs a week, with a potential turnover of £95,000 a day. But while the authorities can take action to prosecute gangs, the rise of internet-based piracy is almost impossible to tackle.

Though at the beginning of the millennium a small number of films were being uploaded to the internet, the people responsible were relatively easy to identify. The movie existed as a file on a single server which could be identified and the file removed or server shut down. But the rise of peer-to-peer (P2P) file sharing has made it almost impossible to remove a film from the internet once it has been uploaded. When a movie is downloaded using a P2P network it is sourced from dozens of places at once and the computer it is downloaded to in turn becomes part of the network supplying other downloaders. Removing the file from one or many computers has little to no effect on the film's availability.

For the most part the industry has chosen to concentrate on prevention. Individual prints and DVD screeners are "watermarked", allowing the studios to trace the sources of illegitimate copies; journalists are frisked for recording equipment before they see movies; and public cinemas are fitted with surveillance equipment and stern warnings played before the main feature. But so far it seems to be a losing battle. P2P file sharing can only really be controlled by the ISP providers (and then only imperfectly), a politically fraught process.

How much does piracy cost the industry? Though vast figures are bandied about – £511 million in 2011 to the UK film industry, between $58 and $250 billion in the US – the answer is that no one really knows. For instance in 2009 the most pirated movie was *Star Trek* with an estimated 10.9 million downloads, but how many of those people would have paid to see the film had no illegal copy been available is impossible to gauge. Given that the long-term decline in studio revenues began at about the same time that piracy became widespread, it's easy to identify it as the one and only cause. But it's not that simple. The rise of the internet, better home entertainment systems, the growth in quality episodic TV such as *The Sopranos* and *The Wire*, and more appealing videogames (now themselves a bigger industry than Hollywood) are all likely to have had an impact on revenue.

What is certainly the case is that the problem of piracy, which is also a headache for the music and increasingly the publishing industry, is a formidably knotty one, and it's not going to be unravelled any time soon.

ROBERT DOWNEY JR

b. 4 April 1965, New York, NY, US

Robert Downey refers to the period in the 80s and 90s when he was addicted to drugs, primarily heroin and cocaine, as "my 21-year coma". By the beginning of the millennium it was looking like one from which he might never emerge, courtrooms and prison cells becoming more familiar territory than sound-stages. After numerous arrests and jail time, he had also become uninsurable, Woody Allen being among the directors who found him impossible to cast for *Melinda and Melinda* (2005). For cinephiles who had watched him in films such as *Chaplin* (1992) and *Natural Born Killers* (1995), his decline was tragic. He has a brace of actor/directors to thank for his rehabilitation: Mel Gibson, a man with his own well-publicized addiction issues, risked casting him in his remake of Dennis Potter's *The Singing Detective* (2003), paying the insurance bond himself. The movie may have been misconceived but it led to further roles for Downey, notably as an obsessed crime reporter in David Fincher's true-life serial killer movie *Zodiac* (2007). But it was Jon Favreau, who followed Gibson's lead by insisting on the star for his *Iron Man* (2008), who cemented Downey's comeback in spectacular fashion, with the role of billionaire industrialist Tony Stark being perfectly calibrated for Downey's slightly off-kilter sensibility – much of the fizzing dialogue was improvised on set, reportedly to co-star Gwyneth Paltrow's annoyance. A shared cab ride to Sting's birthday party (these things happen in Hollywood) introduced him to British director Guy Ritchie, who cast him alongside Jude Law as the lead in his action-oriented adaptation of *Sherlock Holmes* (2009), in which he leavened the Hollywood bombast with typical wit and playfulness. It might be said that the "new" Downey is a little less adventurous in his choices of roles than he had been in the 90s. He seems currently to be almost fully occupied with franchise duties, namely *Avengers Assemble* (2012) and *Iron Man 3* (2013) and a mooted third in the Conan Doyle series. But then, at least he's awake.

Iron Man

2008, US, 126 mins, 12 (UK)

PG-13 (US)

••

cast Robert Downey Jr, Gwyneth Paltrow, Terrence Howard, Jeff Bridges *scr* Mark Fergus & Hawk Ostby and Art Marcum & Matt Holloway *cin* Matthew Libatique *m* Ramin Djawadi *dir* Jon Favreau

Of the pantheon of comic-book superheroes Tony Stark/Iron Man may be the most potentially difficult to bring to the big screen. Unlike Batman he's no tortured soul avenging past wrongs, nor is he subject to the Hulk's spasms of uncontrollable rage or Spider-Man's entertaining genetic mutations. A billionaire playboy whose apparently limitless cash comes from his business as an arms designer, he doesn't even have any actual superpowers, relying instead on technology and guile. His really interesting characteristic, in the original comic books at least, is his alcoholism, a fact about the character stripped from the screenplay for this movie (presumably to safeguard its teen-appropriate rating), and only briefly referenced in the 2010 sequel. How, then, do you make a man whose only life-challenge appears to be how to spend his cash and how to seduce perky assistant Pepper Potts (Gwyneth Paltrow) appealing or dramatically interesting?

The answer, for director Jon Favreau, was in the casting. Though Robert Downey Jr's catastrophic personal problems were behind him – he served a year in jail for drug possession in 2000 – and he had starred in *Good Night, and Good Luck* in 2005 and *Zodiac* in 2007, the notion of putting him in a family-friendly flick was still a risk. Moreover at 43 he was clearly too old to market effectively to the 16- to 25-year-old audience

Stark reality: playboy and maverick engineer Tony Stark (Robert Downey Jr) checks out some of the kit that will transform him into a superhero, in Jon Favreau's playful *Iron Man*.

vital to a summer comic-book blockbuster's box-office success. But Favreau, a former actor whose directing career had taken off with the likeable Will Ferrell vehicle *Elf* (2003), insisted, and his gamble paid off. Downey brings to the role an indefinable charm, and like the greatest contemporary Hollywood stars (Jack Nicholson comes to mind) there's the sense that at a deep level he's in cahoots with the audience and enjoying the ride, and his own jazzy, syncopated performance, as much as we are. He and Favreau also bolstered the anorexic plot with more than a little Roger Moore-era Bondian élan, in the obsession with gimmicky technology and playboy trappings as well as the PG-rated sexual flirtatiousness.

Older cinema patrons may have been surprised to see younger fans glued to their seats during the final credits, atypical behaviour they had also manifested during Marvel flicks *The Incredible Hulk* (2008), *Thor* (2011) and *Captain America* (2011, p.43). Their reward was a brief cinematic *digestif* – in this case Nick Fury (Samuel L. Jackson) informing Stark of the existence of a mysterious "Avengers Project" – which together presaged 2012's *Avengers Assemble*, in which the key luminaries of the Marvel universe were finally united under the SHIELD banner. This momentous development, no doubt opening the way to a infinite variety of future superhero combinations, delighted fans who are either physically or spiritually fifteen-year-old boys, and filled those who feel that the comic-book genre is now pretty much clapped-out with a vague sense of foreboding for the next few summers at the movies.

Juno

2008, US, 96 mins, 12A (UK) PG-13 (US)

··

cast Ellen Page, Jason Bateman, Jennifer Garner, Michael Cera, J.K. Simmons, Allison Janney *scr* Diablo Cody *cin* Eric Steelberg *m* Mateo Messina *dir* Jason Reitman

John Hughes, who died in 2009, was one of the first writer/directors (along with Francis Ford Coppola and his adaptations of the S.E. Hinton novels *The Outsiders* and *Rumblefish*, both 1983) to take teenagers seriously as sympathetic screen characters, rather than treating them as the exploitation fodder of 1950s drive-in pap such as *I Was a Teenage Werewolf* (1957) and even *Rebel Without a Cause* (1955). His legacy lives on as the generation that grew up on *The Breakfast Club* (1985) created a new breed of youth movies, among them *Igby Goes Down* (2003), *Napoleon Dynamite* (2004) and *The Squid and the Whale* (2005). *Juno* was typical of these new hybrids, pitched halfway between the Hughesean style and a new, distinctively 21st-century off-kilter indie sensibility, but refreshingly it takes a teenage girl's travails as its subject matter.

Played with a satisfying measure of feist and easy brio by Ellen Page, Juno MacGuff is a sixteen-year-old high school student living in a Minnesota suburb. We first meet her as she downs gallons of Sunny Delight in order to provide the necessary output for the latest in a series of pregnancy tests, each of which has given the same dismal result. The father is schoolfriend Paulie Bleek (a fantastically reserved Michael Cera), but Juno appears to have been entirely in charge of the unfortunate conception and so intends to make any decisions regarding junior's future. After a brief flirtation with termination – at a visit to the clinic she discovers

A heavily pregnant Juno (Ellen Page) manages to distract awkward Paulie Bleek (Michael Cera), the father of her child-to-be, from the running track.

JASON BATEMAN

b. 14 January 1969, New York, US

Trapped for the better part of the 80s and 90s in American sitcoms of varying quality, Jason Bateman showed not only teen heartthrob appeal but also early directorial ambition, becoming at just eighteen the youngest member of the Directors' Guild of America when he helmed three episodes of *Valerie* (later *The Hogan Family*), in which he starred as eldest son David Hogan. But in was in the 2000s that he finally made his major breakthrough into film and emerged both as a skilful comedy actor often compared to the sadly ailing Michael J. Fox (whom he had replaced in early unsuccessful movie foray *Teen Wolf Too* in 1987), but who also was able to deploy a darker, less eager-to-please aspect. He was enjoyably daft as dimwit sports commentator Pepper Brooks in *Dodgeball: A True Underdog Story* (2004) and was impressive in a purely dramatic role in Peter Berg's unfairly neglected Saudi-set crime procedural *The Kingdom* (2007), in which he played an FBI agent investigating a terrorist attack. In *The Ex* (2006), he starred alongside fellow TV comedy alumnus Zach Braff of *Scrubs* and managed to inject genuine laughs into a mostly dire screenplay with his performance as a scheming wheelchair-bound ex-boyfriend. But it was with *Juno* in 2008 and Jason Reitman's *Up in the Air* (p.247) two years later that he really came into his own, playing in both cases somewhat oleaginous characters with relish: the first a potential adoptive father for the eponymous teenager's baby and in the second a company boss intent on unwanted reorganization. His major TV triumph during the noughties was a return to sitcom but this time with *Arrested Development*, which took the form to new heights before being cancelled after only three seasons, much to fans' vocal displeasure. A movie resurrection of the eccentric Bluth family has thus far been talked about a great deal by both creators and cast but actual development appears to be, ahem, arrested.

to her disgust that they distribute fruit-flavoured condoms and are staffed by employees who seem to treat the process with all the care and compassion of a drive-through fast-food outlet (some pro-choice campaigners felt this revealed the film's bias) – her solution is adoption. And in the small-ads pages of the local paper she finds Mark and Vanessa Loring, an apparently perfect childless couple: wealthy, loving and yearning for a child.

Juno talks with calculated sass, almost as if some genius screenwriter had written her lines for her. "You should've gone to China," she remarks when the prospective parents admit the difficulties thay have experienced adopting. "Because I hear they give away babies like free iPods. They pretty much just put them in those T-shirt guns and shoot them out at sporting events." The dialogue is down to the fantastically monikered ex-stripper and cult blogger Diablo Cody, for which she won a deserved Oscar. In less skilled hands, the character would lurch from funny to irritating pretty quickly, but Page nails perfectly the confusion and vulnerability that lie under the surface, the flip irony and throwaway sarcasm never quite masking the fact that she is all at sea.

She's too young to recognize the profound sadness and disappointment at the heart of this seemingly perfect couple's marriage, a sadness that's only partly to do with their lack of offspring. Jennifer Garner is superb as the tightly wound Vanessa, her face a brittle mask of anxiety, while Jason Bateman subtly plays Mark, a onetime aspiring musician who now pens advertising jingles to pay for the couple's luxurious lifestyle. Here's a man, given what happens, who could be depicted as an out-and-out sleazeball, but Bateman makes him at least a little sympathetic; he's a guy with his own share of disappointments, ones that Juno is too young to fully fathom. Surprisingly then, *Juno* turns out to be a film with as much to say about the adults as it does about the kids. The teen flick's come a long way since Judd Nelson punched the air to the strains of Simple Minds.

The King's Speech

2011, UK/Aus/US, 118 mins, 12A (UK) R/PG-13 (US)

....

cast Colin Firth, Geoffrey Rush, Helena Bonham Carter, Derek Jacobi, Guy Pearce, Michael Gambon, Timothy Spall *scr* David Seidler *cin* Danny Cohen *m* Alexandre Desplat *dir* Tom Hooper

For almost a decade during the 1990s and early 2000s producers Harvey and Bob Weinstein and their production company Miramax dominated the major awards, snatching best film gongs with a regularity that drove Hollywood's more established studios up the wall. But in 2005, in one of the most significant movie business events of the noughties, the siblings walked away from their company and founded the Weinstein Company in its place. Though less prolific, they showed that the old magic was still there with *The King's Speech*, a tale of a buttoned-up, conflicted man rescued by a therapist who persuades him to drop his defences and open up and is thus cured. In its essentials *The King's Speech* is *Good Will Hunting* (another Miramax Oscar winner, from 1998, with which it even shares a title with a dual meaning) goosed with some of the imported British class that had gained them awards success in the past (1998's *Shakespeare in Love*, for example). It's audience-pleasing fluff, but exceptionally skilfully wrought, and elevated to a higher plane by a brace of impressive performances from the perennially reliable Geoffrey Rush and Colin Firth.

Loosely based on a true story, this has Firth as Prince Albert, Duke of York, an incurable stammerer, an embarrassing and frustrating personal disability that becomes a potential national crisis when all-round nincompoop King Edward VIII (Guy Pearce) abdicates and Albert has to step up to both the throne and the newfangled radio microphone and address his subjects. Enter Lionel Logue (Geoffrey Rush), a failed actor and self-declared speech therapist who is hired to help Albert, who insists on informality and, much to the King's surprise, on addressing him as Bertie, a name only used by his close family. Slowly Logue uncovers the details of Bertie's emotionally austere childhood as well as his conflicted views of the monarchy and, as Logue coaches him for his first speech to the nation, the two develop an unusual close friendship.

Director Tom Hooper punches all the right buttons with the precision of a veteran elevator operator. Class divisions are broken down, lifelong friendships forged and Britain marches to war with the clearly enunciated words of their King ringing in their ears. There's even a scene in which a surprised Mrs Logue

Tongue twisters: Coached by therapist Lionel Logue
(Geoffrey Rush), the future King George VI (Colin Firth)
works at overcoming his stammer, supported by his loyal
wife Elizabeth (Helena Bonham Carter), amidst suitably
austere period furnishings.

finds the Royal Family have dropped in for tea – a humble working-class fantasy made real. Timothy Spall puckers and growls entertainingly as Winston Churchill, Helena Bonham Carter is sprightly, kind and stalwart as Elizabeth, Duchess of York (later the Queen Mother). Guy Pearce is especially impressive as duty-free monarch Edward, who in times of crisis is to be found raiding the wine cellar. But it is Firth who really shines, managing to find in an apparently thinly sketched character unexpected depth and emotional resonance. The sequences where he wrestles to get his words out are agonizing and he finds a complex, nuanced expression of the King's fears about the life of public service being demanded of him.

As usual the Weinsteins launched a blitzkrieg Oscar campaign, though it was almost derailed by a row over its American certificate, the MPAA having given it a ridiculous R owing to a single therapeutic outbreak of rude language. Much to almost everyone's dismay, and in typical publicity-generating style, Harvey Weinstein announced that he was cutting the film to achieve a PG-13 rating (which he did in April of 2011). The brouhaha seemed to help rather than hinder his awards push and in 2011 Firth won best actor and, in an unusual double whammy the movie got best film *and* director, sweeping aside the much tipped *The Social Network* (see p.215). The House of Weinstein, the movies' own royalty, had once again seized the crown.

JUDD APATOW

b. 6 December 1967, New York, US

For some reason no film genre defines its decade as indelibly as its comedies. In the 80s Hollywood gave us the broad silliness of National Lampoon, and the 90s erupted in a tsunami of unruly bodily fluids as the gross-out fad splattered its way across cinema screens, typified by the work of the Farrelly Brothers in *Dumb and Dumber* (1995) and *There's Something About Mary* (1998). The noughties, though, brought a new style, taking some of the sexual frankness and juvenile obsession with matters excremental of the 90s and synthesizing them with a new emotional realism; and with it rose a new set of star producers, writers, performers and directors with Judd Apatow indisputably at its helm. His professional beginnings were in TV, notably on the seminal *The Larry Sanders Show* where, he says, he learned to write character-based comedy rather than the gags with which he had been making a living. Though he had previously done uncredited screenplay re-writes on the likes of the much underrated Jim Carrey starrer *The Cable Guy* (1996) and subsequently worked as a producer on many of the decade's most successful comedies, including *Pineapple Express* (2008), *Anchorman: The Legend of Ron Burgundy* (2004, p.13) and *Superbad* (2007), his directorial debut was the *The 40 Year Old Virgin* (2005), a high-concept comedy that deftly avoided the potential crassness of its subject matter with a witty screenplay and a likeable performance from star Steve Carell. *Knocked Up* (2007) was a smash hit, abandoning traditional rom-com conventions for a tale of an unexpected pregnancy and unpredictable love affair between an apparently hopelessly mismatched couple. This frat pack comedy wasn't to everybody's taste: the man-boys epitomized by Seth Rogen – and, in the case of the massively successful *The Hangover* (2009) and its wretched sequel (neither of which involved Apatow), by Bradley Cooper – could sometimes channel a nasty edge of homophobia, racism and cruelty, old bigotries simply repackaged for a new audience. But at its best, with Apatow-produced hits such as *Bridesmaids* (2011), the crudity was seasoned with at least a little warmth and humanity.

Knocked Up

2007, US, 129 mins, 15 (UK) R (US)

••

cast Seth Rogen, Katherine Heigl, Paul Rudd, Leslie Mann, Harold Ramis *scr* Judd Apatow *cin* Eric Edwards *m* Joe Henry, Loudon Wainwright III *dir* Judd Apatow

Judd Apatow's comedy *Knocked Up* is as unkempt and unlikely a hit movie as its star is a leading man. It's flatly shot, at well over two hours at least twenty minutes too long, and occasionally feels not so much carefully crafted as knocked up in the other sense of the phrase. And it is one of the most successful R-rated comedies of all time, making $220 million off a reported $30 million budget. It's certainly sometimes outrageously funny, but the real reason for its incredible success might be its unique appeal to twentysomethings of *both* genders, attracting fans of gross-out (mostly blokes) as well as rom-com (mostly chicks).

On a drunken one-night-stand TV presenter Alison (Katherine Heigl) hooks up with slacker Ben (Seth Rogen), who, along with his unpromising buddies, is lackadaisically developing a website cataloguing cinema's nude scenes, blissfully aware that there are dozens of sites doing just that. Owing to a somewhat implausible misunderstanding in bed, he fails to use a condom (nowhere, by the way, is HIV mentioned), and Alison finds herself up the duff. Having decided to keep the baby, she and Ben must decide if they have a future together...

Oddly, some of *Knocked Up*'s most effective performances may come from its subsidiary characters. Alison's sister Debbie (Leslie Mann) appears to be an unapologetic shrew but, in a couple of beautifully acted moments, one when she finds her husband is *not* cheating on her and another when a club bouncer declares her too old to jump the line, we see the depths of her unhappiness and fears for her future with her emasculated husband (Paul Rudd). It's a counterpoint to Ben and Alison's fragile, sporadic optimism, and it gives the film a dramatic centre that it would otherwise lack. But the film finds its heart, and the majority of its laughs, in the form of *echt* manchild Seth Rogen (a taste the majority of cinemagoers have acquired, much to the bafflement of the few) and his chaotic attempts to assume the mantle of responsibility. For a man whose sole wealth comes from a dwindling road accident settlement that he has eked out for the best part of a decade and who, when an earthquake hits, rescues his bong rather than his girlfriend, this will doubtless be a long haul (and there's a nice cameo from veteran comedy director Harold Ramis as his dad who dispenses comforting, if useless advice).

Knocked Up was a smash hit and gained almost universal critical acclaim. Still, for some the undoubted laughs disguised the film's slightly more troublesome aspects: the discarded condom moment is a case in point, while the subject of abortion is too neatly dealt with, and a few feminist critics have deprecated the film's relentlessly male point of view. But when it comes to comedy you can't argue with the majority, who found in Ben and Alison's unlikely pairing a story that reflected their own attitudes to sex, kids, love and marriage. For younger cinemagoers tired of endless post-*When Harry Met Sally* (1989) dissections of love and friendship, set for the most part in ridiculously unaffordable Manhattan lofts, it took the somewhat dilapidated rom-com by the scruff of the neck and shoved it into the 21st century; it was a film in which Gen Y, struggling with the demands of maturity, saw itself.

Who's a pretty boy? Unkempt slacker Ben (Seth Rogen) decides to take his parental responsibilities seriously. Knocked-up Alison (Katherine Heigl) is unimpressed.

Let The Right One In

2009, Swe/Nor, 114 mins, 15 (UK) R (US)

••

cast Kåre Hedebrant, Lina Leandersson, Per Ragnar *scr* John Ajvide Lindqvist (from his novel) *cin* Hoyte Van Hoytema *m* Johan Söderqvist *dir* Tomas Alfredson

One of the most unexpected but welcome developments in post-millennial horror cinema was the increasing audience interest in international scare-fests, a flowering that occurred against the background of an American industry obsessed with torture porn and dismally unnecessary remakes of 80s franchises. Japan was ascendant in the early part of the decade (see 2003's *Dark Water*, p.62) with Spain later also contributing top-notch terror (2008's *The Orphanage* and *[REC]* being among the best). But who would have thought that Sweden would be the country to deliver the undisputed best horror of the 21st century so far? And as novel as its country of origin was its exploitation of a relatively under-used aspect of the vampire myth, mining the fact that, like double glazing salesmen, vampires have to be invited in in order to wreak their havoc.

Oskar (brilliantly played by the almost translucent Kåre Hedebrant) is a lonely boy living with his divorced mum in an austere, though strangely beautiful, housing estate. We first meet him threatening a tree with a knife. "Are you looking at me?" this mini Travis Bickle says to the dumb spruce. The actual targets of his anger are the bullies at school, who relentlessly pick on him and subject him to physical assaults (face slashed with a birch switch, trousers stolen and copiously pissed on) that he endures with almost heartbreaking stoicism. But one day a mysterious girl, Eli (Lina Leandersson), and what Oskar takes to be her father, move in next door. "I'm twelve, but I've been twelve for a long time," she finally informs a increasingly smitten Oskar, while advising him to stand up with

"You looking at *me*?" Isolated Oskar (Kåre Hedebrant) stoically puts up with the everyday horrors of school – for now – in this extraordinary vampire film set in the Swedish suburbs of the 1980s.

violence to his tormentors. As the two shyly explore their new friendship the newspapers report that a serial killer is stringing his victims up and draining them of their O Negative. The two couldn't possibly be linked, could they?

Let The Right One In is one of the most beautifully shot, atmospheric horror movies of recent times. The housing estate, starkly lit, snow-covered, is surrounded by trees encrusted with ice crystals, while inside a tiny grim café the local boozers huddle and kvetch, perfect fodder for a roaming bloodsucker. Director Tomas Alfredson, who would make his equally impressive English-language debut with *Tinker Tailor Soldier Spy* in 2011, and cameraman Hoyte Van Hoytema imbue each shot with a precise stillness before punctuating the chilly beauty with expertly judged moments of staccato *Grand Guignol*: a sudden glimpse of an acid-sloughed face, a man strung up from a tree, blood spurting from his jugular onto the frozen ground, a vampire combustion in a hospital bed are drop-your-popcorn shocking, while the climactic sequence in a school swimming pool might have you regretting you bought it in the first place.

But despite the grue and gore the real centre of this movie is an exquisitely tender little love story played with restraint and almost supernatural skill by a perfectly cast pair of young actors. The loneliness of adolescence has always been fertile ground for the vampire metaphor – George A. Romero's neglected 1976 masterpiece *Martin* being closest in its depiction of an isolated child – but never has the story been told with such care, love and sympathy. A chaste moment where lonely Oskar, in bed with his freezing new friend, asks her "Will you be my girlfriend?" will melt even the most deeply frozen heart: like spilled blood melts snow.

Little Miss Sunshine

2006, US, 102 mins, 15 (UK) R (US)

∙∙∙

cast Greg Kinnear, Steve Carell, Toni Collette, Alan Arkin, Abigail Breslin, Paul Dano *scr* Michael Arndt *cin* Tim Suhrstedt *m* Mychael Danna, DeVotchKa *dir* Jonathan Dayton & Valerie Faris

When, in 2006, no less a movie luminary than mega-producer Jerry Bruckheimer was asked what screenplay for a movie released that year he wished had crossed his desk, he replied not with a high-octane action extravaganza but with low-key family comedy *Little Miss Sunshine*. Who knows if this sweet-natured tale of a mildly crazy family's road trip to a junior beauty pageant might have featured

Family breakdown: the Hoover clan (Abigail Breslin, Toni Collette, Steve Carell and Greg Kinnear) wait for Dwayne, alongside their increasingly unreliable transport in *Little Miss Sunshine*.

more billowing walls of flame if Bruckheimer had hooked it, but Jerry certainly seems to know what a winner looks like. This $8 million-budget indie-comedy seemed to come from nowhere, pulling in more than $100 million at the worldwide box office, being nominated for four Oscars and winning two. More importantly it effortlessly won the heart of almost everybody who saw it. It's the little movie that could.

One of those Oscar nominations went to nine-year-old Abigail Breslin, playing the seven-year-old Olive Hoover. Slightly plain, slightly pudgy and undeniably adorable, she peers through oversized glasses at a video recording of a toothsome Miss America accepting her tiara, a triumph she recreates for herself endlessly. The Little Miss Sunshine of the title is a junior beauty pageant, one of those uniquely American horror-shows where pre-teens are dolled up to look like, well dolls, but of course Olive doesn't see it like that. She sees princesses and frocks and sparkle – and she fully intends to get herself a piece of it.

She's being trained for her big dance number by Grandpa (the superb Alan Arkin), who has a foul mouth and a heroin habit that's got him kicked out of the Sunset Manor retirement home. Mom (Toni Collette), meanwhile, has come home from the hospital with her brother Frank (a pleasingly dry Steve Carell), America's foremost Proust scholar, who has attempted suicide after a rival Proust scholar stole both his post-grad boyfriend and a research grant, and who will be staying with the family to ensure he doesn't have a second go at his wrists. This is much to the chagrin of dad, Richard (Greg Kinnear), who is trying to sell his nine-point motivational system for success, without much success. Oh, and there's teenage son Dwayne (Paul Dano), a moody emo and wannabe fighter pilot, who has taken a vow of silence and reads nothing but Nietzsche. "Welcome to hell," he writes on a pad for the benefit of a sympathetic Frank. "Thank you, Dwayne," replies Frank. "Coming from you that means a lot." When Olive gets a place in the final, the family pile into their beat-up minibus and point it towards Redondo Beach, California.

The universal appeal, of course, is that most people believe their family to be uniquely insane. Michael Arndt's warm-hearted, consistently funny screenplay captures the conflicting joys and deep frustrations of family life and manages to bear its load of quiet satire on certain American values without drowning out the laughs. It's performed with huge élan by an ensemble cast, each one firing on all cylinders, and helmed by a pair of directors who know not to get in the way. *Little Miss Sunshine* isn't an earth-shaking movie, its ambitions aren't huge and there are no breakthroughs in filmmaking craft from husband and wife team Dayton and Faris, but it is the kind of film you wish would arrive more regularly – one that leaves you smiling with unalloyed pleasure.

The Lives of Others

2007, Ger, 138 mins, 15 (UK) R (US)

··

cast Ulrich Mühe, Sebastian Koch, Martina Gedeck, Thomas Thieme
scr Florian Henckel von Donnersmarck *cin* Hagen Bogdanski *m* Stéphane
Moucha, Gabriel Yared *dir* Florian Henckel von Donnersmarck

Like Harry Caul (Gene Hackman) in Francis Ford Coppola's classic *The Conversation* (1974), Gerd Wiesler (Ulrich Mühe) is a man who listens to people for a living. He is a captain in the Stasi in pre-unification Berlin with expertise in interrogation and surveillance. But instead of being reduced to paranoia and

Welcome to the unforgiving contours of Stasiland: the late Ulrich Mühe gave an intense performance as Gerd Wiesler, a ruthless Stasi captain who eventually sees the error of his ways.

insanity by the things he hears, Wiesler is unexpectedly brought to life. The year, appropriately enough, is 1984 and the captain is ordered by Minister Bruno Hempf (Thomas Thieme) to listen to the bugged apartment of playwright Georg Dreyman (Sebastian Koch) and his actress girlfriend Christa (Martina Gedeck). In fact, Hempf is less interested in the couple's politics than in getting Dreyman out of the way so he can move in on his girlfriend, whom he is already blackmailing for sex. Wiesler, a cold, intensely loyal apparatchik whose emotional life consists of rendezvous with well-endowed prostitutes, at first approaches the task with his customary zeal. But slowly that simple act of listening to people expressing their thoughts freely, to a couple devoted to each other and to their art, leads him to begin the potentially deadly process of questioning both himself and the Party.

Von Donnersmarck's film is particularly effective at evoking the surrealities of living under a police state: when questioning a suspect who protests his innocence Wiesler says, "So you think our human system arrests people on a whim? That'd be reason enough to arrest you." These Stasi overlords exist in a state of bureaucratic ecstasy where everything is known. We see the vast mechanized card catalogues containing the minutiae of every citizen's life; when Wiesler senses he has been spotted bugging a home by a woman across the hallway, without missing a beat he threatens her daughter's acceptance to medical college. Every part of ordinary existence is observed and controlled, human love and loyalty exploited ruthlessly.

The film has been accused by those who were there of underplaying the terrible realities of living in East Germany, author and Stasi historian Anna Funder pointing out that there is not a single example of an officer behaving in anything like the noble way Wiesler finally does. These considerations aside, *The Lives of Others* remains a fantastically tense political thriller beautifully acted by a cast of Germany's most talented actors. Mühe in particular brings a compelling reality to his role as the glacially loyal Party man reassessing everything about his life.

A coda set in Berlin after the fall of the Wall is a little contrived, providing the kind of reassuring, uplifting moment that no doubt appealed to the Academy (it won an Oscar for best foreign film). There is a better, more satisfying, conclusion a few minutes before, one based more firmly in the realities of history. Dreyman encounters the fat, vile Minister Hempf outside a performance of his play. Hempf delights in informing him that his flat was bugged all along, giving him a vulgar critique of the couple's overheard lovemaking. "To think that people such as you ruled our country," Dreyman says, then turns and walks off into the night. And in the New Germany, there is absolutely nothing Hempf can do about it.

The Lord of the Rings: The Fellowship of the Ring

2001, NZ/US,182 mins (208 mins

extended edition), PG (UK) PG-13 (US)

••

cast Ian McKellen, Christopher Lee, Elijah Wood,
Dominic Monaghan, Billy Boyd, Andy Serkis, Sean
Astin, Sean Bean, Viggo Mortensen, Cate Blanchett
scr Fran Walsh & Philippa Boyens & Peter Jackson
(from the novel by J.R.R. Tolkien) **cin** Andrew Lesnie
m Howard Shore **dir** Peter Jackson

Without any doubt the single most important event
in popular cinema of the 21st century so far, *The Lord
of the Rings* trilogy stands in relation to American
cinema in the 2000s as the *Star Wars* (1977) series did
to it in the 1970s and early 80s. It turned a generation
on to film; radically altered the kinds of films that
were being made (almost every aspiring summer
blockbuster began to pack itself with dense cod
mythology and running times became even more
unjustifiably extended); has been resold, pimped
out and marketed to within an inch of its life; and,
whisper this, is probably not *quite* as good as even
those who celebrated it remember it.

J.R.R. Tolkien's original epic trilogy divides readers
into two distinct and mutually uncomprehending
groups: those who can take seriously books that have
elves in, and those who cannot. Both awaited the
arrival of Jackson's $300 million epic trilogy with some

PETER JACKSON
b. 31 October 1961, Wellington, New Zealand

A decade or so after the event, it's easy to forget
what a risk *The Lord of the Rings* trilogy was both for
budget studio New Line (then perhaps best known
for being the home of Freddy Krueger), who financed
the $300 million sixteen-month shoot, and for Peter
Jackson, charged with bringing a sprawling book,
jealously guarded by its fans, to the screen. Jackson
was hardly a conventional choice; better known
for splatter horror with a sense of humour, such as
Braindead (1993), or entertainingly offensive puppet
atrocity *Meet the Feebles* (1992), his only mainstream
hit had been 1995's *Heavenly Creatures*, a dark tale of
childhood fantasy and murder with little suggesting
the epic scope that *LotR* would demand. The result, of
course, was a triumph both artistically and, happily for
New Line, commercially, their investment rewarded
with a world box-office take touching $3 billion. And
if his output post-*LotR* has been a little anticlimactic,
that's surely not his fault. Any director would have
trouble following what is without doubt the defining
popular cinematic event of its decade. *King Kong*
(2005), an ambitious attempt to remake the 1933
classic, and presumably banish all memory of the 1976
Dino De Laurentiis misfire, was a movie of two halves
(fun on scary Skull Island, less so back in New York).
But *The Lovely Bones* (2010) was a copper-bottomed
stinker, a cloying, fatally misconceived adaptation
of Alice Sebold's novel, narrated by a raped and
murdered child from heaven (to make matters worse,
Jackson could not blame the solid performances from
Mark Wahlberg, Rachel Weisz and Saoirse Ronan). He
had previously resisted helming the planned *Hobbit*
movies, handing over director duties to Guillermo
del Toro, but a long-running studio row together with
union disputes in New Zealand held up production
and del Toro left. After the critical walloping that had
greeted *The Lovely Bones*, Middle-earth must have
seemed like a good place to hole up and Jackson took
up the reins, stoking fan anticipation to a feverish,
and possibly unsatisfiable, pitch. *The Hobbit: The
Unexpected Journey* will be released at the end of 2012,
with *The Hobbit: There and Back Again* due to arrive
in 2013.

Small but perfectly formed: four intrepid Hobbits – Merry (Dominic Monaghan), Frodo (Elijah Wood), Pippin (Billy Boyd) and Sam (Sean Astin) – take on the forces of darkness in an awe-inspiring New Zealand setting.

trepidation. In fact, neither had to worry about having their minds changed: to the convert Jackson's rendering of the tale of the One Ring, ultimate source of evil in his Manichean world, is technically magnificent, thoroughly exciting; to the sceptic it boasts many of the flaws of its source material – it is bloated, juvenile and oddly charmless. As usual the truth is somewhere in the middle.

The performances are entirely serviceable, often enjoyable, but rarely inspired (with the exception of Andy Serkis's/Weta's Gollum, a harbinger of an entirely new kind of acting in which the skills of performer and digital artist are seamlessly integrated). Ian McKellen barely breaks a sweat as the mostly twinkly-eyed, pipe-puffing wizard Gandalf; saucer-eyed Elijah Wood and co are appropriately inoffensive as those most inoffensive of creatures, Hobbits, and Christopher Lee mugs satisfyingly in a mildly pantomimic performance as evil wizard Saruman. This is a triumph of precision casting rather than the thespian craft. Then again, the real stars are not the actors, but the screenplay, the groundbreaking special effects and, perhaps most of all, the magnificent landscapes. Story-wise the constipated, repetitive nature of the material is negotiated with great skill by Jackson and his co-authors, its acres of pitiless historical exposition concentrated into a few efficient montages. And if it can't quite dispel the feeling that the relentlessly linear structure is really just a case of one damned Orc after another, it moves the pace on effectively enough to paper over the cracks.

The effects, which propel the Ray Harryhausen monster aesthetic of *Clash of the Titans* (1981) into the 21st century, established antipodean outfit Weta as a significant rival to George Lucas's Industrial Light & Magic. But *Fellowship* and the two films that followed are at their best and most emotionally affecting when they set their tiny, all too vulnerable characters against New Zealand's vast, stunning and infinitely varied landscapes: verdant meadows give way to rolling plains which in turn transform into bleak volcanic outcrops and jagged, snow-covered mountains. (Some of the more artificial vistas can be less effective: the cutesy bucolic Shires of the Hobbits is akin to a multimillion-dollar version of one of those pottery cottages your grandma used to have.)

For their fans, which number in the hundreds of millions, the *Rings* films are quite simply the greatest movies ever made: the word is overused, but they are beloved. In that sense the carpings of the few unconvinced film critics, or Tolkien sceptics, are an irrelevance. One wonders though, if the first of the two *The Hobbit* films, to be directed by Jackson after a chaotic and extended period of pre-production that at one point had Guillermo del Toro attached to direct, can be anything other than a mild disappointment.

VIRTUAL UNREALITY

How performance capture is changing the way movies are made

Sometime in the early 2000s Peter Jackson, deep in pre-production for his groundbreaking *Lord of the Rings* trilogy, pondered the problem of Gollum. How would he bring the sinister Stoor-Hobbit, described by Tolkien as "a small slimy creature ... as dark as darkness, except for two big round pale eyes in his thin face", to the screen? Eschewing prosthetic make-up, puppetry and even stop-motion, he decided to try to push the rapidly developing technology of performance capture to its very limits. The result was this millennium's introduction of a new form of performance, a seamless fusion of the deeply human and the height of technology. And it's a technology that actors and directors still have only scratched the surface of, and that audiences, awards organizations and some critics struggle to fully understand.

Motion capture is essentially a sophisticated form of a much older animation technique called rotoscoping, in which animators would trace their drawings on top of film of real images to make their work's movement more accurate and lifelike. Patented in 1917 by Max Fleischer, mo-cap's first real star was his brother Dave dressed in a clown costume. The resulting character, Koko, appeared in a number of *Out of the Inkwell* episodes in the early 1920s and animators ever since have used rotoscoping in one form or another. But by the 1970s computers were beginning to be used for what would become known as "performance capture". This has comprised different techniques, and the technology is still developing, but the principle remains the same. An actor is covered with dozens of tiny reflective markers and filmed by digital cameras while he or she performs a scene. The movement of these individual markers, often including facial ones, is recorded in detail and this data used to generate a 3D digital representation of the original performance, a kind of virtual armature on top of which skilled computer animators can model an almost unlimited range of characters: from a slimy creature with big round eyes (Gollum) to a thoroughly annoying Ebonics-spouting eight-foot-tall space-newt (the *Star Wars* prequels' Jar-Jar Binks).

The use of the new technique wasn't without its teething troubles. In 2004 Robert Zemeckis became the first director to shoot an entire film using performance capture and to use it to create mundane human rather than animal or fantastic characters. *The Polar Express*, a Christmas confection about a boy boarding a train to the North Pole, starring Tom Hanks, was branded a failure, the technology seemingly subtracting from the performances rather than adding to them: "creepy", "lifeless", "dead-eyed"

and "frightening" being among the harsh words critics flung at the digital renderings. It was a problem that hadn't been solved seven years later when Steven Spielberg's *The Adventures of Tintin: The Secret of the Unicorn* (2011) faced similar brickbats, with the Belgian boy-detective being described as looking "like a Ronseal marionette". For the moment it seems creating believable humans is beyond even the most powerful software.

But Andy Serkis's performance as Gollum in *The Fellowship of the Ring* (2001) was a revelation. Realistic, nuanced and utterly believable, it almost instantly rendered the previous technologies of puppetry, prosthetics and stop-motion redundant, and in Serkis created its most famous and skilled practitioner. Serkis would go on to refine his work in two more *Rings* movies and, seemingly making a speciality of playing simian roles, would bring a wounded humanity to the giant ape in Peter Jackson's *King Kong* (2005) and a revelatory moment of transformation from ape to super-ape as Caesar in Rupert Wyatt's *Rise of the Planet of the Apes* (2011).

But the new technology has brought with it its own controversies. Not only is it often misunderstood (even in 2011, some critics were describing Jamie Bell as merely having "voiced" Tintin), some feel that it dilutes the craft of acting or compromises a performance's integrity, with the actor merely a kind of provider of raw original movement for a sophisticated special effect. And who is responsible for the final result? The actor or the droves of digital animators? In 2012 Serkis's *Apes* co-star James Franco called for the performer to be considered for a best supporting actor Oscar nomination, saying: "this is not animation so much as it is digital make-up" and comparing Serkis's performance to John Hurt's in *The Elephant Man* (1980). How the Weta effects team felt about having their groundbreaking work so dismissed goes, probably thankfully, unrecorded.

Serkis, though, is in no doubt about who is at the heart of these half-human half-machine "cyborg" performances. "I think there is a woeful lack of understanding," he said in 2011. "If you don't get the performance on the day, you can't enhance the performance. What you can do with visual effects is enhance the look of the character, but the actual integrity of the emotional performance and the way the character's facial expressions work, that is what is going to be created on the day with other actors and the director." The day when the best performance Oscar is given to a special-effects company is a way away yet.

Lost in Translation

2004, US, 102 mins, 15 (UK) R (US)

••

cast Bill Murray, Scarlett Johansson, Giovanni
Ribisi, Anna Faris *scr* Sofia Coppola *cin* Lance Acord
m Kevin Shields *dir* Sofia Coppola

Sofia Coppola's follow-up to her impressive debut *The
Virgin Suicides* (2000) is a movie with a secret. For a
start it eludes easy categorization. Is it a love story?
A cinematic tone poem about alienation, loneliness
and ennui? A beautifully photographed Japanese
travelogue? Or is it all just about a really nice hotel?
Whatever it is, it is a movie of rare delicacy; it leaves
you agreeably sad, wreathed in a strange melancholy.

We meet Bob Harris (Bill Murray), a Hollywood
action star who is in Tokyo alone to film a lucrative
commercial for a Japanese whiskey, as he peers out
of his car on the way to the hotel at the garish view,
which may as well be of a city on another planet. Jet-
lagged, disoriented and unable to sleep, he retires
to the hotel bar where he meets Charlotte (Scarlett
Johansson), a young woman in Japan with her
celebrity photographer husband (Giovanni Ribisi).
Or rather she is occasionally next to him but not
with him very much at all. They seem strangers after
two years of marriage. Bill and Charlotte begin to
chat, and meet again by chance the next day before
embarking on a low-key Japanese odyssey involving
karaoke bars and student parties. Slowly the tendrils
of some unexpressed need, much more subtle and
oblique than the desire for a mere May–December
fling, extend themselves. The nature of this relationship is indefinable, more
than friendship, not in the end sexual, but undeniably profound and intense. The
strangeness of Tokyo, its towering cliffs of neon, deafening pachinko parlours and

SOFIA COPPOLA

b. 14 May 1971, New York, NY, US

When, in 1990, Winona Ryder dropped out of *The
Godfather Part III* (1991) in order to star in *Edward
Scissorhands* (1991), a wise decision as it would turn
out, director Francis Ford Coppola conducted what
one critic described as "an extensive casting call of his
immediate family" and put his daughter Sofia in the
role. The movie was a critical disaster and, though she
would crop up in the occasional role subsequently, it
seems to have put paid to her acting ambitions. By
the late 90s she had moved behind the camera and
delivered her first feature, *The Virgin Suicides* (2000),
based on the novel by Jeffrey Eugenides. Delicate,
mysterious and subtly erotic, in both tone and subject,
as it examines the reactions of a group of girls to their
burgeoning adolescence, it brings to mind Peter Weir's
masterpiece *Picnic at Hanging Rock* (1976). Three films
have so far followed, all scripted by Coppola herself:
Marie Antoinette (2006) divided critics, with some
celebrating its dynamic attitude while others found not
much more than a teen movie gussied up with big wigs.
But her two key films were *Lost in Translation* (2004)
and *Somewhere* (2010), both concerning movie stars
in posh hotels. This superficially unpromising trope is
doubtless autobiographical. Coppola spent much of
her childhood in the world's fanciest hotels and seems
to have soaked up some of their capacity to induce a
kind of ennui; the characters in these films are ever so
slightly tranquillized, floating along in a not entirely
unpleasant haze. In *Lost in Translation* an oblique love
story plays out against the alien neonscapes of Tokyo,
while in the less seen but no less impressive *Somewhere*
a film star, played with militant understatement by
Stephen Dorff, has his life almost changed by the arrival
at his hotel home of his eleven-year-old daughter.
The unhurried tone to both films is reminiscent of
Tom DiCillo or Gus Van Sant and there's a beguiling
elusiveness and sense of unresolvable mystery – an
atmosphere that owes absolutely nothing to her
father's more bombastic, direct style.

odd little ceremonies (all beautifully captured by star indie lenser Lance Acord) offers an alien background against which both Bob and Charlotte's lives are thrown into relief. Charlotte is unsure of what she wants out of life and beginning to suspect that her marriage might have been a mistake. Bob has resigned himself to a wife more interested in carpet samples than his middle-aged dissatisfactions. They draw comfort from the fact that someone out there feels as deeply ambivalent about existence as they do.

Coppola is too sharp a writer/director not to allow Murray, a man who rations his movie appearances to perfection, to stretch his comedy muscles a little: there's a funny scene with a prostitute sent to his room by the booze executives, he does a bit of business channeling Buster Keaton with a running machine in the gym, but for the most part he's laconic, tired, quietly resigned to his lot. Johansson's Charlotte, a woman frightened that she might never discover something to become passionate about, is an old head on young shoulders. Her moments of quiet, looking out of the window on a bullet train speeding to Kyoto, wandering around a Japanese garden where she sees a wedding, are amongst the film's most affecting.

Lost in Translation ends with a cinematic masterstroke. Meeting Charlotte for a final time after a last-minute run through a crowded street – the nearest thing to a romantic cliché in the film, and even so Coppola makes it work – he grabs her and whispers in her ear. The audience does not hear what he says, but as he retreats he is smiling, and so is she. This Tokyo story, as delicately spun as Japanese silk, concludes with a moment too personal for us to share. It is a movie that keeps its secret to the end.

The delicately sketched friendship of laconic Bob (Bill Murray) and uncertain Charlotte (Scarlett Johansson) is thrown into relief by the alien surroundings of Tokyo in Sofia Coppola's subtle, ambiguous film.

Midnight in Paris

2011, US/Sp, 94 mins, 12A (UK) PG-13 (US)

••

cast Owen Wilson, Rachel McAdams, Adrien Brody, Corey Stoll, Kathy Bates, Marion Cotillard **scr** Woody Allen **cin** Johanne Debas, Darius Khondji **m** Stephane Wrembel **dir** Woody Allen

Ever since Woody Allen performed a surprising volte-face, abandoned the Manhattan that had been the location for almost all of his films since 1975's *Love and Death*, and embarked on what might be called his later European phase, his increasingly despondent fans became like loyal supporters of a once great football team now languishing in the lower divisions, turning up every week only to see hope regularly trounced five-nil by experience. Even if some considered the critical opprobrium heaped on *Match Point* (2006) a little excessive, and *Vicky Cristina Barcelona* (2009) was actually quite good, there was still the genuinely dire *Scoop* (2006), Ewan McGregor's Cockernee outrage in *Cassandra's Dream* (2008) and the utterly negligible *You Will Meet a Tall Dark Stranger* (2011). It seemed to increasingly resigned audiences that not only were Allen's best films behind him, his moderately good ones were too. And then came *Midnight in Paris* and, joy to behold, the filmmaker had returned to spectacular form.

Gil (Owen Wilson) is a hack Hollywood screenwriter vacationing in Paris with his fiancée (Rachel McAdams) and her carping family. Enchanted by the city, and less so by them, he wanders off one night only to get hopelessly lost. As midnight tolls an ancient roadster pulls up and a mysterious figure beckons in the curious American, only to whisk him to a wildly exciting party which, he slowly realizes, is happening in the 1920s. (It's a gloriously graceful way of avoiding ten minutes of time travel exposition and the best use of a car as temporal

MARION COTILLARD

b. 30 September 1975, Paris, France

It takes *cojones* for a Frenchwoman to take on the role of the country's legendary crooner Edith Piaf. Or maybe you just need to *be* a bit nuts. "The idea of Piaf to me was completely crazy," Cotillard said in 2007 of her role in biopic *La vie en Rose* (2007). "But then I read the script and I wanted to be as crazy as [director Olivier Dahan] was." Crazy turned out to be a good call and seems to have served her well ever since. Her performance as the legendary singer was a revelation (as was the stunning make-up by veteran Didier Lavergne), convincingly portraying the troubled singer from her youth to her untimely death at a ravaged 47, and snagged her an Oscar, making her the first person to win best actor or actress for a French-language performance (a feat echoed by Jean Dujardin in *The Artist* in 2012, if his two words count). Her most visible project in the 90s was the comedy/action *Taxi* trilogy, created by Luc Besson (1998, 2000 and 2003), in which she played the girlfriend of pizza delivery boy turned supercharged cabbie Samy Naceri. In Hollywood she had a small role in Tim Burton's typically whimsical *Big Fish* (2004) and subsequently turned up in Ridley Scott's soapy adaptation of Peter Mayle's *A Good Year* (2006) opposite Russell Crowe. But her Oscar success as Piaf was a turning point in terms of her American career. Though Rob Marshall's attempt to recapture *Chicago*'s (2003) success with musical *Nine* (2009) was underwhelming (though -Cotillard got the movie's few critically approving nods as the wife of Daniel Day-Lewis's blocked film director), she harnessed her inner crazy again as Mal Cobb, a nasty wrinkle in Leonardo DiCaprio's subconscious in Christopher Nolan's *Inception* (2010, p.141). Woody Allen cast her perfectly as Picasso's muse and Hemingway's lover, or maybe it's the other way around, in his delightful *Midnight in Paris* (2011). She cemented her place in Christopher Nolan's growing repertory company when he cast her as Miranda Tate in his *The Dark Knight Rises* (2012), an intriguing new character to the franchise.

deus ex machina since *Back to the Future*'s Delorean.) There he meets his literary and artistic heroes, Ernest Hemingway (Corey Stoll), Salvador Dali (Adrien Brody) and Gertrude Stein: a bracingly straight-talking Kathy Bates, who offers to critique his magnum opus, a novel uncoincidentally about a man who works in a nostalgia shop. Gil is of course delighted, and begins to fall for artistic muse Adriana (Marion Cotillard), who is the key to the movie's moral: in the end we must all live in our own present; nostalgia is a beguiling trap.

Midnight in Paris's pleasures are many – moody, smoky cinematography, half a dozen sparkling performances – but its chief delight is Owen Wilson's irresistible turn as Allen *manqué* Gil. Stepping into Allen's shoes has always been a fraught business for any actor: play the dialogue too closely and you look like an impersonator, stray too far away and the lines lose their unique tang. But Wilson makes them his own, eschewing Allen's syncopated anxiety for his own, mildly nasal, ever so slightly dude-ish cadences. It really shouldn't work, but it really does. And he has in spades what even Woody himself at his best struggles for: an easy, unforced charm.

Midnight in Paris might not quite be in the league of the timeless classics of the 1970s, the *Annie Hall*s (1977) and *Manhattan*s (1979), but as you walk out of the cinema with a goofy smile, and the director's recent indifferent output fades in the memory, it's easy to imagine that we're back in the 1980s, when Allen regularly delivered beautifully crafted cinematic love letters such as *The Purple Rose of Cairo* (1985) or *Radio Days* (1987). In that, it's a little piece of time travel of its own.

An American in Paris: Gil (Owen Wilson) accompanies Adriana (Marion Cotillard) on a nighttime stroll in Woody Allen's glorious return to form.

Milk

2009, US, 128 mins, 15 (UK) R (US)

....

cast Sean Penn, Josh Brolin, James Franco, Emile Hirsch, Diego Luna *scr* Dustin Lance Black *cin* Harris Savides *m* Danny Elfman *dir* Gus Van Sant

Sean Penn (alongside Emile Hirsch) makes himself heard in the face of opposition as legendary gay activist Harvey Milk.

Gus Van Sant's gripping biopic of activist Harvey Milk, the first openly gay man to be elected to public office in the United States, begins with archive footage. At first we see grainy black-and-white newsreel of men being arrested during a raid on a gay bar sometime in the 1960s. Some hiding their faces, others staring defiantly at the camera, the men are loaded into paddy-wagons, many of their lives and careers no doubt already ruined. Then we cut to the exterior of San Francisco City Hall on a November night in 1978 and the announcement, to a shocked crowd, that Milk, together with Mayor George Moscone, has been assassinated by a disgruntled politician. In the decade or so between these two dates the battle for

gay rights was at its height in the US, scoring key victories while coming under sustained attack from the Christian right. It was a febrile, fascinating period both in San Francisco and elsewhere and Van Sant and screenwriter Dustin Lance Black perfectly capture its triumphs and tragedies.

The Oscar-winning screenplay neatly stresses both Milk's unlikely origins as a political activist – he was forty before he moved to the run-down Castro district of San Francisco and began a career in political campaigning – and his almost preternatural political instincts, exemplified by a talent for forging unlikely coalitions. Teamsters angry at union-busting Coors beer (which Milk got removed from every gay bar in the Castro), senior citizens alarmed about safety on the streets, and almost everybody enraged by the amount of dog dirt on San Francisco's sidewalks were recruited to his campaigns.

Penn's performance is perfectly calibrated, a gratifying surprise from an actor better known for channelling wounded, often uncompromising machismo. He captures the fey, archly camp nature of Milk's personality without once coming anywhere near caricature, revealing that Milk's playful jokiness and capacity to disarm – when asked if two men are capable of procreation he replies "no, but we sure keep trying" – was underpinned with a will of steel and an absolute determination to raise the visibility of gays in local and national politics. Josh Brolin, in another strong turn, depicts Milk's assassin as a tormented character, without friends in politics, and whose depths of rage and anguish Milk perhaps misjudges. The suggestion is made that he is a repressed homosexual, which feels a little glib and unnecessary.

Some critics complained mildly that the film verged too close to hagiography, that the more complex, messy elements of both Milk's life and the gay milieu of the 70s were tastefully airbrushed out of the picture. (San Franciscan bathhouse culture, a key element of gay life, and one that Milk was personally familiar with, is mysteriously absent, while Milk is presented as essentially monogamous: he wasn't and he was open about it.) They may be right, but then Hollywood is notorious for softening the less attractive sides of its biopic subjects, so why should Harvey Milk be any exception to having the biographical light adjusted to show his best side? What is worth noting is that 32 years after Milk's murder, Sean Penn accepted his fully deserved Oscar in a state that had just passed Proposition 8, banning gay marriage, and in front of an audience containing not a single out gay A-list star. It really isn't difficult to imagine what Harvey Milk would have to say about that.

Moneyball

2011, US, 133 mins, 12A (UK) PG-13 (US)

....

cast Brad Pitt, Jonah Hill, Philip Seymour Hoffman, Robin Wright *scr* Steven Zaillian and Aaron Sorkin (story by Stan Chervin from the book by Michael Lewis) *cin* Wally Pfister *m* Mychael Danna *dir* Bennett Miller

If *Moneyball*, a slick, exciting sports movie in the traditional mould, is anything to go by, the old saying about Hollywood – "nobody knows anything" – applies to America's national sport as much as it does to the dream factory. Perhaps it's why Hollywood was drawn to this story in which the certainty of statistics replaces the vagaries of gut instinct or whether or not a player has, for instance, a "baseball face" or an ugly girlfriend ("shows he has no confidence" a scout unimpressed with a proposed player says). If Hollywood could apply the same mathematical certainties to films, where comparable voodoo seems to determine gazillion-dollar production decisions, it'd be a studio exec's dream, and this kind of classy, intelligent, popular film would be ten a penny at the multiplex instead of the rarity they are.

Based on a book by journalist Michael Lewis (who usually writes about financial scandals), *Moneyball* charts the true story of the Oakland A's, a struggling California baseball team whose best players are regularly poached by bigger, richer outfits. In response to a particularly catastrophic season general manager and failed player Billy Beane (a perfectly cast Brad Pitt, more and more beginning to resemble Robert Redford in his middle period) hires flabby Yale-educated economist Peter Brand (played with skill and understatement by Jonah Hill, making a welcome detour from his usual comedic roles). Brand is a maths nerd who holds the Warren Buffet-ish "true value" view that by mining the data in order to find undervalued players, a team can be put together on the cheap that might look damned odd to ball aficionados, but nevertheless has a good chance to win. Bemused and enraged by this new approach are the leathery old club scouts as well as chief coach Art Howe, a shaven-headed and slightly underused Philip Seymour Hoffman. Buried underneath the locker-room headbutting is Billy's conviction, expressed in tightly edited flashbacks, that, urged on by scouts, he made the wrong decision as a young man, and that college would have been a better choice than the baseball diamond. In one of the movie's many keenly judged moments he asks Brand if he would have recruited him: the answer is no.

The odd contradiction at the heart of *Moneyball* is that this is a film about hard numbers replacing guts, instinct and passion. It's a direct rejection of the strident romanticism of most sports movies in which heart and soul trump cold reason. But apart from this oddity it sits squarely in the underdogs beating the reigning champs tradition of the trad Hollywood sports movie, in which ones are won for the Gipper and The Mighty Ducks reign supreme. What makes it special is the burnished till it gleams quality of every aspect: Steven Zaillian and Aaron Sorkin's screenplay is an object lesson in unobtrusive exposition and propulsive structure; Bennett Miller (who had previously only directed one film, 2006's *Capote* with Philip Seymour Hoffman) expertly paces the story, minimizing the sporting action in favour of off-field drama, and has a gimlet eye for the telling dramatic moment. Pitt meanwhile manages to deliver a performance that is both movie-star appealing and yet complicated and subtle enough to be more than superficially interesting. Auteur theory be damned: great Hollywood moviemaking, like baseball, turns out to be all about the team.

Off-field drama: team manager Billy Beane (Brad Pitt) teams up with genius numbers man Peter Brand (Jonah Hill).

Moon

2009, UK, 97 mins, 15 (UK) R (US)

cast Sam Rockwell, Kevin Spacey **scr** Nathan Parker (story Duncan Jones) **cin** Gary Shaw **m** Clint Mansell **dir** Duncan Jones

Duncan Jones's exciting and acclaimed directorial debut eschews the flashy, action-oriented post-*Matrix* (1999) cyberpunk that has come to dominate the genre, returning instead for its influences to a golden age of sci-fi movies, a period that ran roughly from the mid-1960s to the mid-70s. It echoes some of the themes and the intelligent tone of films such as *2001: A Space Odyssey* (1967), *Solaris* (1972), *Silent Running* (1972) and even John Carpenter's *Dark Star* (1974) to fashion a thoughtful, gently melancholic meditation on loneliness, isolation and the deeper question of what it might mean to be human.

Sam Bell (Sam Rockwell) is a man who is as alone as it is possible to be. Stuck on the dark side of the moon, he's the only inhabitant of a lunar mining outpost; giant remotely controlled machines do the actual digging, while Sam runs maintenance. His only companion on the base is GERTY, a somewhat shambolic-looking robot (voiced expertly by Kevin Spacey, channelling more than a little of Douglas Rain's HAL) whose role is to look after Sam's physical needs, something he does with paternal concern. Direct communication with Earth is impossible, as a vital communications satellite has been malfunctioning since before

Ground control to Major Sam: Sam Rockwell as the loneliest man in the world in Duncan Jones's thought-provoking, 1970s-style *Moon*.

SAM ROCKWELL

b. 5 November 1968, Daly City, CA, US

"I aspire to do what Dustin Hoffman did in the 70s maybe, or Jon Voight or Jeff Bridges," Sam Rockwell declared back in 2007. "Ideally kind of do both character parts and leading man parts." If nothing else it's an ambition that shows that he has exquisite taste, but Rockwell does indeed have much of the eccentric, off-beam charisma and unpredictable energy of those titans. And if leading man roles have been thinner on the ground than he might hope, this is not a symptom of any failing on his behalf but of the sad fact that big sophisticated Hollywood dramas of the late 60s and 70s – *The Graduate*, *Midnight Cowboy* – are now for the most part a distant memory, replaced by the indie fare in which he has flourished. He made his name in small movies in the late 1990s, notably *Lawn Dogs* (1997), in which he played with wit and charm a gardener who forms an unlikely friendship with a lonely ten-year-old, and *Jerry and Tom* (1998), a black comedy in which assassins moonlight as used-car salesmen. He was perfectly cast in George Clooney's biopic of Chuck Barris, *Confessions of a Dangerous Mind* (2003), giving the loopy game-show host/self-declared undercover spook/fabulist exactly the right blend of goofball fun and unpredictable danger. Subsequently he turned up as the more amusing half of a pair of con men (the other was Nicolas Cage) in Ridley Scott's thriller *Matchstick Men* (2003), and in Ron Howard's *Frost/Nixon* (2009) as investigative journalist James Reston Jr. He joined the equally quirky Robert Downey Jr on *Iron Man 2* (2010) as unprincipled rival arms manufacturer Justin Hammer. But his key achievement of the millennium was his performance in Duncan Jones's restrained, mysterious science fiction tale *Moon* (2009). As the sole miner on the desolate lunar surface, Rockwell conjured a palpable sense of wounded, lonely humanity. It's a role that the Hoffmans, Voights and Bridges would have relished and Rockwell gives a performance as nuanced, powerful and finally moving as any of them might have.

Sam arrived. But things aren't too bad: he gets regular taped messages of his wife and child back on Earth, and with only two weeks left to go of his three-year contract he is looking forward to returning home. But when he wakes up, following an accident, to find a second, seemingly identical, Sam Bell in the base with him, his and his doppelgänger's perceptions of who or what they are begin to change.

Given that it was made for just $5 million, *Moon* is a wonder: Jones's decision to use miniature models for the lunar exteriors is a masterstroke, adding to the sense that this is a film with its heart very much in the 70s, while Clint Mansell's score is spare, evocative and at times effectively sinister. Sam Rockwell meanwhile gives a brace of thoroughly worked-out performances, speedily dispatching any suspicion that having one actor play the two Sams is any kind of gimmick (though a table tennis game between the two mischievously plays with the audience's "how did they do that?" curiosity). Discussing the themes of the film might give away too much of the ingenious plot, but suffice it to say that one of its subjects is corporate ethics. What, it asks, are vast conglomerates willing to do in their ceaseless search for profit, particularly if no one can see them?

On *Moon*'s release, the world's film press made sure no one missed the fact that Jones's father is David Bowie. The director himself has worked hard to forge an independent path, starting with ditching his original name, but even so, is there a nod to dad in the son's debut movie? Can it really be accident that this intelligent, humane science fiction film, in many ways reminiscent of yet another classic of the genre from the 70s, ends with the image of a man falling to Earth?

LONG LIVE THE NEW FLESH #3:

Ten directors who made their debuts in the 2000s...

ZACK SNYDER Debut: *Dawn of the Dead* (2004)
George Romero's zombie trilogy has been the victim of drive-by remakes before, but Zack Snyder's re-imagining of the second, always more interesting, film captured both its creative and plentiful gore and its wit, replacing the first movie's political satire with gooey black humour. Snyder subsequently became a fanboy favourite with sword-and-sandal hokum *300* (2007) and *Watchmen* (2009), both adapted from graphic novels, and sets Superman soaring again in the forthcoming *Man of Steel*.

MATTHEW VAUGHN Debut: *Layer Cake* (2004)
Vaughn started his career as a producer, notably of Guy Ritchie's mockney smash *Lock, Stock and Two Smoking Barrels* (1998). His own directing debut was also a crime caper and featured a mesmerizing performance from a pre-Bond Daniel Craig as a criminal embarking on that always tricky "one last job". Densely plotted and stylishly directed, together with cult comic-book adaptation *Kick-Ass* (2010), it impressed Hollywood enough to hand him the keys to one of their most valuable franchises with *X-Men: First Class* (2011).

RIAN JOHNSON Debut: *Brick* (2006)
Dashiell Hammett meets *Fast Times at Ridgemont High* (1982) in Rian Johnson's thrillingly original *film noir*/high-school movie mash-up which has Joseph Gordon-Levitt as a teenager investigating the death of his girlfriend. One of those movies that really doesn't work on paper, it gained Johnson the chance to direct Gordon-Levitt again in *The Brothers Bloom* (2010) and alongside Bruce Willis in sci-fi *noir Looper* (2012).

STEVE MCQUEEN Debut: *Hunger* (2008)
A Turner Prize-winning conceptual artist who often utilized film in his work, McQueen's debut feature was a coolly merciless account of conditions in the Maze Prison in Northern Ireland and the death of hunger-striker Bobby Sands (Michael Fassbender in the role that rocketed him to international attention). McQueen's next film was the perhaps over-praised but still skilfully directed account of sex addiction, *Shame* (2012), again with Fassbender.

JUAN ANTONIO BAYONA Debut: *The Orphanage* (2008)
If Bayona's spooky Spanish story of a young boy living in an ancient orphanage has distant echoes of Guillermo del Toro's *The Devil's Backbone* (2001), it certainly didn't seem to bother del Toro, who acted as an executive producer on the film. Deeply unnerving, skilfully plotted and directed and in its ending unexpectedly uplifting, it gives yet another reason, if one were needed, *never* to go into the cellar...

SAM TAYLOR-WOOD Debut: *Nowhere Boy* (2009)
A member of the famous/infamous group of conceptual tyros known as the YBAs (Young British Artists), Sam Taylor-Wood displayed an interest in John Lennon with her early portraiture. Her feature debut was this Lennon biopic that surprised some critics with its conventionality but pleased audiences with its straightforward account of Lennon's early life in Liverpool and a likeable performance from unknown Aaron Johnson, to whom she later became engaged despite the much remarked on 23-year age difference.

BEN WHEATLEY Debut: *Down Terrace* (2010)
Essex-born Wheatley spent his early career directing advertising and viral clips before graduating to features with this thrillingly black family crime dramedy set among Brighton lowlife, which showcased his talent for acid dialogue and hairpin plot turns. *Kill List* (2011) brought his burgeoning skills to a gritty horror flick with a uniquely grim atmosphere and queasy sense of moral rot.

OREN MOVERMAN Debut: *The Messenger* (2011)
A touchingly acted and sensitively directed example of the "War at Home" movies generated by the wars in Iraq and Afghanistan, Moverman's debut had Woody Harrelson and Ben Foster as US soldiers whose job it is to deliver the worst news to military families. His sophomore effort, *Rampart* (2012), a violent crime drama again starring Woody Harrelson as a brutal cop, was equally impressive.

JOHN MICHAEL MCDONAGH Debut: *The Guard* (2011)
McDonagh's brother Martin had already given us his hugely entertaining *In Bruges* (2008) but John rivals it with this rude, crude and hilarious Irish crime caper/buddy movie/fish-out-of-water tale. Brendan Gleeson is on top form as a rotten policeman not averse to stealing drugs from dead road accident victims who has to team up with an uptight FBI agent (Don Cheadle) to get to the bottom of a drug-ring.

RICHARD AYOADE Debut: *Submarine* (2011)
Known to British TV comedy fans from *The IT Crowd*, Ayoade made the move behind the camera and to the big screen with this winning adaptation of the coming-of-age novel by Joe Dunthorne. Craig Roberts stars as a duffel-coated teenager attempting to both save his parents' marriage and shed his virginity before his sixteenth birthday. Ayoade directs with sympathy, wit and visual flair: it gained a BAFTA for outstanding British debut in 2012.

Mulholland Drive

2002, US/Fr, 146 mins, 15 (UK) R (US)

....

cast Naomi Watts, Laura Harring, Justin Theroux, Ann Miller *scr* David Lynch
cin Peter Deming *m* Angelo Badalamenti *dir* David Lynch

Mulholland Drive, a strange, beguiling masterpiece from America's greatest surrealist David Lynch, has much about it of a waking dream. It's febrile and mysterious and vaguely hallucinatory. Despite being apparently set in the present it's drenched in the richly textured atmosphere of old Hollywood and *film noir* and goosed with a hefty slug of repressed, and then not very repressed, eroticism. And for anyone who likes their films to make sense, for loose ends to be neatly knotted off, motives sketched, uppances comed, it must seem like some exquisite form of torture.

It seems to be a story about a wannabe actress who might be called Betty (Naomi Watts), who arrives in Hollywood in the opening minutes of the film. She's blonde and bright and perky and hopelessly naive, a promising morsel on which Hollywood might chew. But when she arrives at her aunt's beautiful apartment she finds a girl who probably isn't called Rita (Laura Harring) already in situ. Rita is apparently suffering amnesia after a road accident and as the two try to find out who she is and why she has a purse stuffed with dead presidents and a strange blue key, they find themselves plunging into a maze populated by gangsters and cool film directors, *femmes fatales* and inept hit men. Instead of making more and more sense as it goes on, *Mulholland Drive* makes less and less. It's full of strange moments that seem like they might be clues but then lead nowhere. Betty announces at one point that she arrived in Hollywood after winning a jitterbug competition. Many wannabe starlets no doubt did, but more than fifty years ago. That blue key seems to change shape and then a smooth blue box that it might fit turns up. What's inside? Characters suddenly vanish or seem to recombine in new and different forms.

The miracle of Lynch's film, certainly among his very best, alongside *Eraserhead* (1977) and *Blue Velvet* (1986), is that it doesn't drive you up the wall. Instead, its odd, ever so slightly tranquillized tone seduces and hypnotizes. Its many moods glide seamlessly into one another, the exciting almost Nancy

A wilderness of mirrors: reflections of Rita (Laura Harring) – and Betty (Naomi Watts) – in David Lynch's beguiling, symbol-laden cinematic riddle.

Drew-ish investigation embarked on by the two girls (and it deftly sketches the kind of sudden friendship you're only really capable of when you're young), the hardboiled world of weary gumshoes and thugs. Suddenly it lurches into a kind of bloody comedy worthy of the Coens, with a botched robbery featuring an ever-increasing body count, and then it becomes a work of cool symbolism along the lines of Fellini. Audiences spent hours attempting to unpick it, to force it to reveal its secrets. Is it one long dream sequence? Is it two? Where does reality begin and end? Are we witnessing the shards of a fractured life flashing by at the moment of death? It's precisely the wrong thing to do. Prod it crudely like that and, like an exotic sea anemone, it simply withdraws its delicate tendrils and closes itself up. It is best enjoyed as a kind of tone poem, a richly seductive meditation on movies and *noir*, identity and fate, and about the nature and importance of stories themselves. David Lynch's *Mulholland Drive* ain't a place then; it's a state of mind.

No Country for Old Men

2008, US, 122 mins, 18 (UK) R (US)

. . . .

cast Tommy Lee Jones, Josh Brolin, Javier Bardem *scr* Joel Coen
& Ethan Coen (adapted from the novel by Cormac McCarthy)
cin Roger Deakins *m* Carter Burwell *dir* Joel Coen & Ethan Coen

Sheriff Ed Tom Bell's (Tommy Lee Jones) despairing opening
voiceover, delivered over a series of stark Texan landscapes, sets
the tone for the Coen brothers' bleakest and most brilliant film to
date. Remembering a murderer he sent to the electric chair, for
an offence some described as "a crime of passion", he says "[He]
told me that he'd been planning to kill somebody for about as long
as he could remember. Said that if they turned him out he'd do it
again. Said he knew he was going to hell. 'Be there in about fifteen
minutes.' I don't know what to make of that, I sure don't."

In essence *No Country for Old Men* is the Coens' other crime
masterpiece, *Fargo* (1996), turned inside out. If *Fargo* is at its
chilly heart a reassuring comedy in which the bad guys get their
comeuppance and order is restored, then *No Country for Old Men*
is its tragic twin. The most obvious inversion is the setting: *Fargo*'s
frozen Minnesota has been swapped with the sun-blasted Texan
desert. But there are deeper resonances. In place of *Fargo*'s inept
kidnappers we get Javier Bardem's conjuring of pure anarchic
evil in Anton Chigurh, a hit man for whom murder and chaos
are their own rewards. The ordinary man corrupted by money in
Fargo is the hapless Jerry Lundergaard (William H. Macy) who, in
the tradition of comedy, is allowed to live. In *No Country for Old*

Josh Brolin having a blast as Llewelyn Moss, a man with a suitcase of money and a
hit man closing in on him, in the Coen brothers' crime masterpiece.

JOSH BROLIN

b. 12 February 1968, Los Angeles, CA, US

On seeing his own performance in the 1986 skateboarding film *Thrashin'*, former *The Goonies* (1985) star Josh Brolin declared it to be so rancid that he forswore film acting forever. Thankfully his self-imposed cinematic exile was not to be permanent and in the mid-noughties he emerged from theatre and television, where he had spent the bulk of the intervening time, not as the leading man that Hollywood had once seemed determined to make him, but as one of its most versatile character actors, specializing in subtle depictions of flawed alpha males. His real break came when the Coen brothers cast him as thief on the lam Llewelyn Moss in *No Country for Old Men* (2008), a role to which he gave what would become a typical complexity. He worked with the Coens again on their Western remake *True Grit* (2011), in which he played a murderer on the run, and has worked with Oliver Stone twice: once as a corrupt banker in *Wall Street: Money Never Sleeps* (2010), an underpowered companion piece to the 80s classic to which he couldn't add much, and more impressively playing President George W. Bush in Stone's biopic *W.* (2008). It was a part he was initially reluctant to take. "When Oliver asked me, I said, 'Are you crazy? Why would I want to do that with this moment in my career?'" he told *The Los Angeles Times*. Reassured that the film wasn't just "a far-left hammering of the president" he took the job and, despite the film's other imperfections, was convincing as a man trying to prove himself to a sceptical family. He was equally subtle in another political biopic, this time as councilman Dan White, Harvey Milk's assassin in Gus Van Sant's *Milk* (2009, p.172). He gave the role nuance, and even sympathy, controversially revealing in a key scene with Sean Penn what might have been deeper motives than simple professional jealousy. Previously unseduced by the lure of summer blockbuster, he nevertheless took over from Tommy Lee Jones as the grumpier half of *Men in Black*'s double act opposite Will Smith for the franchise's rebirth in 2012. Retirement, then, seems to be a thing very much of the past.

Men it is Llewelyn Moss (Josh Brolin), whose single act of altruism – returning to the scene of a drugs deal gone awry from which he has stolen a case-full of greenbacks, in order to give water to a wounded dealer – sets in motion the trail of events that will lead to his bloody demise.

If anything lends warmth to this desolate picture of humanity, and offsets a little of the film's palpable sense of impending violence and doom, it's Tommy Lee Jones's perfectly judged performance as Sheriff Ed Tom Bell, a man who sees the world as *almost* hopelessly rotten. "Who *are* these people?" he wonders as he works methodically to track down Chigurh. His tone is one of dismay, but not nihilism; without his very thin sliver of optimism this wouldn't be a country fit for anyone at all.

Some critics seemed afraid to touch on the film's moral foundation, perhaps fearing the inevitable accusations of pretension and over-reading. But this is a work of art concerned with the big questions, of the possibility of good in a fallen world. At the end of the film, sitting in his modest home, beginning a retirement you feel he might regret, Ed Tom Bell delivers a monologue that recalls the opening of the movie, and describes a dream he has had of his dead father holding a light in the darkness. In this faint but real possibility of redemption and peace *No Country for Old Men*, the Coens' first to win a best picture Oscar, reveals itself to be a film of serious moral passion: and it's as good as cinema gets in this or the previous millennium.

Oldboy

2004, S. Kor, 120 mins, 18 (UK) R (US)

••

cast Choi Min-sik, Yu Ji-tae, Gang Hye-jung, Chi Dae-han, Oh Dal-su, Kim Byeog-ok *scr* Hwang Jo-yun, Lim Joon-hyung and Park Chan-wook (from the manga by Garon Tsuchiya and Nobuaki Minegishi) *cin* Chung Chung-hoon *m* Shim Hyun-jung *dir* Park Chan-wook

A terrified man clutching a poodle is dangled by his tie over the edge of a tall building. The assailant, his face a study of rage, stares into his victim's eyes. "I want to tell you my story," he says. It's hard not to think of the opening moments of Park Chan-wook's super-charged masterpiece as a metaphor for the director

Hammer time: Choi Min-sik about to exact bloody retribution for his fifteen-year captivity in Park Chan-wook's crazy, stylish tale of violence and epic revenge.

daring us not to be fascinated by his crazy tale of violence and epic vengeance. (The poodle? Well you'll have to figure that out for yourself.) And the story Oh Dae-su (Choi Min-sik) has to tell *is* an utterly gripping one. Fifteen years ago, after a drunken night on the town, he was abducted and kept in a secret prison. Not told of the reason for his captivity he is finally released, only to be given a suitcase of cash and a challenge – find the person who did this to him, and why, in just five days.

Much happens along the way. Dentistry is performed with claw hammers, a hand becomes detached from its arm, love is fallen in, and a live octopus is eaten. *Oldboy* was quite rightly given an ecstatic welcome by critics but there was an odd reluctance to enjoy it on its own terms, its admirers loading it with a literary provenance it couldn't really sustain. Unnecessary references to Greek tragedy and Russian literature popped up, as if this maniacally constructed puzzle couldn't be enjoyed for what it is: a fantastically dressy B-movie; a trashy tour de force that has at its heart that old, satisfying staple, the riproaring rampage of revenge.

What can't be argued over is Park's incredible visual style. A fight sequence in one long take, the camera only moving horizontally back and forth along a corridor as Oh Dae-su beats up two dozen heavies, is a bloodily balletic standout. A slo-mo showdown amid the shattered glass of a minimalist penthouse is another. There are knowing nods to Buñuel as ants erupt from his body while he goes crazy in his prison cell (dolled up, in a final act of cruelty, to look like a cheap hotel room – will he be presented with a fifteen-year bill?), and to Hitchcock with a sequence in which he follows his younger self through an abandoned school, a crazy patchwork of Dutch angles and Escher-style staircases. Meanwhile Choi Min-sik, in a bravura performance, moves from the drunken buffoonery of the opening scenes through bewilderment, inchoate rage and finally horrified realization as his ghastly fate works itself out. And frankly any actor prepared to eat a live octopus (or rather four, the notorious scene requiring multiple takes) can't be accused of any lack of commitment. Nor, of course, can the octopuses.

With an idea as good as this it was inevitable that the ever-hungry maw of Hollywood would begin to drool. An English-language remake was almost immediately mooted with Steven Spielberg to direct Will Smith, much to the film's hardcore fans' vocal disgust. That project died only to be replaced by Spike Lee in the director's chair and Josh Brolin in the lead. Fans weren't much happier. And with the American Humane Association's interests no doubt extending to the cephalopod family, how will that symbolic eating of a live creature be achieved? Will some chichi oyster bar in Malibu Beach really cut it?

Pan's Labyrinth

2006, Sp/Mex/US, 120 mins,
15 (UK) R (US)

••

cast Sergi López, Ivana Baquero, Ariadna Gil,
Maribel Verdú, Doug Jones **scr** Guillermo del Toro
cin Guillermo Navarro **m** Javier Navarrete
dir Guillermo del Toro

Guillermo del Toro, in 2006 better known to English-speaking audiences for films such as comic-book adaptation *Hellboy* (2004), doodled designs and ideas for *Pan's Labyrinth*, his most ambitious celluloid excursion – and he has said he believes the most wholly successful realization thus far of his vision – for nearly twenty years before bringing it to the screen to almost universal critical acclaim. (Though the film was nearly stymied when he accidentally left his precious notebooks in the back of a London cab. They were returned after a couple of days.) An ambitious mingling of the fantastical and the horrifically real, it's an astonishing act of pure imagination, lushly designed and beautifully acted.

Set for the most part in mid-1940s Francoist Spain, the first ten minutes establish us as simultaneously in fairy tale territory with a prologue in which we learn the tale of Princess Moanna who, curious about the human world, enters it, only to forget her real identity. As the sumptuous fantasy visuals fade, we meet Ofelia (Ivana Baquero), an unhappy young girl on the cusp of puberty and still immersed in her fairy tale books which she carries with her in a bundle, being taken by her pregnant mother (Ariadna Gil) to a new life and a new stepfather in Captain Vidal

GUILLERMO DEL TORO
b. 9 October 1964, Guadalajara, Mexico

"The movie nerd's movie nerd" was a widely held early perception of Mexican-born del Toro. From childhood he has had a macabre sensibility; at the age of five he requested mandrake root for Christmas for the purposes of voodoo and in his spare time roamed the local sewers in search of slugs on which to pour salt. The son of a psychic and a businessman who won the national lottery (del Toro populated the resulting mansion with rats and snakes), he was an inveterate horror fan and finally founded his own special effects company. His first film, *Cronos* (1994) was a ferociously imaginative vampire story filled with alarming, often surreally beautiful imagery, and was successful enough for veteran spotters of foreign talent, the Weinsteins of Miramax, to offer him the chance to direct *Mimic* (1998), which again drew on his special effects know-how in its gooey tale of killer insects in New York. *Blade II* (2002) was an efficient entry in the hip vampire franchise while *Hellboy* (2004), featuring a perfectly cast Ron Perlman as the scarlet demon on the side of the angels, is one of the more imaginative comic-book adaptations. But he soon started alternating these fantasy movies, which were often based on previously published material, with his own stridently original fantastic visions. The critically lauded *Pan's Labyrinth* (2006) has rather overshadowed his other, equally excellent Spanish Civil War-set tale of the supernatural, *The Devil's Backbone*, which he made five years earlier. His recent projects have been bedevilled by false starts and budget difficulties. He was set to direct both *Hobbit* movies but dropped out after extended delays, while his mooted adaptation of H.P. Lovecraft's *At the Mountains of Madness* was nixed by Universal due to concerns over its $150 million budget. But with *Pacific Rim* – "a beautiful poem to 25-storey-high robots beating the crap out of 25-storey-high monsters", as he puts it – coming up he remains one of Hollywood's most in-demand directors. Which must suit Mexico's slugs just fine.

(Sergi López). A Fascist military commander, Vidal is tasked with hunting out the remaining rebels in the surrounding hills and is interested only in the son he believes his new wife Carmen is carrying. Vidal's brutal, sadistic character is revealed when he savagely beats a captured man to death, stoving his face in with a bottle, and shooting his son. It's a moment of horrifying, explicitly shot violence, and of course immediately renders the film unsuitable for children. Ofelia meanwhile finds a rotting stone labyrinth that reveals various magical beings including a faun (Doug Jones) who suspects that she may in fact be the spirit of the lost Princess and, in true fairy tale tradition, gives her three tasks that must be completed if she is to prove herself to be of this fantastical otherworld, and not the other, "real" and utterly dispiriting one.

Whatever else there is to say, what can't be doubted is del Toro's ambition: he has attempted to fuse war and fantasy, the end of childhood innocence, politics, Spanish history, violence and tragedy into an incredibly audacious, dark, twisted piece of virtuoso dream-making. Technically it couldn't be bettered: the fantasy effects, for the most part achieved with costume and make-up, are among the best the medium has to offer, while Eugenio Caballero's production design is uniformly superb, capturing both the magical realm and the darkly atmospheric camp with equal aplomb. And it's indubitably beautifully acted: López is coldly terrifying as Captain Vidal, Gil quietly affecting as the ailing mother and Baquero miraculously manages to channel a luminous purity without the tiniest hint of cloying sentimentality. There are a few sceptical of the mingling of the tragically real and fantastical, for whom *Pan's Labyrinth* couldn't be anything other than a courageous, and undoubtedly sincere, folly. But for those who are untroubled by the notion of the imaginary colliding with the appallingly real it is a masterpiece of imagination, a maze, both terrifying and beguiling, full of horrors and surprises: it's a movie to get lost in.

The elaborately designed faun (del Toro regular Doug Jones) on his throne is typical of the director's lush, fantastic vision in *Pan's Labyrinth*, a clash of fairy tale and wartime horror.

WORLD HOTSPOTS #3: THE AMERICAS
Beyond Hollywood...

Such is Hollywood's domination of the American market that it's easy to forget that there are thriving industries north of the 49th Parallel and south of the Rio Grande. Indeed, such were the facilities and cash incentives in Canada in the 21st century that many studio projects continued to be shot there with Canadian locales doubling for urban and rural US locations alike. These films provided work for local crews but did little to help the nation's directors, although established auteurs like David Cronenberg (*A History of Violence*, 2005, p.127), Atom Egoyan and Guy Maddin continued to reach their niche audiences, as did such Quebecois talents as Denys Arcand, who won the Oscar for best foreign film with the poignant social satire *The Barbarian Invasions* (2003), and Jean-Marc Vallée, who followed the hit comedy of gay sexual manners *C.R.A.Z.Y.* (2006) with the Hollywood period biopic, *The Young Victoria* (2009).

The language barrier proved beneficial to the film industries of Latin America: allowed to develop without being swamped by Hollywood productions, each country developed its own specific genres. But, while cult followings grew up around Mexican Rodolfo Guzmán Huerta (who made more than fifty pictures as the masked wrestler El Santo between 1958 and 1982), Brazilian José Mojica Marins (who frequently appeared in his own bizarre horror movies as the evil exploiter Coffin Joe) and the Chilean Alejandro Jodorowsky (whose distinctive brand of violent surrealism reached its peak in the 1970 anti-Western, *El Topo*), few Latin movies were renowned outside the region. Moreover, the many right-leaning repressive regimes imposed strict censorship, which restricted the screening of the politicized works of Third Cinema to ideologically sympathetic countries like Cuba.

However, things changed as military dictatorships were replaced by moderate democracies and, by the turn of the century, new waves were breaking in Mexico, Brazil and Argentina, while smaller nations like Peru, Colombia and Uruguay started making an international impact for the first time. Even Chile could finally claim home-produced pictures like Pablo Larraín's hyper-violent *Saturday Night Fever*-themed serial killer flick *Tony Manero* (2009), instead of those made by such exiles as the French-based maverick Raúl Ruiz and documentarist Patricio Guzmán.

Such has been the effect of *nuevo cine mexicano* that directors Alfonso Cuarón, Alejandro González Iñárritu and Guillermo del Toro have become major players in Hollywood. Iñárritu got the ball rolling with *Amores Perros* (2001), which became known as "the Mexican Pulp Fiction", while Cuarón made an impressive stylistic leap in going from the erotic road movie *Y Tu Mamá También* (2002) to *Harry Potter and the Prisoner of Azkaban* (2004, p.119). But del Toro produced the most consistently excellent work in alternating between classy Spanish Civil War fantasies such as *The Devil's Backbone* (2001) and Hollywood genre fodder like *Hellboy* (2004).

The unexpected vogue for Mexican cinema sent a *buena onda* (or "good vibe") into South America. Brazil was the first to respond, with Walter Salles building on the success of his quaint 1999 drama *Central Station* with *The Motorcycle Diaries* (2004), a picaresque profile of Che Guevara as a young man. However, ever since the *cinema novo* movement of the 1960s, Brazilian film has always had a strong social realist streak and Fernando Meirelles captured the poverty, violence and crime of the favela shanties above Rio de Janeiro in *City of God* (2003, p.52), while Hector Babenco and José Padilha respectively tackled prison squalor and police corruption with uncompromising compassion in *Carandiru* (2004) and *Elite Squad* (2008).

Elsewhere on the continent, New Argentine Cinema emerged from the recession that had ended the brief boom of the 1990s. Capturing the mood of the nation, films were either cynical, like Fabián Belinsky's con thriller *Nine Queens* (2002), or sentimental, like Carlos Sorín's canine odyssey *Bombón: El Perro* (2005). But they were also stylistically innovative, with Pablo Trapero putting a new spin on neo-realism in the road movie *Familia Rodante* (2005), and thematically daring, with Lucrecia Martel denouncing bourgeois social and religious conservatism in *The Headless Woman* (2010). But the standard bearer of the Latin surge was José Juan Campanella's *The Secret in Their Eyes* (2010), a murder mystery that flashes back to the 1970s as a novelist investigates a Dirty War conspiracy, which won the Academy Award for best foreign film.

Persepolis

2008, Fr/US, 96 mins, 12A (UK) PG-13 (US)

. . . .

cast Chiara Mastroianni, Catherine Deneuve, Simon Abkarian, Danielle Darrieux, Gabrielle Lopes Benites *scr* Marjane Satrapi and Vincent Paronnaud (from the comics by Marjane Satrapi) *m* Olivier Bernet *dir* Marjane Satrapi and Vincent Paronnaud

Published in 2000, Marjane Satrapi's *Persepolis* comics (the title refers to the ancient capital of Persia) told the story of Satrapi's childhood in Iran before and during the 1979 revolution and the subsequent Iran–Iraq war, a conflagration that cost more than a million lives. Like Art Spiegelman's *Maus* before it, it helped the continuing process of "legitimizing" the graphic novel (or in this case graphic "augmented memoir") as a genuine art form. This film adaptation, by Satrapis in collaboration with fellow graphic artist Vincent Paronnaud, preserves the spirit of the comics, deftly fusing the political and the personal into a universal coming-of-age story told with wit and warmth.

Beginning in the present day, and in muted colour that contrasts with the remainder of the film's black and white, we see an adult Marjane at one of Paris's airports as she is denied entry onto a plane for Tehran: asked for her ticket, she sadly shakes her head. As she sits disconsolately in the busy terminal she catches sight of a sprightly little girl and is soon remembering her own childhood in Tehran in the 1970s, before the overthrow of the Shah. The nine-year-old Marjane is irresistibly feisty: we first see her practising her terrifying Bruce Lee moves at a dinner party, then later she becomes enamoured with forbidden Western pop music (a somewhat ludicrous dissident currency in which shady-looking men with their collars turned up furtively deal in tapes of Abba and Julio Iglesias). She paints "Punk Is Not Ded" on the back of her T-shirt, which stands in stark rebuke to the headscarf she must wear and raises the ire of the increasingly intolerant neighbours. In contrast her family and their friends, sophisticated, educated and almost continually smoking, discuss the revolution, certain that it will bring democracy and peace. Their impotent dismay as what emerges is not freedom but vicious religious repression and a devastating, pointless war, is one of the film's most powerful elements. Sent to school in Austria by her parents after a dangerous ideological run-in with her teacher, Marjane finds it equally hard to fit in with the student poseurs who talk of anarchy and rebellion, but whose actual experience of the sharp end of politics is limited to just that: talk. Unhappy, she returns to Iran

The past is another country: Marjane's childhood amongst the Iranian intelligentsia, drawn in deceptively simple black and white, ill prepares her for the political repressions to come.

only to find it hopelessly changed by the religious zealots who have taken over and again finds herself an outcast and dissident in her own home country. Finally she decides to leave for good.

Persepolis is a wonderfully lucid account of recent Iranian history, but it's also a compelling personal story: Satrapi's skill is in balancing these elements, never letting the sometimes depressing historical facts get in the way of the lively human tale. The simply drawn characters are a delight, particularly Marjane's grandmother (Danielle Darrieux), clearly the most important influence in her life, a source of compassion, common sense and useful bra-care tips in a harsh and repressive world. But as well as being a political primer and personal narrative, *Persepolis* has at its heart a shared experience – coming of age and the youthful struggle to find oneself that almost everyone can identify with and, as an adult, seeing one's youth vanish slowly over the horizon. Much later, as she sits reminiscing in the airport, Marjane longs to return not just to pre-revolutionary Iran, but to a carefree and happy childhood surrounded by people who loved her and whom she loved: and that's a return journey for which, sadly, we are all denied a ticket.

Pirates of the Caribbean: The Curse of the Black Pearl

2003, US, 143 mins, 12A (UK) PG-13 (US)

. . . .

cast Johnny Depp, Geoffrey Rush, Orlando Bloom, Keira Knightley *scr* Ted Elliott & Terry Rossio (story Ted Elliott & Terry Rossio and Stuart Beattie and Jay Wolpert) *cin* Dariusz Wolski *m* Klaus Badelt *dir* Gore Verbinski

It's easy to forget, nearly a decade later, after three sequels and a franchise box-office total nudging $4 *billion*, that *Pirates of the Caribbean* was considered at the time one of Disney's greatest risks. Here was a movie based on, of all things, a theme park ride. Not only that but a pirate-themed ride; as any exec would be more than aware, all previous attempts at resuscitating the swashbuckling genre had become expensive debacles (Polanski's *Pirates* in 1986 and Renny Harlin's 1995 *Cutthroat Island* being the most notorious). And then there was Johnny Depp; he might have arthouse and cult appeal, but he was no Will Smith or Tom Hanks. To put the tin lid on it the director was planning to slap the cinematic equivalent of a "you must be this tall to ride" notice on the film in the form of a PG-13 certificate, the first in Disney's history.

They needn't have worried. What emerged after a reportedly pressured shoot was a riotously enjoyable example of Hollywood big-budget blockbusterdom at its best. Orlando Bloom channels his inner Errol as the dashing blacksmith in love with plucky British governor's daughter Elizabeth Swann (Keira Knightley); Geoffrey Rush's timbers are gloriously shivered as curse-afflicted pirate captain Barbossa (sporting a monkey rather than a parrot); and director Gore Verbinski delivers three or four unforgettable set pieces, the highlight being a sword fight amid shards of moonlight that reveal the cursed pirates' real nature as decaying skeletons. It's a thrillingly original conceit worthy of early Spielberg.

But it is of course Depp's outrageously entertaining turn as Captain Jack Sparrow that is at the heart of the film's effortless appeal. His early observation that since pirates were, as he put it, the rock stars of their day, he would include a fair measure of Keith Richards in his shambling, eccentric performance was a masterstroke. It was, however, a decision that would further alarm the already

JOHNNY DEPP

b. 9 June 1963, Owensboro, KY, US

Johnny Depp has been a renegade presence in Hollywood ever since his escape from TV series *21 Jump Street* and his apparent fate as teen pin-up via John Waters' *Cry-Baby* in 1989. But it is in the 21st century that he broke through to multiplex recognition mainly via his astonishingly entertaining turn as dyspeptic pirate captain Jack Sparrow in *Pirates of the Caribbean: The Curse of the Black Pearl* (2003) and its successively less amusing sequels. His major achievement there, and with roles such as Inspector Frederick Abberline in Jack the Ripper drama *From Hell* (2001) and Peter Pan creator James Barrie in *Finding Neverland* (2004), has been to preserve a delicate oddness and whimsy that seems gloriously at odds with contemporary Hollywood tastes. His major continuing collaboration has been with director Tim Burton, which produced his fey turn as Willy Wonka in Burton's *Charlie and the Chocolate Factory* (2005), and a performance that delighted some as the murderous tonsorialist in Burton's musical *Sweeney Todd: The Demon Barber of Fleet Street* (2007). He might be forgiven his disappointing role as Imaginarium Tony 1 in *The Imaginarium of Doctor Parnassus* (2009) – a film that would have been better abandoned after the death of its original star Heath Ledger. It was nice to see him ease off on the idiosyncrasy just a little and reprise the more "earthly" kind of performance he gave as real-life cocaine smuggler George Jung in Ted Demme's superior crime flick *Blow* (2001) as legendary gangster John Dillinger in Michael Mann's *Public Enemies* (2009). His second outing playing his friend gonzo journalist Hunter S. Thompson (after Terry Gilliam's hit *Fear and Loathing in Las Vegas* in 1998), *The Rum Diary* (2011) was less successful and sank at the box office, and so it was back to audience-pleasing pantomime – as an ancient bloodsucker awoken in 1972 in Tim Burton's vampire comedy *Dark Shadows* (2012), and then as Tonto in Disney's long-gestating *The Lone Ranger*, directed by *Pirates of the Caribbean*'s Gore Verbinski, which is scheduled finally to be released in 2013.

twitchy Disney executives. "[They] were going, 'What's wrong with him? Is he, you know, like some kind of weird simpleton? Is he drunk? By the way, is he gay?'", Depp said. (His reply that "all my characters are gay" can't have done much to calm them.) But, in the end, like its namesake, *Pirates of the Caribbean* is a ride worth queueing for.

Which makes what happened next all the more baffling. First one and then another sequel (*Dead Man's Chest* and *At World's End* in 2006 and 2007) appeared and utterly failed to capture the unforced charm of the original. After a decent interval Disney replaced Verbinski with Rob Marshall, threw Bloom and Knightley overboard, and had another go with *On Stranger Tides* in 2011, again with little success. The breezy storytelling of the first film had been replaced with gobbets of indigestible cod mythology, its enchanting visuals and inventive set pieces replaced by the infernally loud, mostly incoherent action sequences that bedevil the genre. There are no sword fights amid beams of moonlight here. It was a sorry sight: Captain Jack Sparrow marooned in a sea of Hollywood mediocrity. Screenwriter William Goldman once famously remarked of Hollywood's inability to predict success that "nobody knows anything". It seems that when it does accidentally stumble on the secret of great moviemaking, it's quite capable of forgetting it almost immediately. Not encouraging then for the next Bruckheimer/ Verbinski/Depp collaboration, the budget-busting, on-again-off-again *The Lone Ranger*, in which Depp is set to play Tonto.

A Prophet

2010, Fr/It, 155 mins, 18 (UK) R (US)

••

cast Tahar Rahim, Niels Arestrup, Adel Bencherif, Hichem Yacoubi *scr* Thomas Bidegain and Jaques Audiard (from an original screenplay by Abdel Raouf Dafri and Nicolas Peufaillit) *cin* Stéphane Fontaine *m* Alexandre Desplat
dir Jacques Audiard

Following up on his BAFTA-winning crime drama *The Beat That My Heart Skipped* (2005), director/writer Jacques Audiard has stayed with crime, but with *A Prophet* he harks back to the socially committed crime movies that Hollywood produced in the 1930s, such as *I Am a Fugitive from a Chain Gang* (1932), and like them combines a moral message with gripping, plot-driven entertainment. Itself a BAFTA winner and Oscar nominee, it boasts a meticulously researched screenplay, sure-handed direction and, in virtually unknown Tahar Rahim, one of the finest debut performances in international cinema this millennium.

Ordered by Corsican mobster César to murder a fellow inmate, Malik (Tahar Rahim) prepares for the meeting with a razor blade inside his mouth, in one of *A Prophet*'s tensest moments.

He plays Malik, a nineteen-year-old petty criminal whom we meet at the beginning of a six-year prison sentence for assaulting a police officer. Shy, terrified, his face paradoxically a picture of innocence, we watch as he endures the grim rituals and humiliations of entering prison. Like many in his position his plan appears to be to keep his head down and do his time without attracting anyone's attention. It is, of course, not to be. Within days he has been approached by the Corsican gangs, headed by César (the excellent Niels Arestrup, who looks disconcertingly like British TV chef Antony Worrall Thompson's evil twin, and whose dead eyes and occasional sudden violence are chief weapons of intimidation). César tells him that he is to murder a fellow inmate whose testimony the Corsicans wish to prevent. If he refuses, he himself will be killed. When, shaking with fear, he presses his cell buzzer to ask for a meeting with the warden, the Corsicans arrive instead and thrust a polythene bag over his head before savagely beating him, leaving no doubt as to who is really in charge. What follows is the story of Malik's survival and ascendancy within the prison system. His careful studying of the ecology of the place, with its constantly shifting loyalties and influences, and his virtual invisibility as "just another dirty Arab", serve him well, and finally the apprentice is in a position to take on his master.

Audiard's direction shifts seamlessly from a kind of docu-drama using handheld cameras and long lenses to record the minutiae of prison life – the doling out of the daily baguette, the currency of violence, both actual and threatened, as well as the virtual absence of prison officers as figures of meaningful authority – to more impressionistic sequences: the ghost of Malik's victim appears at intervals and talks to him, sporting a livid scar, and at one point, mysteriously, on fire. Malik's occasional forays outside prison let fresh air into the movie and in a sense are among the most affecting: his delight at walking through an airport and taking his first flight are set in contrast not only to his brutalized existence in jail, but also to the carefree, uncomplicated life we might hope for him after release but suspect, given his increasing immersion in more and more serious crime, is rapidly becoming an impossibility.

A Prophet's central point, of course, is the pretty much unarguable observation that if reform is an aim of sentencing then prison is in most cases absolutely the worst place for an unformed petty criminal. Malik arrived a blank slate (a point reinforced by Audiard's decision to cast a relative unknown against the instantly recognizable Arestrup) and the jail that, in the final shot, recedes into the background, has in a real sense made him; that innocence so apparent in his face in the opening scenes is a distant memory. Exactly what it has transformed him into is a question this visceral, strikingly humane and psychologically fascinating film leaves unanswered.

Punch-Drunk Love

2003, US, 95 mins, 15 (UK) R (US)

●●●

cast Adam Sandler, Emily Watson, Philip Seymour Hoffman, Luis Guzmán *scr* Paul Thomas Anderson *cin* Robert Elswit *m* Jon Brion *dir* Paul Thomas Anderson

Punch-Drunk Love is a love story about anger. Or is it an anger story about love? There's certainly plenty of both on display in this wilfully eccentric film from arthouse darling Paul Thomas Anderson and king of the knuckle-dragging multiplex comedy Adam Sandler. Sandler plays Barry Egan, a self-employed distributor of novelty lavatory plungers whom we meet as he nervously peers out of his business unit early in the morning like a frightened rodent. It is typical either of his character, or more likely the director's, that when two dramas enact themselves simultaneously in front of him – a spectacular, unexplained car wreck and the mysterious dumping of a harmonium at his feet, thrown out of a speeding van like a returned hostage – Egan focuses his attention on the latter.

We get to understand a little of how Barry became so cowed when we meet his seven bullying sisters (some played by real-life relations), who are relentlessly dismissive of him; at a dinner party they laugh about how as children they used to call him "gayboy", an epithet which then caused him to take a hammer to the windows. They profess to be surprised when he ends the gathering by given a sudden repeat performance. Buried under the fear, then, are vast wells of repressed anger that manifests itself in wall-punching, bathroom-trashing outbursts. To put it bluntly, he's nuts. Love and potential catastrophe enter his life, the latter in the form of an ill-advised (and hilariously unerotic) sex-line call

PHILIP SEYMOUR HOFFMAN
b. 23 July 1967, Fairport, NY, US

Amateur cinematic talent-spotters might well have singled out Philip Seymour Hoffman as one to watch in Al Pacino crowd-pleaser *Scent of a Woman* (1993). While co-star Chris O'Donnell was perfectly adequate as the clean-cut preppie charged with looking after a shouty Pacino, it was Hoffman who stood out in his few scenes as a weaselly rich boy. In the 90s he continued to make an impact with subsidiary roles in Paul Thomas Anderson's *Boogie Nights* (1998) as a porn movie sound man with a crush on Mark Wahlberg, and then in *Magnolia* (2000) as a sympathetic cancer nurse for Jason Robards. He was effective as Tom Ripley's doomed nemesis Freddie Miles in Anthony Minghella's otherwise somewhat limp 2000 adaptation of *The Talented Mister Ripley*. In the 2000s he has continued to pursue an eclectic range of parts, bringing a ferocious commitment and impressive versatility to each of them. He was winsomely entertaining as legendary rock scribe Lester Bangs in Cameron Crowe's autobiographical *Almost Famous* (2001), but brutish and scary as bullying sex line owner Dean Trumbell in *Punch-Drunk Love* (2003). Leading roles have been thinner on the ground, but his two greatest achievements have been in films whose success hung on his performance. In Bennett Miller's 2006 biopic *Capote* he surmounted the obvious physical discrepancies – Capote was an elfin 5' 3" while Hoffman stands a chunky 5' 10" – with an uncanny depiction of the legendary author as he composed his masterpiece of narrative non-fiction *In Cold Blood*. In Charlie Kaufman's outrageously ambitious and unpronounceable *Synecdoche, New York* (2009, p.228) he delivered an irresistible, tragicomic picture of a man struggling to find meaning over the course of an entire life. He played baseball manager bad guy in 2011's *Moneyball* (enraging real-life coach Art Howe, who said "He was a little on the heavy side. And the way he portrayed me was 180 degrees from what I really am") and was predictably succulent as a political spin doctor in George Clooney's *The Ides of March* (2011). He returns to work with Paul Thomas Anderson in the 1950s-era *The Master*, as enigmatic guru Lancaster Dodd, alongside Joaquin Phoenix as his troubled acolyte. Comparisons to Hollywood's favourite cult – Scientology – have already been made.

The ever reliable Philip Seymour Hoffman gives a gutsy performance as sleazy sex-line proprietor Dean Trumbell in Paul Thomas Anderson's angry love story.

that attracts the attention of carpet store owner Dean Trumbell (a magnificently sleazy Philip Seymour Hoffman, his garish shirt pulled tightly over a protruding stomach – rarely has a pot-belly been so brilliantly deployed in the service of character), who decides to blackmail him. Love, on the other hand, arrives in the charming form of Lena (a winning Emily Watson), who is inexplicably drawn to this odd homunculus. Their pillow-talk, proof of the old aphorism that there really is someone out there for everyone, seems to have come from a Scorsese movie. "I'm lookin' at your face and I just wanna smash it. I just wanna fuckin' smash it with a sledgehammer and squeeze it," he coos. "I want to chew your face, and I want to scoop out your eyes and I want to eat them," she whispers back.

Punch-Drunk Love marks a fascinating point in the careers of both star and director. Anderson follows an apparently conventional narrative structure, abandoning the loose episodic structure of *Boogie Nights* (1998) or *Magnolia* (2000), but retaining some of their air of unpredictability and vague magical realism. Nothing in *Punch-Drunk Love* happens quite as the genre demands, and yet in its tones, structure and finally its optimism, it clearly nods to the classic Hollywood romantic comedy. Adam Sandler, on the other hand, seems to be interested not so much in expanding the *schtick* that has made him his millions, but exploring its depths, seeing how his familiar character reacts to situations unavailable to him in the likes of *Happy Gilmore* (1996). It's a brave piece of experimentation from both, and the result is a funny, alarming, idiosyncratic movie unlike anything else you're likely to see.

The Road

2010, US, 112 mins, 15 (UK) R (US)

● ●

cast Viggo Mortensen, Kodi Smit-McPhee, Charlize Theron, Robert Duvall, Guy Pearce *scr* Joe Penhall (from the novel by Cormac McCarthy) *cin* Javier Aguirresarobe *m* Nick Cave and Warren Ellis *dir* John Hillcoat

The end of the world has traditionally been an excuse for Hollywood destruction on an epic scale – think of Michael Bay's *Armageddon* (1998) or Roland Emmerich's *The Day After Tomorrow* (2004, p.64). But in this adaptation of Cormac McCarthy's bleak modern classic, the apocalypse arrives not in the shape of an asteroid or tsunami but as a few flickers of light from behind a bedroom curtain. A young husband (Viggo Mortensen) is woken, peers out, is bathed in an eerie orange glow then goes to the bathroom and turns on the taps. "Why are you having a bath?" his wife sleepily asks. "I'm not," he says. And so the world ends.

Australian director John Hillcoat was no stranger to placing fragile human beings in brutal landscapes having delivered blood-drenched Aussie Western *The Proposition* in 2005, but he excels himself in this harrowing, almost wholly grim tale of a man and boy surviving in a desolate post-apocalyptic world. His anguished wife having left the family presumably to die, Man and Boy (they are never named) embark on a 100-mile walk to the coast for not much other reason, it seems, than there is nowhere else to go. (Special mention must go to Charlize Theron, who plays Wife, seen only in increasingly brief flashbacks – it's a rare Hollywood actress who would take on such a bleak and superficially unsympathetic role.)

VIGGO MORTENSEN

b. 20 October 1958, New York, NY, US

Possibly the only actor to gain a lasting career boost from Peter Jackson's *Lord of the Rings* trilogy (in contrast with Orlando Bloom, Elijah Wood and other assorted Hobbits, all of whom have floundered), Viggo Mortensen, an actor with a pleasing solidity and rough-hewn sex appeal, had spent the late 80s and 90s honing his craft in an array of films ranging from the unapologetically trashy (*Young Guns II* and *Leatherface: The Texas Chainsaw Massacre III*, both in 1990) through to much more interesting work, particularly with the underappreciated British director Philip Ridley on *The Reflecting Skin* (1990) and strange fairy tale *The Passion of Darkly Noon* (1996) and with Gus Van Sant on his quixotic/pointless *Psycho* remake (1999). He smouldered effectively in Jane Campion's *The Portrait of a Lady* (1996) and deployed his cleft chin and impressive physique in Tony Scott's crass *G.I. Jane* (1997) opposite Demi Moore. But it was his performance as the heroic Aragorn in Jackson's Tolkien adaptation (replacing Stuart Townsend, who was booted off the film after just four days of shooting) that propelled him onto the A-list. Subsequently he was compelling in David Cronenberg's hit *A History of Violence* (2005, p.127), giving a cool, mysterious performance that obviously impressed co-star Ed Harris enough for him to cast him in Mortensen's second Western (after 2004's *Hidalgo*). Harris's *Appaloosa* (2008) was a laid-back affair that pleased some traditionalist fans of the genre but left others snoring. In Cronenberg's London-set thriller *Eastern Promises* (2007) he topped off a layered performance with a spectacular fight sequence, a more than usually startling spectacle since it was performed entirely in the nude. He returned to work with Cronenberg a third time as founder of psychiatry Sigmund Freud opposite Michael Fassbender's acolyte turned rival Carl Jung in *A Dangerous Method* (2012). Based on a stage play by Christopher Hampton, the film was overly talky, and though both actors acquitted themselves admirably the script failed to put them on screen together enough to generate the anticipated intellectual fireworks. His crowning achievement thus far though is without a doubt his wrenching performance in John Hillcoat's adaptation of Cormac McCarthy's *The Road* (2010).

Javier Aguirresarobe shoots in what might best be described as Despair-O-Vision: all is dusty greys or brown, the world caked in grime and shrouded in a thin, milky mist. Hillcoat makes effective use of modern digital effects to render devastation on a vast scale – this is probably the most convincingly rendered desolation in movie history. Blasted forests, deserted highways and ruined cities are the background against which pockets of survivors scrabble for food and fuel, trudging occasionally over now worthless hundred-dollar bills.

Occasionally it all lurches a little too close to George Romero territory to entirely keep its credibility. Gangs of cannibals roam the countryside, and in one grotesque sequence Man and Boy discover an apparently abandoned house whose cellar turns out to be a live human meat locker, while the jerry-rigged vehicles unfortunately bring to mind *Mad Max* (1979). (Of course, these sequences are in the novel, too, but film inevitably renders them in a literal way that can't help but conform to genre movie expectations.) But not much of this matters, since the heart of the movie is the tender relationship between father and son growing up in a world turned upside down.

Viggo Mortensen is staunch and believable as a man whose most treasured possession is a gun with two bullets – one for him and one for his son – while the frankly miraculous Kodi Smit-McPhee seems incapable of delivering a wrongly judged moment. "It's bubbly!" he delights when given a can of Coke, for him a rare sliver of pleasure, for his father a reminder of very different times. There's not been a more convincing performance by a child actor since Christian Bale in *Empire of the Sun* (1987). In a tiny masterstroke Hillcoat eschews music over the final credits in favour of the sounds of a suburban street: the lawnmowers and dogs, indistinct chatter and cars passing by. You find yourself glued to your seat, listening in wonder.

Hug a hoodie: Viggo Mortensen and Kodi Smit-McPhee's father and son try to survive in the blasted, brown and grey landscapes of John Hillcoat's *The Road*.

WES ANDERSON

b. 1 May 1969, Houston, TX, US

The most common complaint by those not won over by Wes Anderson's instantly recognizable, intricately wrought cinematic whimsies is that his films are "all the same". It's an odd angle of attack. After all, isn't it possible to instantly spot a Hitchcock or for that matter a Tony Scott? Born in Texas, he met frequent collaborator Owen Wilson at the state's university where they worked together on the screenplay for *Bottle Rocket* (1996), a heist-themed caper that established their arch, calculatedly eccentric universe. Wilson also co-wrote Anderson's sophomore effort, *Rushmore* (1999), a bittersweet coming-of-age saga that introduced then unknown Jason Schwartzman to audiences as an overachieving, lovestruck teenager and was appealing enough to harness the services of the great Bill Murray as the third corner of an implausible love triangle. Murray remained a frequent collaborator with Anderson, appearing in *The Royal Tenenbaums* (2002), which boasted a heavyweight accompanying cast, and *The Life Aquatic with Steve Zissou* (2005), in which he played the eponymous scubanaut (based on one of Anderson's childhood heroes, Jacques Cousteau) as he relentlessly pursued an elusive shark in an off-kilter retread of *Moby-Dick*. Jason Schwartzman and Owen Wilson returned for the slightly less successful *The Darjeeling Limited* (2007), about three brothers taking a train trip across India after the death of their father, a film some found culturally condescending. His adaptation of Roald Dahl's *Fantastic Mr Fox* (2009) was a departure in technique, being hand animated, but his whimsical style remained, as did a sense of peril and sorrow missing from most family films. Anderson has occasionally been a controversial figure: in 2012 he enraged his fans by directing a series of commercials for Hyundai. Typically, and unlike most other feature directors' commercial work, his style was unmistakeable and loud whispers of "sell-out" could be heard. With luck his latest, *Moonrise Kingdom* (2012), which brings Bruce Willis into the Anderson fold alongside Murray and Schwartzman, will silence them.

The Royal Tenenbaums

2002, US, 110 mins, 15 (UK) R (US)

••

cast Gene Hackman, Anjelica Huston, Bill Murray, Ben Stiller, Owen Wilson, Luke Wilson, Gwyneth Paltrow, Alec Baldwin *scr* Wes Anderson & Owen Wilson *cin* Robert Yeoman *m* Mark Mothersbaugh *dir* Wes Anderson

The Royal Tenenbaums takes place in a Manhattan that seems to have been ripped from a *New Yorker* story from years past. Its vision of the city is slightly dreamy and yet arch; the larger-than-life characters that populate it might have walked out of a John Irving adaptation (there's something of the odd, sad atmosphere of *The Hotel New Hampshire*). It's a heady confection and thus, as with the rest of the director's work, it's a Marmite movie: as with the British yeast spread you either can't get enough, or its appeal is totally baffling.

The Tenenbaums are a dazzling brood of geniuses à la J.D. Salinger's Glass family. We meet them in their prime twenty years ago via an extended montage and monologue delivered by Alec Baldwin. Chas (played as an adult by Ben Stiller) is a financial whizz at the age of twelve and invents "Dalmatian mice" (which infest the house); adopted daughter Margot (Gwyneth Paltrow) is already a playwright; and Richie (Luke Wilson) is a tennis champ and aspiring artist who lives in a tent in the ballroom and appears only to be able to draw pictures of his adopted sister: "He failed to develop as an artist," Baldwin deadpans. But slowly their individual promise peters out. Richie's tennis career ends after an inexplicable meltdown the day after said sister's marriage; Margot loses a finger, acquires a wooden one and finds herself mired in seven years of writer's block; Chas's wife is killed in a plane crash that everyone else, including the dog, survives. Eventually they wind up back in the family home along with the estranged, now broke paterfamilias Royal Tenenbaum (Gene Hackman). Twenty-two years later, as the narration puts it, "all memory of the brilliance of the young Tenenbaums had been erased by two decades of failure, betrayal and disaster".

Second childhood: Gene Hackman is deliciously anarchic as head of the tragicomic Tenenbaum family.

Anderson's formal, playfully literary tone and eccentric wit doesn't disguise the melancholy at the core of the movie: this is a story about failure, about great expectations disappointed. The Tenenbaums are a family hopelessly trying to recapture their glittering past when all was promise – or at least retrieve something from the wreckage. It's all beautifully played by a stellar ensemble cast. Hackman is delicious as the terrible father, a man who, when his eight-year-old daughter asks for his opinion on her play, tells her that "it just didn't feel very realistic to me", and who takes his grandchildren out to dog fights. Anjelica Huston is airily likeable as the relatively sane, bemused matriarch who has to abandon her bridge parties to care again for her unusual brood; Gwyneth Paltrow is remote and chilly as the secret smoker, blocked playwright and serial adulterer; and Owen Wilson (who co-wrote) employs the sly, slightly ironized little-boy charm – which he then seemed, inexplicably, to abandon in favour of a string of underpowered comedies – as family friend Eli Cash, a stetson-wearing literary sensation with a raging drug problem.

The Royal Tenenbaums is a movie that feels like it takes place inside a delicately wrought snow-globe and its maximum-octane whimsy is certainly not for everyone. But for those who do "get it", this is an enchanting, loveable film. It's difficult to resist being drawn into the strange, tragic and funny world of these modern-day Magnificent Ambersons.

Shaun of the Dead

2004, UK/US/Fr, 99 mins, 15 (UK) R (US)

....

cast Simon Pegg, Nick Frost, Kate Ashfield, Lucy Davis, Dylan Moran, Penelope
Wilton, Bill Nighy *scr* Edgar Wright & Simon Pegg *cin* David M. Dunlap
m Daniel Mudford, Pete Woodhead *dir* Edgar Wright

For some millennial reason or other, a passing comet maybe, the 2000s soon
revealed themselves to be the Decade of the Living Dead. Danny Boyle's effectively
bleak low-budget effort *28 Days Later* (2002) was leader of the noisome pack,
while a couple of superior international entries, *[REC]* (Spain, 2008) and *Dead*

Come and get it: Simon
Pegg as Shaun with Dylan
Moran, Kate Ashfield (left)
and Lucy Davis (right),
tooled up to take on the
walking dead in Edgar
Wright's zom-rom-com.

Snow (Norway, 2009) – which gave us zombified SS Stormtroopers – showed at least some originality. But the necrotic revival soon got tiresome: zombies after all are among the least inherently interesting of horror cinema's outrages, so perhaps it wasn't that surprising that it was the *comic* potential of the reanimated deceased that produced the best movies. Ruben Fleischer's *Zombieland* (2009) took its chainsaw-wielding cast on a chaotic road trip, extracting maximum gruesome slapstick from the hapless corpses, but Simon Pegg and co-writer/director Edgar Wright's sleeper hit *Shaun of the Dead* is the best of the lot: a loving tribute to George A. Romero's seminal *Night of the Living Dead* (1968) as well as being a nimbly written, surprisingly affecting depiction of male friendship.

At the age of 29, electronics salesman Shaun (Simon Pegg) is stuck in an indefinitely extended student existence whose twin poles are the sofa in front of his PlayStation and his local pub, the Winchester Tavern. Stuck between the urge to make something of his life and the equally powerful instinct to do bugger all that every male can, at some level, identify with, he attempts to hold onto both his girlfriend Liz (Kate Ashfield) and his enduring friendship with the unconflicted slob Ed (real-life pal Nick Frost), whose main personal achievement is to have perfected an unnervingly good chimpanzee impression. When their London suburb is invaded by the animated dead, at first Shaun is too hungover to notice, but when finally he and Ed do wake up to the catastrophe they arm themselves with a cricket bat as well as unwanted items from Shaun's LP collection (Sade is an early casualty) and determine that the only place of safety for them and their loved ones is, inevitably, the pub.

The screenplay is economical, pacy and polished, letting no gag or set-up outstay its welcome and generating some genuinely original laughs: a sequence in which these suburban refugees have to mimic zombies to make it to the safety of the saloon bar is a highlight. Pegg himself embodies an irresistible, low-wattage likeability: "now who would like a peanut?" is a typical response when the survivors actually make it to the Winchester, only for it to emerge that this is the end rather than the beginning of Shaun's crisis planning. Penelope Wilton and Bill Nighy add thespian class and, in the former case, a nicely judged note of genuine tragedy, as Shaun's mum and grouchy stepdad.

Wright and Pegg's subsequent collaboration, action movie spoof *Hot Fuzz* (2007), delivered more of the same, though was slightly less winsome – perhaps a result of the pair not being as devoted to Bruckheimeresque high-octane as they were to Romeroesque horror – but it was still a vast improvement on Hollywood's laddish comedy offerings which, in films such as *The Hangover* (2009), wallowed in cynical childishness seasoned with a dose of homophobia and borderline racism. Blokesploitation seems to be that rare cinematic phenomenon: something the Brits do best.

Shutter Island

2010, US, 138 mins, 15 (UK) R (US)

....

cast Leonardo DiCaprio, Ben Kingsley, Mark Ruffalo, Max von Sydow, Emily Mortimer, Michelle Williams *scr* Laeta Kalogridis (from the novel by Dennis Lehane) *cin* Robert Richardson *dir* Martin Scorsese

After Scorsese had finally achieved his long delayed Oscar for best director (see *The Departed*, p.67), he appears to have been in a mood to celebrate. And for Scorsese celebrating took the form of a deliriously indulgent paean to one of his, and any true cinephile's, favourite genres: *noir*. *Shutter Island* is an expertly assembled and shamelessly enjoyable mash-up of genre staples: mysterious islands, storm-wracked lunatic asylums, overgrown cemeteries, lonely lighthouses, and surreal dream sequences. And if things weren't Gothic enough, Max Von Sydow turns up as a creepy German psychiatrist. This is pure pulp bliss.

It's 1954 and Teddy Daniels (a chunky, permanently vexed-looking Leonardo DiCaprio) is a US Marshall sent to a prison for the criminally insane on the titular island – a grim lump of granite whose single jetty is the only way on or off – to investigate the apparent escape of a prisoner. Trapped there by a violent storm, along with his partner Chuck Aule (Mark Ruffalo), he finds the psychiatric staff, headed by Dr Cawley (Ben Kingsley at his most succulently sinister), strangely uncooperative. Teddy is also plagued by nightmares not only of the horrors he saw when, as a GI, he was involved in the liberation of Dachau, but also of the death of his wife (Michelle Williams) in a house fire. Oddly, these dreams begin to merge with what seem to be the memories of Rachel Solando, the inmate he

LEONARDO DICAPRIO

b. 11 November 1974, Los Angeles, CA, US

Indisputably now one of Hollywood's most compelling talents and, in an age where they are increasingly rare, one of its brightest stars (see box, p.111), Hollywood-born DiCaprio's key achievement in the 2000s has been to survive the success of James Cameron's *Titanic* (1998). Before the big boat sank he'd been a promising character actor with the likes of *What's Eating Gilbert Grape* (1994) and *Romeo + Juliet* (1997) behind him. But the half-decade following *Titanic* showed him struggling a little to escape the teen pin-up trap before he finally emerged in the mid-noughties as a Hollywood heavyweight capable of both big action and high drama. Though his early choices of director and material were impeccable – Danny Boyle's *The Beach* (2000); Steven Spielberg's tale of serial hoaxer *Catch Me if you Can* (2003); Martin Scorsese's *Gangs of New York* (2003) – unluckily for him, these proved not to be their directors' best work. Things started looking up with Martin Scorsese's Howard Hughes biopic *The Aviator* (2005), for which he gained an Oscar nomination. His further collaborations with Scorsese have been the most significant for the director since his legendary films with Robert De Niro. *The Departed* (2006, p.67) saw him as part of Scorsese's Oscar-baiting dream cast, and while Ed Zwick's *Blood Diamond* (2007) was somewhat patience-testing, he was convincing as a gem-smuggler. He was impressive, too, in Sam Mendes' 50s-set portrait of a failing marriage *Revolutionary Road* (2009) alongside *Titanic* love interest Kate Winslet. He gave a convincingly tortured performance in Scorsese's *Shutter Island* and Christopher Nolan's *Inception* (both 2010, p.141), playing essentially the same role, an anguished alpha male with a faltering grip on reality and a vexatious dead wife, in both. His biggest risk thus far will be his role as Jay Gatsby in Baz Luhrmann's 3D adaptation of *The Great Gatsby* (2012); while the casting may be spot-on, the director has a reputation for the superficial and his last film, *Australia* (2008), was a notorious flop. He has wisely hedged against this risk by collaborating with Quentin Tarantino on his much anticipated *Django Unchained* (2012) and returns to Scorsese for *The Wolf of Wall Street*, a true tale of financial excess and hubris set in the 1990s.

is trying to track down, who murdered her three children. And then there is the mysterious Ward C, where Teddy suspects that secret government experiments are being carried out…

Everything in *Shutter Island* is deliciously overwrought: Dante Ferretti's lush rococo design and Sandy Powell's costumes ratchet up the overstated sense of place and time; Robert Richardson's cinematography is luxuriously atmospheric and plays with some of the colour and perspective tricks that Hitchcock used to disquiet audiences. And even more than usual for a Scorsese movie, this is a perfect opportunity to play spot the film reference, with Charles Laughton's *The Night of the Hunter* (1955), Kubrick's *The Shining* (1980), Hitchcock's *Vertigo* (1958), Sam Fuller's *Shock Corridor* (1963) and even Dario Argento's *Suspiria* (1977) just a few of the titles that Scorsese pillages for *Shutter Island*'s arresting imagery, while in using avant-garde European composers rather than an original score he nods to Kubrick's *2001* (1968), right down to the Ligeti.

Even after a (much recommended) second viewing, some critics found holes and contradictions in *Shutter Island*'s insanely convoluted plot: no matter. *Noir* plots are notorious for making no sense on closer examination; it is a style of filmmaking more concerned with mood and psychological state than quotidian storytelling. And anyway the key to the movie, and its apparent fractured, crazy narrative, might be given in a throwaway line delivered by Teddy's partner Chuck in a storm-ravaged crypt after they have been quizzing the booby-hatch's residents. "I dunno boss, how d'ya believe a crazy guy?" he says. Ask yourself from whose perspective this story was being told. On Shutter Island the inmates might have taken over more than the asylum.

Pure pulp bliss: an anguished Teddy Daniels (Leonard DiCaprio), observed by partner Chuck (Mark Ruffalo), struggles to find the truth in Scorsese's atmospherically shot paean to *film noir*, *Shutter Island*.

THE LITTLE MOVIES THAT COULD
Ten American indies that punched way above their weight...

IGBY GOES DOWN (Burr Steers, 2003)
"Ferris Bueller's Year Off" is how one critic described this sharply written and played coming-of-age drama, but its roots may go further back into American cultural history. Kieran Culkin is the eponymous Igby, a privileged Upper East Side teen who, along with his brother (a well-cast Ryan Phillippe), weathers his mother's cancer, his father's insanity and an affair with an older woman. Holden Caulfield, meet the 21st century...

SHATTERED GLASS (Billy Ray, 2003)
Between career-destroying appointments as Anakin Skywalker in George Lucas's *Star Wars* prequels, Hayden Christensen played journalist hoaxer Stephen Glass in this gripping true-life drama about the notorious hack who fabricated articles for *The New Republic*, "the in-flight magazine on Air Force One". Sharp on both journalism and office life it features great support from Hank Azaria as Glass's increasingly suspicious editor. Oh what might have been...

ABOUT SCHMIDT (Alexander Payne, 2003)
Some preferred Payne's Californian wine-country flick *Sideways* (2005), but this is at least as good. Jack Nicholson, playing effectively against type, is a just-retired Omaha widower who embarks on a road trip to discourage his daughter from getting married, all the while corresponding with a six-year-old African orphan called Ndugo whom at one point he blithely advises to "join a fraternity". Sharply observed and warm without being cloying, it's Nicholson's best performance of the millennium.

GARDEN STATE (Zach Braff, 2004)
Scrubs star Braff's feature debut recalls *The Graduate* (1967) in its story of twentysomething ennui. Braff is Andrew Largeman, a zoned-out 26-year-old aspiring actor who returns to his small hometown for his mother's funeral and reconnects with his old friends. A painfully on-the-nose soundtrack aside, it nevertheless conjures a loose, likeable atmosphere and features a great performance from Natalie Portman as Andrew's similarly adrift love interest.

AMERICAN SPLENDOR (Shari Springer Berman & Robert Pulcini, 2004)
Paul Giamatti excels in this eccentric biopic of cult cartoonist Harvey Pekar, whose identically titled comic books examine the minutiae of his superficially boring and dissatisfied life. Documentarians Berman and Pulcini toy gently with postmodernism, the real Pekar occasionally turns up, as do other people from the artist's life, and effectively convey the quotidian subject matter, the doctor's appointments and minor emotional crises that populate Pekar's quirky work.

KINSEY (Bill Condon, 2005)
Liam Neeson is on top form as the tormented biologist whose classic, and at the time notorious, study of "Sexual Behaviour in the Human Male" shocked America in the late 1940s and partially paved the way for the sexual revolution of the 60s. Condon's humane screenplay carefully examines this unlikely revolutionary's complicated motives and unique methods, while John Lithgow is excellent as Kinsey's sternly disapproving preacher father.

THE WOODSMAN (Nicole Kassell, 2005)
Few actors would take on the role of a child-molester without second thoughts, but the often underestimated Kevin Bacon gives a nuanced performance as Walter, a convicted paedophile who on being released from prison attempts to rebuild his life. A couple of sequences are necessarily gruelling, particularly one in a park when Walter meets a young girl, but Kassell's direction eschews dramatic exploitation and the result is an intelligent, restrained film about an agonizing subject.

THE SQUID AND THE WHALE (Noah Baumbach, 2006)
Noah Baumbach's autobiographical film about a New York family unravelling is a little reminiscent of early Woody Allen but with a sharper bite. A pre-*The Social Network* Jesse Eisenberg is excellent as the sixteen-year-old Walt, who helplessly watches as his parents' marriage implodes. It's acutely observed, funny and moving, and features a barnstormer of a performance from Jeff Daniels as the arrogant, clueless paterfamilias whom Walt, naturally, idolizes.

BEFORE THE DEVIL KNOWS YOU'RE DEAD (Sidney Lumet, 2008)
From the veteran director of classics such as *12 Angry Men* (1957) and *Dog Day Afternoon* (1975), the late Sidney Lumet's last movie features great performances from Philip Seymour Hoffman and Ethan Hawke, while Kelly Masterson's complex, unpredictable screenplay continually wrong-foots the viewer, starting out as a classic heist gone wrong flick but spinning off into a blistering family drama. Pretty impressive stuff from a guy who was 83 when he directed it.

PARANORMAL ACTIVITY (Oren Peli, 2009)
Poltergeist meets *The Blair Witch Project* (still the most profitable independent film of all time) in this chilling contemporary haunted house tale from director Oren Peli, who spent a year preparing his own home and a week shooting his wildly successful feature debut. Using mostly static cameras, it cranks up the tension by exploiting what doesn't happen rather than what does. But still, never has a door slamming been so terrifying...

A Single Man

2010, US, 101 mins, 12A (UK) R (US)

••

cast Colin Firth, Julianne Moore, Matthew Goode, Nicholas Hoult, Jon Kortajarena *scr* Tom Ford & David Scearce (from the novel by Christopher Isherwood) *cin* Eduard Grau *m* Abel Korzeniowski *dir* Tom Ford

It's fair to say that when news broke that Tom Ford, the then 48-year-old Texan-born fashion designer and former creative director at Gucci, was not only to make his debut as a feature film director but that he was financing the project himself and had chosen Christopher Isherwood's classic to set out his stall, there was a fair amount of critical scepticism. Was this some kind of vanity project? What, after all, would a man who made gazillions out of handbags and suits know about cinema? But in fact Ford's film is a skilfully made, understated picture, and one of the most assured debuts in recent memory.

Set on an American college campus in the early 1960s, *A Single Man* has George (Colin Firth), an English Literature lecturer besieged by grief after the death of his long-time partner Jim (Matthew Goode, whom we see in occasional flashbacks) in a car accident. He has, it quickly emerges, determined to commit suicide and, on the single day during which the film takes place, he goes about the necessary chores: there is a visit to his safety-deposit box to put his affairs in order, the buying of a gun and bullets. But as he does so he encounters flickers of remaining hope in his

Model T Ford: Matthew Goode and Colin Firth recline on the beach in monochrome flashback in Tom Ford's cool and classy debut.

COLIN FIRTH

b. 10 September 1960, Hampshire, UK

An inspiration to actors approaching middle age who still aspire to Hollywood stardom, Colin Firth was 35 when he first made an overnight impact, smouldering fit to set off the nation's smoke alarms as Mr Darcy in the BBC's 1995 TV adaptation of *Pride and Prejudice*, although in fact he'd been a jobbing telly actor for at least a decade. The films that followed have somewhat unimaginatively exploited his reputation as the educated woman's crumpet, notably as the amusingly monikered Mark Darcy in *Bridget Jones's Diary* (2001) and *Bridget Jones: The Edge of Reason* (2004), but until recently he seems to have been for the most part happy to oblige and has scored impressive box-office doing so with a string of smash hits. In *Shakespeare in Love* (1999) he donned ruff and earring as the Earl of Wessex (though the girl got to wear it when he starred in *The Girl with the Pearl Earring* in 2004). He pleased his core audience as a jilted author who learns to speak Portuguese to propose to his housekeeper in Richard Curtis's vapid but much seen *Love Actually* (2003), did so again as one of Meryl Streep's wedding guests in *Mamma Mia!* (2008), and was solid support for Emma Thompson as a widower in need of an au pair in the unexpected family hit *Nanny McPhee* (2005). But more recently he's begun to specialize in reserved, damaged Englishmen – with huge critical and box-office success. "My primary instinct as an actor is not the big transformation," he has said. "Often it's a case of witnessing a big party piece but wondering afterwards, where's the substance?". You get to see what he means in both Tom Ford's *A Single Man* (2010) and his Oscar-winning role in *The King's Speech* (2011, p.151). The more interesting work continues: in *Tinker Tailor Soldier Spy* (2011) he was suitably chilly as double-agent Bill Haydon, a role he says he based on real-life traitor Kim Philby, and he has been cast in Atom Egoyan's *Devil's Knot*, a dramatization of the notorious Robin Hood Hills murders, the subject of Joe Belinger and Bruce Sinofsky's incomparable *Paradise Lost* documentary in 1996.

life: there's his best friend Charley (Julianne Moore), a rambunctious, ever so slightly gin-sodden socialite with whom it seems he had a fling in the distant past; the flirtatious attentions of an absurdly pretty young student (Nicholas Hoult); and an unexpectedly soulful encounter with a hustler (Jon Kortajarena). Is there enough in these flashes of a future to save his life?

Perhaps unsurprisingly everything about Tom Ford's movie is exquisite. (Ford was apparently even meticulous enough to insist on the particular aftershaves the actors wore.) A few critics voiced reservations about this excess of design and, true, a sequence shot in Ansel Adamsish pellucid black and white, in which George and his lover recline on a rocky beach, would only need a heavily accented voiceover whispering "Pour Homme" to serve as an ad for one of Ford's posh scents. (One of his other directorial flourishes, the muted frame suddenly flooding with colour and moments of human warmth, was a delight for some and too theatrical for others.) But this studied, somewhat chilly beauty is perfectly judged in terms of George's emotional state: the world around him is frozen, he walks through it as if trapped in an aquarium (indeed the opening image is of naked male bodies drowning). And for that matter why should we not simply take cinematic beauty on its own terms and enjoy it?

Ford's masterstroke was the casting of Colin Firth, who here gives the performance of his career. He is a man in the grip of overwhelming pain, but unable both through character and convention to express it. Thus Firth's magnificent performance is all in the eyes, which Ford accentuates by framing them with heavy-rimmed spectacles. It's at its best and most emotionally devastating when a friend of his lover calls to inform him of the accident. Thank you for telephoning, he says, after being told that he will not be welcome at the funeral. His voice, calm, cultured, gives away nothing. But his eyes say it all. It is in his wonderful performance of subtlety and deep humanity that *A Single Man* reveals itself as a singularly memorable film.

The Skin I Live In

2011, Sp, 120 mins, 15 (UK) R (US)

....

cast Antonio Banderas, Elena Anaya, Marisa Paredes, Jan Cornet *scr* Pedro
Almodóvar and Agustín Almodóvar (from a novel by Thierry Jonquet)
cin José Luis Alcaine *m* Alberto Iglesias *dir* Pedro Almodóvar

For the first twenty minutes or so of *The Skin I Live In* you'd be forgiven for
thinking you had wandered into the wrong movie by mistake and were watching
a David Cronenberg flick rather than a Pedro Almodóvar one. After all, here
are all the Canadian auteur's familiar tropes. There are the fetishistic shots
of surgical equipment, scalpels and petri dishes in a spotless lab. At medical
conferences suave surgeons talk of face transplants and a mysterious process
called "transgenesis" in hushed voices. But then a man dressed as a tiger arrives,
bares his bottom to reveal his identity, revolvers are produced and time and
identity begin to become alarmingly fluid. Oh, and the home furnishings are all
aggressively sumptuous. Now we are unmistakeably in Almodóvar country.

The Spanish master's first venture into something like horror takes a crazy,
overheated plot that 50s exploitation movie hacks might have felt to have been a
bit ripe and treats it with the utmost seriousness; the result is a movie that perches
thrillingly on a knife-edge between a fevered nightmare and a wicked joke.
Antonio Banderas is smoothly plausible as Dr Robert Ledgard, an urbane plastic
surgeon who is publicly developing a new kind of incredibly strong human skin
but who secretly, in his luxurious mansion decorated with giant classical nudes
and complete with its own operating theatre, has imprisoned a young woman
called Vera (Elena Anaya). Trapped in a sparsely furnished upstairs room, and
wearing nothing other than a kind of flesh-toned body-stocking, she spends her
days performing yoga and occasionally half-heartedly attempting suicide, carving
away at her unusually flawless skin, much to her perfectionist captor's irritation.
Ledgard, it turns out, in the spirit of Dr Victor Frankenstein, or perhaps Dr Frank
N. Furter, has hatched a diabolical plan to use his surgical skills to transform Vera
into a simulacrum of his ex-wife who committed suicide after being horribly
burned in a car accident. But who is, or rather was, Vera? What is the compliant
housekeeper's (Marisa Paredes) part in the plan? And who is the gun-toting thug in
the tiger suit? Via flashbacks we find out the alarming truth about Vera's previous
life and discover that Ledgard's plan is rooted in a grief and guilt more complex
than we first comprehended.

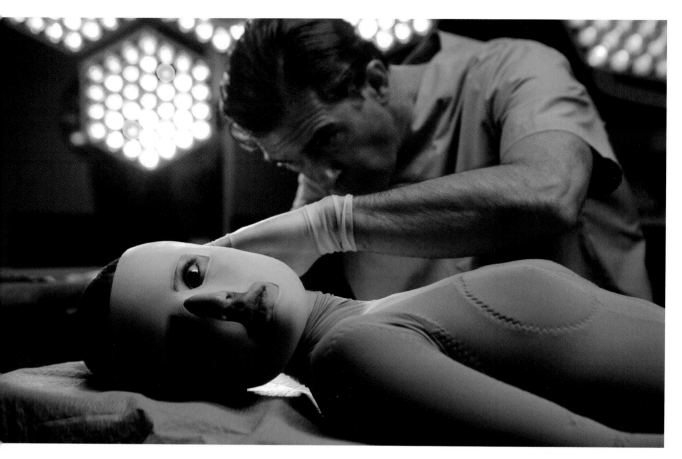

Operating theatre of
the absurd: Dr Ledgard
(Antonio Banderas)
wields the scalpel on
captive Vera (Elena
Anaya) in Almodóvar's
dark, twisting tale.

It's often difficult to tell whether Almodóvar is winking at us with this distinctly
gamey stew – or rather when and for how long. Certainly there are moments
(impossible to describe without giving the film's loopy but highly effective plot
twists away) of what can only be described as black comedy. But as well as the
melodrama Almodóvar's beautifully shot and designed film might touch on a few
more profound questions. Are we defined forever by our physical appearance,
the skin that we in some sense inhabit? Or is the alterability of skin and flesh
and bone a route to human mutability; change it and do we ourselves become
something radically different? Almodóvar delivers an ambivalent ending that
draws no firm conclusions (and it is worth mentioning that many feminists
were enraged by some elements of what might be called the film's Hitchcockian
attitude towards women). It's that tease, the sense that it seems to have much
more going on under its exquisite surface, but then again it might *just* be surface,
skin, and nothing more, that underpins *The Skin I Live In*'s utterly perverse
pleasures.

The Social Network

2010, US, 120 mins, 12A (UK) PG-13 (US)

••

cast Jesse Eisenberg, Andrew Garfield, Jusin Timberlake, Armie Hammer *scr* Aaron Sorkin (from a book by Ben Mezrich) *cin* Jeff Cronenweth *m* Trent Reznor, Atticus Ross *dir* David Fincher

For a movie that is at least partly concerned with algorithms, computer code and virtual networks, *The Social Network*'s key pleasures are comfortingly old-fashioned. This is a tale of privileged teenagers who stumble, by accident more than design, upon a billion-dollar secret, the outrageous success of which tears them apart. It's the old story of the rock band that hits the big time only to implode spectacularly under the pressure, only this time the keyboards have @ keys.

David Fincher directs this high-end soap with his familiar technical aplomb; almost every aspect drips quality. Aaron Sorkin (*The West Wing*) deploys his talents in both the trademark rat-a-tat dialogue and an ingenious structure. Driving the story at a trot, he dips in and out of two court depositions – Mark Zuckerberg is being sued by both ex-best friend Eduardo Saverin, played by Andrew Garfield complete with big hair, and the patrician Winklevoss twins (both played by Armie Hammer), who accuse him of stealing their idea – as well as flashing back to Facebook's early days as a project founded by a peeved undergraduate just dumped by his girlfriend (a detail the real Zuckerberg strenuously challenges). Fincher's regular cinematographer Jeff Cronenweth makes the most of the Ivy League locations, the cosy dorm

DAVID FINCHER

b. 28 August 1962, Denver, CO, US

The most common criticism of David Fincher, an ex-rock-promo director whose early films such as *Se7en* (1995) and *Fight Club* (1999) displayed a gloomy, neo-noirish sensibility, is that he is a master film technician: a wizard with cameras, computers and precision editing but lacking in heart. But after a wobbly start to the 2000s with *Panic Room* (2002), a well-wrought but mostly unengaging thriller starring Jodie Foster, he seemed to take the criticism on board and was drawn to stories with more convincingly human characters. He may even have swung too far in the other direction with *The Curious Case of Benjamin Button* (2008), the story of a man who ages backwards, which delivered a triumph of digital effects make-up – ageing and reverse-ageing Brad Pitt – but in the service of a sentimental Oscar-baiting tale laced with the kind of cod profundity that recalled Robert Zemeckis's *Forrest Gump* (1994). But two of his other recent films, both based on true stories, have delivered richly conceived characters as well as plentiful intellectual stimulation. *Zodiac* (2007) was a gripping account of the pursuit of the eponymous San Franciscan serial killer that didn't shy away from the open-ended nature of the narrative (the killer was never caught), and featured powerful performances from stars Robert Downey Jr and Jake Gyllenhaal. While his account of the founding of Facebook, *The Social Network* (2010), was criticized by some for distorting the facts, its entertaining fallings-out and feudings concealed among other themes a subtle attack on the soulless net generation from its elders, an unusual recasting of the state of play in the generation wars. The film was tipped for Oscar success, but was eventually beaten to the podium by *The King's Speech* (p.151). His eagerly anticipated adaptation of Stieg Larsson's *The Girl with the Dragon Tattoo* (2012), with Daniel Craig, was dark and violent, and critically generally well received, but for some reason failed to connect with audiences at the box office, throwing further Hollywood iterations of Larsson's *Millennium* trilogy into doubt.

rooms and crisp autumnal quads, while Trent Reznor and Atticus Ross's beautifully spare score invokes a kind of wistfulness, perhaps for a time just a few years ago when these baby moguls weren't at each other's throats. At the centre of this 21st-century Jacobean comedy is the fascinating, ambiguous figure of Zuckerberg himself, played with amazing skill by Jesse Eisenberg. He presents Zuckerberg as a fearsomely intelligent, mouthy smart alec whose motives are unclear, though anger at being excluded from Harvard's snootier clubs is certainly a factor. There is more than a suggestion of Asperger's syndrome, both in his almost Olympian levels of social ineptitude and the formidable focus and mastery of detail required to launch his invention upon an unsuspecting world.

If the simple pleasures of this maelstrom of hubris and *schadenfreude* aren't enough, there's another interpretation of the film, one that gives it a little more critical bite. Is *The Social Network* at its core a social satire created by two middle-aged men who grew up on rock'n'roll and radical politics, which takes careful aim at a passionless, zoned-out internet generation? Almost everybody involved is pretty unappealing: Zuckerberg, accurately or not, is portrayed as a young man willing to sacrifice friendships whenever they conflict with his grand project; Eduardo Saverin is a CFO who is dumb enough to sign away his entire investment in the fledgling company ("I can't look at my father!" he wails at one point); the Winkelvosses are a pair of cartoonish privileged posh boys whose disbelief at being got the better of is one of the movie's more satisfying threads; while interloper Sean Parker (an effectively reptilian Justin Timberlake) plays Yoko, sowing the seeds of discontent between the co-founders. In the midst of all this intrigue our heroes closet themselves in dorm rooms and Silicon Valley mediaplexes, transforming real-life flesh and blood relationships into status updates, news feeds and digital marketing opportunities. Welcome, *The Social Network* seems to say, to the ultimate revenge of the nerds. Like?

Friends forever? Andrew Garfield and Jesse Eisenberg as Facebook co-founders Eduardo Saverin and Mark Zuckerberg enjoying happier times at Harvard in David Fincher's *The Social Network*.

Spirited Away

2003, Jpn, 125 mins, PG (UK) PG (US)

cast Rumi Hiiragi, Miyu Irino, Mari Natsuki, Bunta Sugawara *scr* Hayao Miyazaki *cin* Atsushi Okui *m* Joe Hisaishi *dir* Hayao Miyazaki

Connoisseurs of Japanimation had long known that Studio Ghibli, headed up by veteran manga creator and animator Hayao Miyazaki, produced classics of the genre, but *Spirited Away*, made after his threatened retirement, thrust anime into the mainstream. Not only a smash hit in Japan, displacing *Titanic* (1998) at the top of the all-time box-office charts, it also conquered the US – where Pixar's head honcho John Lasseter supervised its English dubbing – and Europe. Purists of reading age should of course see it in its original (subtitled) version, but in any language it's an hour and a half of pure, exhilarating magic.

After her parents make an unwise detour on the way to their new house, they turn up at a strange, apparently deserted theme park. Unhappy ten-year-old Chihiro (Rumi Hiiragi) wanders off and, as night falls and the abandoned park lights up, she finds herself trapped in a building filled with odd characters, while her parents, after tucking into a banquet they come across, are transformed into gobbling pigs. Finding help in the shape of a young boy, Haku (Miyu Irino), she discovers that this is the Bathhouse of the Gods, where eight million deities come to scrub away the dust of the day. To avoid the wrath of the human-hating boss Yubaba (Mari Natsuki), and to stand any chance of rescuing her enchanted parents, Chihiro must find work and beware of forgetting her human name, which Yubaba confiscates as part of her employment contract.

A towering edifice, the bathhouse is an alarming establishment, likewise its staff and patrons: vast piles of what looks like shambling dung – Stink Gods – occasionally turn up demanding to be cleansed; a spectral masked figure called No Face wanders around producing gold nuggets at will and occasionally eating the staff; hyperactive toads and slugs scurry with towels and plates piled with food. But it's also a busy, exciting place packed with fascinating, unpredictable characters. Unlike the straightforwardly evil witches and innocent fawns of classic Disney, Miyazaki's characters are complex and unpredictable and their motives often mysterious; they're very much as adults must often appear to children. Kamajî (Bunta Sugawara), the six-limbed boiler-room operator who dresses in a Victorian frock coat and sunglasses and marshals hordes of smuts of soot who reluctantly

carry coal to the giant boilers (talk about recycling), is gruff at first but turns out to be sympathetic; Haku is mercurial, sometimes kind, sometimes brusque, occasionally a dragon. Yubaba, a squat hag with a vast face and a bureaucratic attitude, is interested only in the bottom line and coddling her alarmingly oversized baby.

Miyazaki's animation is simple but incredibly expressive. A train trip across a vast flood plain into the evening is a delicious highlight; it's a sequence that encapsulates the strange, enchanted, constantly surprising mood of this perfectly wrought little masterpiece. But amidst the charm there is always the sense that the magic could run out of control: with all that slopping water and animated inanimates, the dangerously anarchic spirit of the Sorcerer's Apprentice movement of *Fantasia* (1940) is never far away. As she becomes ever more immersed in this beguiling world, Chihiro has to remind herself of her humanity if she is to rescue her parents from their porcine fate; sometimes she struggles to remember that there is a world outside that must be returned to. Sometimes, as we are transported by this spellbinding film, so do we.

Heroine Chihiro with her companion Haku: simple, expressive animation blends the ordinary with the magical in Miyazaki's complex and mysterious world.

The Station Agent

2004, US, 90 mins, 15 (UK) R (US)

••

cast Peter Dinklage, Bobby Cannavale, Patricia Clarkson, Raven Goodwin,
Michelle Williams *scr* Thomas McCarthy *cin* Oliver Bokelberg *m* Stephen Trask
dir Thomas McCarthy

Devotees of 90s American indie cinema might remember seeing Peter Dinklage,
this movie's four-foot, five-inch star in Tom DeCillo's classic *Living in Oblivion*
(1995), raging against the lazy use of dwarfs to signify dream sequences. "Have

you ever had a dream with a dwarf in it? ... *I* don't even have dreams with dwarfs in them," he bellows at director Steve Buscemi. "The only place I've seen dwarfs in dreams is in stupid movies like this!" It was a *cri de coeur* obviously heard by first-time writer-director Thomas McCarthy, who in Finbar McBride has created a role that would be a gift to an actor of any stature, and in *The Station Agent* one of the most shamelessly sweet-natured films of the noughties.

Fin is a handsome, dignified man (with, it has to be noted, an initially disconcertingly deep voice), whose response to a lifetime of stares and dumb comments – when he walks into a convenience store the woman behind the counter pulls out a camera and takes his picture, and there is the humiliation of literally being overlooked at a supermarket counter – has been to develop a hard-as-nails defensive shell and a permanent scowl, and to bury himself in his great passion: railways. After a friend dies and leaves him a piece of land in rural New Jersey, complete with an abandoned train depot ("It's beautiful but there's nothing there, nothing," the lawyer tells him, much to Fin's approval), he heads out of town to escape the pointing and sniggering and indulge his solitary passion. But he soon finds himself befriended, initially much against his will, firstly by Joe (an irresistible Bobby Cannavale), a puppyishly energetic young hot-dog and coffee vendor who parks up outside the deserted depot, and then by Olivia (the consistently excellent Patricia Clarkson), a divorcee who, after managing to almost run him over twice, slowly begins to emerge from the cocoon of grief in which she has encased herself after the death of her young son. Then there's Emily (Michelle Williams), a young librarian who has noticed that Fin is good-looking and certainly a nicer guy than her scumbag

Brief encounter: librarian Emily (Michelle Williams) falling for railway enthusiast Fin (Peter Dinklage) in Thomas McCarthy's sweet-natured, laid-back *The Station Agent*.

MICHELLE WILLIAMS

b. 9 September 1980, Kalispell, MT, US

The female stars of *echt* 90s TV show *Dawson's Creek* seem to have had a much better time of it in the 21st century than the boys. Of course Dawson's (James Van der Beek) sometime main squeeze Katie Holmes went off and became Mrs Tom Cruise and found herself starring both in that drama and the odd half-decent movie. But as for Dawson and best pal Pacey (Joshua Jackson), well, with the exception of Van der Beek's *The Rules of Attraction* (2003), the less said about their movie careers the better. It was Michelle Williams who established herself as a fully fledged star. Arthouse audiences first noticed her as Peter Dinklage's librarian love interest in *The Station Agent* (2004) and alongside Ryan Gosling in *The United States of Leland* (2005). But Hollywood sat up and took notice in 2006 when she played Heath Ledger's unhappy wife in Ang Lee's *Brokeback Mountain* (2006, p.41), after which she seemed unstoppable. Meanwhile, her burgeoning relationship with Ledger, which had begun on set, provided much paparazzi fodder and, after his tragic death, sadly more. Todd Haynes cast her as Coco Rivington, a channelling of aristocratic youthquaker Edie Sedgwick in his unconventional Bob Dylan movie *I'm Not There* (2007), she was affecting as Philip Seymour Hoffman's love interest in *Synecdoche, New York* (2009, p.228), and it was as another woman trapped in an unhappy marriage à la *Brokeback* that got her an Oscar nomination for *Blue Valentine* (2011, p.31). But it was in the daunting role of the greatest star of them all, Marilyn Monroe, in *My Week With Marilyn* (2011), that she has made her greatest impact. It was a role she nearly didn't take. "As soon as I finished the script, I knew that I wanted to do it, then I spent six months trying to talk myself out of it," she told *Vogue*. Thankfully she failed and delivered an astonishing portrayal of the damaged, vulnerable and often incredibly annoying actress, gaining her second Oscar nomination along the way. Aspiring filmmaker Dawson would no doubt approve – wherever he is.

boyfriend, and Cleo (Raven Goodwin), a twelve-year-old as yet unembarrassed enough to ask Fin if he is "a midget" without malevolent intent.

It would be easy for a concoction filled with as much whimsy as this to deliquesce into syrupy mawkishness, and with different actors and a different director maybe it would have. But McCarthy's screenplay is a masterclass in understatement, his filmmaking style is unhurried and unafraid of long, companionable silences and quiet moments – like Fin, it's confident enough to spend a great deal of time just wandering down railway tracks saying nothing in particular. The performances he extracts from his key troika of performers (an actor in dozens of films himself, he apparently wrote the screenplay with them in mind, and it shows) are subtle and utterly unaffected. None of these characters asks for sympathy, either each other's or ours, but each develops slowly and naturally, reaching out to one another before recoiling, then trying again, and finally, unexpectedly, wonderfully, finding in each other a warmth and human contact, a salve for the different lonelinesses that afflict them all. *The Station Agent* – made on a shoestring budget for just over a million dollars and proving that indie cinema was still alive, if ailing – is a movie that leaves you feeling unaccountably happy. Small? Maybe, but almost perfectly formed.

Sunshine

2007, US/UK, 107 mins, 15 (UK) R (US)

....

cast Cillian Murphy, Chris Evans, Rose Byrne, Hiroyuki Sanada, Michelle Yeoh *scr* Alex Garland *cin* Alwin Küchler *m* John Murphy *dir* Danny Boyle

The near future: our sun is dying and with it, of course, Earth. A desperate mankind has already sent one space mission, somewhat hubristically named *Icarus*, to try and reignite our life-giving star, but it vanished mysteriously into the soundless void. A second and, we are led to believe, last possible mission, is now under way. *Icarus II*, then, is a vast spaceship with only one purpose, to deliver its payload to the failing sun and thus explode it back into life: it's the interstellar equivalent of applying the electric paddles. Its crew, "eight astronauts strapped to the back of a bomb", as mission physicist Capa (Cillian Murphy) puts it, are equally dedicated to this single goal, and though there is a hypothetical plan to return them home, none are in any real doubt that this is a suicide mission. The future of all of us depends on their success.

So far, so, well, *meh*. There's not much that sci-fi fans will be unfamiliar with in the set-up. After all, replace the sun with an asteroid and you've got the plot to *Armageddon* (1998). But what makes *Sunshine* a very good, and nearly a truly great, sci-fi movie is the presence of Danny Boyle, a director whose work is shot through with an irrepressible humanism. He takes this slightly foxed plot and loads it with a kind of woozy, swoony romanticism coupled with a melancholic sense of finality. Though it obviously owes *2001: A Space Odyssey* (1968) a debt (it's difficult to think of a subsequent serious space-set film that doesn't), it stresses the human rather than the technological, and it's squarely on our side – it's Kubrick played with soul.

DANNY BOYLE
b. 20 October 1956, Bury, Lancashire, UK

Like one of his many cinematic heroes Martin Scorsese, Danny Boyle, among the best of the new wave of British directors and certainly the most consistently surprising, was originally destined for the priesthood. However, unlike Scorsese's early work, Boyle films don't manifest any angsty spiritual darkness: in many ways he's closer in spirit to Frank Capra, putting his characters through the emotional grinder before providing an uplifting, crowd-pleasing ending. His breakthrough films in the 90s – *Shallow Grave* in 1995 and *Trainspotting* the year after, both with Ewan McGregor – showed a dedication to an exuberantly kinetic style of filmmaking and youthful subject matter long missing from British cinema and launched a mini-renaissance (Guy Ritchie with his *Lock, Stock and Two Smoking Barrels*, 1998, being a key beneficiary). *The Beach* (2000), from a hit novel by frequent writing collaborator Alex Garland, was a debacle; perhaps the controversial casting of a post-*Titanic* (1998) Leonardo DiCaprio (which led to Boyle falling out with McGregor, who had previously starred in his uncharacteristically leaden attempt at screwball rom-com *A Life Less Ordinary* in 1997) was to blame. The new millennium, though, has been almost all good news: gritty, lo-fi zombie flick *28 Days Later* (2002) was in the top rank of the reanimated genre, *Millions* (2005), his nearest thing to an autobiographical film, about a seven-year-old Catholic boy who talks to the saints, might have slipped under many cinemagoers' radar but was still whimsically enjoyable, and *Sunshine* (2007) showed a facility for dazzling visuals as well as emotional heft. His biggest commercial hit was Hollywood/Bollywood hybrid *Slumdog Millionaire* (2009), a Mumbai-set rags-to-riches tale perfectly calibrated for both box-office and Oscar success. He's also enjoyed success in theatre, notably with an inventive production of *Frankenstein* in which Jonny Lee Miller and Benedict Cumberbatch alternated in the role of the doctor and his ghastly creation. The pulpit's loss, then, has definitely been the multiplex's gain.

Reminders of the sensual joys of Earth are everywhere aboard the *Icarus II*. In the spaceship's "oxygen garden", life-giving water cascades over the verdant plant life. In the "Earth room" – a kind of holographic immersion chamber that simulates the sensation of being back home – familiar scenes can be conjured for homesick astronauts. A seaside promenade is recreated, and three laughing women struggle with their umbrellas in the gusting wind as the waves crash up the sea wall, drenching them. On seeing this mission engineer Mace (Chris Evans playing steely macho) grins with delight, but it's a joy etched with sadness – will he ever feel the sting of sea-spray against his skin again? Will any of us? "Again," he says, and the sea obeys.

Augmenting this sense of sensual immersion is Boyle's use of colour, which is just a little trippy – the greens of the oxygen garden are a tad oversaturated, as are the roiling yellows and oranges of the dying sun. Everything is about *sensation*,

Break out the factor 20: Danny Boyle's gloriously sensual sci-fi film pits eight astronauts (led by Cillian Murphy) against a dying sun.

about the experience of being human and still alive even in the depths of space. Boyle often shoots his characters in hyper-close-ups, observing flickering eyes and beads of sweat, tiny human details set in vertigo-inducing contrast to the immense, majestic and often more than a little terrifying FX shots of *Icarus II* – which itself resembles a giant umbrella, its golden canopy pointing towards the fiery surface of the sun.

So why a *nearly* great sci-fi movie? Well, it's the ending. For the last twenty minutes or so Alex Garland's screenplay does a screeching handbrake turn into what might charitably be described as WTF? territory. What had been a science-fiction movie both meditative and tense bizarrely resolves itself into more of a horror outing. A pity of course, but nowhere near misjudged enough to squander the sense of wonder and sadness so carefully built in the first two thirds. For the most part Danny Boyle's fantastic voyage dazzles.

J.J. ABRAMS

b. 27 June 1966, New York, NY, US

J.J. Abrams's offices in Santa Monica don't bear the name of his company, Bad Robot, but instead are adorned by a large sign reading "National Typewriter Company". A small sign next to the small, glowing green doorbell simply reads "Are you ready?" It's typical of the essential playfulness and love of mystery that animates the man who created *Lost*, the hit TV series that alternately delighted and infuriated its fans between 2004 and 2010. (That playfulness might also cause the occasional embarrassing emergency: the toilet in his office is hidden behind a fake bookshelf with the prospective user needing to know which specific volume acts as the handle.) Born in New York, Abrams was brought up in Los Angeles with Hollywood in his blood, attending early screenings of films such as *Escape from New York* (1981) with his producer parents, and at one point was charged with the conservation of Steven Spielberg's 8mm film collection. After leaving college he started writing screenplays and co-producing films such as *Regarding Henry* (1991), *Forever Young* (1993) and Jerry Bruckheimer's *Armageddon* (1998). His feature debut came with *Mission: Impossible 3* (2006), the Tom Cruise vehicle that had been resting since its second entry in 2000. Though it divided the critics, with some finding the brand tired by now, it featured a glowering performance from villain Philip Seymour Hoffman and Abrams proved himself an adept director of action. He produced *Cloverfield* (2008, p.54), which showcased his taste for mystery and hucksterism, while *Super 8* (2011) was a heartfelt homage to his childhood hero Steven Spielberg. With his reboot of another franchise, *Star Trek*, which had been dormant since the disastrously poor *Star Trek: Nemesis* in 2003, he took the story back to its beginnings, populating the newly built USS *Enterprise* with a youthful, sexy crew including Chris Pine as James T. Kirk, Zachary Quinto as Spock and, entertainingly, Simon Pegg as Scotty. The movie was a hit with critics, and possibly more importantly with the vocal Trekker community, who were impressed enough to consent to a sequel to be directed by Abrams, due in 2013.

Super 8

2011, US, 111 mins, 12A (UK) PG-13 (US)

....

cast Joel Courtney, Riley Griffiths, Elle Fanning, Ryan Lee, Kyle Chandler *scr* J.J. Abrams *cin* Larry Fong *m* Michael Giacchino *dir* J.J. Abrams

J.J. Abrams's *Super 8* opens at a funeral in a small American town sometime in the summer of 1979. Inside the modest shingle-clad house adults chat quietly while outside a young teenage boy sits disconsolately on a swing. A female mourner looks at him through the window and worries about the boy and the future he will have with his now widowed father. "I don't think he really *knows* Joel," she says of the bereaved man's relationship with his son. But the boy has his friends, film fans who are busily completing their 8mm masterpiece, a zombie movie. When they sneak out to a train station one night to snatch some of their director Charles's (a likeable Riley Griffiths, reminiscent of Jerry O'Connell's Vern in 1986's *Stand By Me*) much vaunted "production value" they witness a spectacular train crash. But what were those strange noises from one of the cars? Why have the military turned up? And what happened to all the town's dogs?

Hold on. Strange goings-on in small-town America? The military chasing an extraterrestrial who might just want to go home? Daddy issues? If it all sounds a bit familiar then that's because J.J. Abrams's *Super 8* is probably the most extended, heartfelt homage by one director to another in movie history. Steven Spielberg is the recipient of this celluloid *billet-doux* (made by his own company, Amblin) and at its best it reminds us just how almost supernaturally good early Spielberg could be. At its worst – and it never gets anywhere near bad – it reminds us of exactly the same thing.

This cinematic cap-doffing doesn't stop with the story or themes. Michael Giacchino's soaring score is a credible imitation of John Williams's emotion-freighted compositions, while Larry Fong's precise widescreen compositions are flooded with the deliberate lens flare that marked out Spielberg's early work, and horizons and starscapes are much in evidence à la *Close Encounters of the Third Kind* (1977). More vitally Abrams casts his film impeccably: the kids are both natural and likeable, particularly Joel Courtney and Elle Fanning, who manage to be sweet without ever tipping over into saccharine. But after an hour or so things derail, if only a little. Its action-packed final act seems oddly disconnected from the first. There's nothing fundamentally wrong with it, the chaos is well handled, but it reminds you of just how skilfully *E.T.* (1982), the Spielberg masterpiece that *Super 8* nods to most often, seamlessly handled these transitions from drama to action and back again.

Some asked who this movie is primarily made for: kids out for a summer popcorner, or jaded fortysomethings keen to relive the movies that seduced them in the first place? There's no reason it can't be a joy for both. For the adults, the first hour or so at least is an unashamed wallow in nostalgia for a time when the ice cream in the usherette's tray was King Cone and the Kia-Ora too orangey for crows. For anyone, it's a refreshing, almost unique, example of a summer movie that caresses rather than assaults the senses, delivering emotional as well as pyrotechnic wallop and which leaves you with a sense of the joyful possibilities of story and cinema rather than a bad case of tinnitus.

An explosion marks the start of mysterious goings-on in smalltown America: set in the summer of 1979, *Super 8* harks back visually and narratively to early Spielberg.

Synecdoche, New York

2008, US, 124 mins, 15 (UK) R (US)

....

cast Philip Seymour Hoffman, Samantha Morton, Michelle Williams, Catherine Keener, Hope Davis, Dianne Wiest, Emily Watson *scr* Charlie Kaufman *cin* Fred Elmes *m* Jon Brion *dir* Charlie Kaufman

Baffling, brilliant and finally emotionally devastating, *Synecdoche, New York* without a doubt established its writer/director Charlie Kaufman as not just an eccentric postmodern jester working for a small audience of devoted fans, but an utterly unique cinematic voice, a major American filmmaker with a world-view unlike any other. His previous screenplays, such as 1999's *Being John Malkovich* and *Eternal Sunshine of the Spotless Mind* (2004, p.88), had shown us his intellectual nimbleness and playful self-referentiality as well as giving us an oblique insight into the obsessions and neuroses of their creator. But in no way do they prepare you for *Synecdoche, New York*, Kaufman's directorial debut. This is filmmaking at the highest, most exhilarating level. Here goes: it's not completely outrageous to mention it, in terms of its cinematic ambition at least, in the same breath as *Citizen Kane* (1941).

It all begins, for a Kaufman story, conventionally enough. Caden Cotard is a forty-year-old playwright on the verge of great success with an unorthodox adaptation of Arthur Miller's *Death of a Salesman*. But at home his life is slowly drifting off the rails. His artist wife Adele (Catherine Keener), who paints portraits so minuscule they have to be viewed through magnifying glasses, is distant, admitting to their therapist (a great cameo by Hope Davis) that she fantasizes about him dying and her starting afresh. He begins to develop odd physical symptoms including pustules on his face and inexplicable tremors. Eventually Adele leaves him but simultaneously he receives an apparently infinite grant and determines to create a work of art that is "nothing less than the brutal truth". In an impossibly vast hangar he begins his project, a sprawling play starring thousands and performed on life-sized sets of New York (at one point a zeppelin flies through the skyscrapers) into which he inserts himself as one of the characters. But slowly art and life slide into one another, and as he desperately and hopelessly tries to create the perfect work of art, real life inexorably vanishes over the horizon.

It's virtually impossible to describe *Synecdoche, New York*, let alone adequately review it. In its huge ambition it resembles one of the heavyweight "great American novels" – John Irving, or John Updike's *Rabbit* cycle come to mind. It's packed with bizarre, surreal details. To wit: box-office salesgirl Hazel (Samantha Morton) is shown around a house by a real-estate agent who assures her that it's perfect for a single person. Yes, she replies, but I'd be afraid of the fire. And indeed the house is, and for the forty-year span of the whole film, will remain on fire.

In lesser hands all this riddle-setting, intellectual pirouetting and allusion (the name Cotard, for instance, may well refer to Cotard's syndrome, a rare neurological condition in which the sufferer believes themselves to be dead, and it *may* be a clue to unravelling the film) would rapidly become irritating, but Kaufman is no cinematic performing seal. At the heart of his film is a single man (played over four decades with astonishing control by Philip Seymour Hoffman) and his anguish, the truth of his life eluding him at every turn despite his Herculean efforts to capture it. The title of this intoxicating masterpiece refers to a figure of speech where a part of something stands for the whole. In this sprawling, heartbreaking film Caden Cotard's hopes, fears, his reckless dreams and finally his magnificent failure represent at the deepest level what it is to be one of the human species. Caden Cotard is all of us.

Philip Seymour Hoffman playing everyman Caden Cotard and Tom Noonan playing an actor playing Caden Cotard in Charlie Kaufman's magnificently strange *Synecdoche, New York*.

Team America: World Police

2004, US/Ger, 98 mins, 15 (UK) R (US)

....

cast Trey Parker, Matt Stone, Kristen Miller, Daran Norris *scr* Trey Parker & Matt Stone & Pam Brady *cin* Bill Pope *m* Harry Gregson-Williams *dir* Trey Parker

Strings definitely attached: gun-happy Team America destroy more than they save in Trey Parker and Matt Stone's hilarious, scatological satire.

It says something or other about the state of either film or politics, or probably both, that some of the most acute, penetrating insights about post 9/11 geopolitics and the world's reaction to it have been made by badly animated eighteen-inch marionettes. *South Park* creators Trey Parker and Matt Stone's puppet-based satire – which reportedly began as a plan to remake disaster movie *Armageddon* "because he doesn't know it but Jerry Bruckheimer makes comedy" – takes typically enthusiastic aim at almost everything to do with the "War on Terror" and scores an impressive hit rate.

Team America are a *Thunderbirds*-style outfit (rendered in "Supercrappymation" according to Parker, though cinematographer Bill Pope also shot *Spider-Man 2* and 3 as well as *The Matrix*, the cheap and cheerful look apparently requiring great technical skill) complete with a base located inside Mount Rushmore and an array of spiffy stars-and-stripes-decorated vehicles. They charge all over the world defeating terrorists with machine guns and laser-guided missiles and inevitably leave more carnage than the terrorists: the Eiffel Tower and Egypt's pyramids are a couple of the World Heritage Sites that they manage to destroy. But to defeat a plot masterminded by South Korea's Kim Jong Il, recast as a Bondian villain with a pot belly, a Mao suit and a voice suspiciously similar to Cartman's, they recruit Gary Johnston, a Broadway musical actor (and performer of one of the movie's many beautifully observed songs, "Everyone Has Aids" from the musical *LEASE*), intending that he masquerade as a terrorist to infiltrate the gang.

If American militarism is a key target of Parker and Stone's acid satire, Hollywood liberalism is as ferociously sent up. "As actors it is our responsibility to read the newspapers and then say what we read on television like it's our own opinion," blethers Janeane Garofalo (voiced, as is almost everybody else, by Parker) to a chuntering gathering of the bleeding-heart Film Actor's Guild. (Crunch the acronym and you get a feel for the impressively juvenile level of much of the movie's humour.) Sean Penn constantly reminds everybody that he's "been to Iraq", Matt Damon appears to be able to only say his own name, while "socialist weasel" Michael Moore is transformed into a hot-dog-scoffing liberal suicide bomber – no doubt provoking the ire of Moore, whose worthy polemic *Fahrenheit 9/11* came out in the same year. Small wonder that many impeccably liberal critics, unused to this scorched-earth form of satire and unsure what to make of having their own prejudices lambasted alongside the easier targets, opted to criticize the film for its relentless blow-job gags, extraordinarily extended projectile vomiting sequence and a main theme consisting for the most part of the lyric: America – fuck yeah!

In fact, as with *South Park*, much of the humour comes from the pair's forensic understanding of the genre they're ripping into and its various lazy tropes and clichés. Harry Gregson-Williams' score is a perfect synthesis of the bombast and easy emotion regularly provided by the likes of Hans Zimmer (and comes complete with that keening *ay-ay-ayyy!* ululation that every contemporary thriller slams on the soundtrack when someone vaguely Arabic-looking walks on). Each location title is helpfully provided with its exact distance from the only country that matters (eg, North Korea, 5945 miles west of America).

Team America: World Police calls down a pox on everybody's house, is consistently hilarious while doing so and features cinema's first, and likely only, hardcore marionette sex scene. Can you really argue with that?

WAR! WHAT MOVIES IS IT GOOD FOR?
How 9/11 didn't change Hollywood

Only a few days after the tragic events of 11 September 2001, satirical magazine *The Onion*'s front page carried a picture of the twin towers wreathed in billowing flame with the headline "LIFE TURNS INTO BAD JERRY BRUCKHEIMER MOVIE!" It was a bold piece of satire, too close to the bone for some readers, but it did crystallize the strange, surreal nature of the day: as some noted at the time, the atrocity, watched endlessly on screens of varying sizes across the world, in its outrageousness and spectacle had a kind of alternative-cinema quality to it. Given that those few moments would in many ways define politics and world affairs for the subsequent decade and beyond, it might seem strange that real cinema has treated the subject gingerly, if at all.

The physical events of 9/11 have been covered in a handful of dramas of varying quality: Paul Greengrass's subdued, gruelling account of events aboard the only plane not to hit its target, *United 93* (2006, p.244) captured some of the horror of what it might have been like to have been on board, while Oliver Stone's *World Trade Center* (2006) was a more emotionally manipulative and sentimental account of the rescue of two Port Authority policemen trapped in the buildings' wreckage. (And by 2012 there has apparently been enough distance for events of that day to be used as background for the likes of Stephen Daldry's icky *Extremely Loud & Incredibly Close*.)

Movies about the subsequent wars in Iraq and Afghanistan have been equally scarce, though there have been a number of excellent documentaries, including Tim Hetherington (who was subsequently killed covering the Libyan civil war) and Sebastian Junger's *Restrepo* in 2010; Janus Metz's account of a Danish platoon's experiences in *Armadillo* the same year; and veteran documentarian Errol Morris's *Standard Operating Procedure* (2008), a horrifying exposé of the abuses at Abu Ghraib. Kathryn Bigelow's Oscar-winning *The Hurt Locker* (2009, p.134) is probably the most notable fictional war film, while Paul Greengrass's *The Green Zone* (2010) was an uncomfortable blend of Hollywood heroics and war commentary that perhaps tried to achieve some of the same mildly surreal tone as David O. Russell's *Three Kings* (2000) had with the Persian Gulf War, but failed.

If there's been a relatively small number of conventional war movies, or even "war-is-hell" movies about the post-9/11 world, there have been a few more "war at home" films. Jim Sheridan's *Brothers* (2010) starring Tobey Maguire, Jake Gyllenhaal and Natalie Portman was typical of the sub-genre. Set in working-class middle America, it used the capture of a Marine Captain in Afghanistan (Maguire) to probe questions of loyalty, patriotism and family dynamics as his brother (Gyllenhaal) attempts to comfort the wife (Portman) and becomes too close. Oren Moverman's thoughtfully directed and beautifully acted *The Messenger* (2011) had Woody Harrelson and Ben Foster as a pair of soldiers charged with the job of breaking the worst possible news to various military families, while Paul Haggis's *In the Valley of Elah* (2008), starring Tommy Lee Jones as a devastated war vet who searches for answers about the mysterious death of his son in Iraq, was both taut and compelling but also more critical of the war than you might expect for a mainstream Hollywood film (Jones gained an Oscar nomination for his quietly heart-wrenching performance). All these films explored the hidden damage to families and society that being at war wreaks, but which rarely makes the news headlines.

Bizarrely, some of the most notable post-9/11 films have been comedies. *Four Lions* (2010), Christopher Morris's acid satire about a group of British Muslims ineptly plotting the bombing of the London Marathon, made the point that just because suicide bombers are frightening doesn't mean they're not idiots ("he was in heaven before his head hit the ceiling," one wannabe jihadist remarks approvingly of a colleague at one point), while Trey Parker and Matt Stone's *Team America: World Police* (2005, p.230) deployed badly animated marionettes in its blunderbuss mockery of post-9/11 American foreign policy and liberal Hollywood's response to it. Sacha Baron Cohen's *The Dictator* (2012) used Saddam Hussein as a template for his crazy displaced despot to entertaining effect.

While there are few war movies either of the gung-ho type or *Platoon*-style (1986) dispatches from the trenches sub-genre, it should be noted that it took Hollywood a good decade to approach the topic of Vietnam after that war's end, and much World War II moviemaking was in the service of propaganda. And if this strange silence makes our cinema seem somehow distant and disconnected from the world, perhaps that's the point. In times like these people look to films for escape and comfort, not a reminder of the apparently endless chaos and misery afflicting the world outside. Audiences, it seems, demand any kind of film but a war film. They'll even watch a bad Jerry Bruckheimer movie.

There Will Be Blood

2008, US, 158 mins, 15 (UK) R (US)

....

cast Daniel Day-Lewis, Paul Dano, Kevin J. O'Connor *scr* Paul Thomas
Anderson (based on the novel *Oil!* by Upton Sinclair) *cin* Robert Elswit
m Jonny Greenwood *dir* Paul Thomas Anderson

Like its protagonist, Paul Thomas Anderson's turn-of-the-century epic is vastly
ambitious, grimly compelling and in the end fatally flawed, but still it represents a
giant step forward for one of America's most promising filmmakers. Commencing
with a crashing discordance of strings, a kind of orchestral howl of pain, *There
Will Be Blood* introduces silver-prospector Daniel Plainview (Daniel Day-Lewis)
as a man quite literally in a hole. Over a gruelling, extended sequence we see
the trials of a man attempting to make his fortune, his determination evidenced
not only by the brutal physicality of his labours but by his solitude. His almost
pathological single-mindedness (which will eventually reveal itself as a devastating
character fault) is demonstrated when, after a catastrophic accident in which he
breaks his legs, he drags himself to town to cash in his small find. A few years
later, having struck oil, and somewhat unexpectedly adopted the son of a dead
friend, he engages in a battle of wills with an equally avaricious preacher (Paul
Dano) who, via his congregation, controls the rights to land on which Plainview
wants to build a pipeline. Anderson's film charts Plainview's life as he obsessively
expands his business – and, more vitally, tries to gain independence from the
major oil companies – to a violent, anguished conclusion which makes good on
the prophecy of the film's title and then some.

Anderson's previous films tended towards urban, contemporary subjects – his
breakthrough *Boogie Nights* only went back as far as the late 1970s – and loose
episodic screenplays that reached their apex in *Magnolia* (2000). Here, however,
he attempts epic tragedy, a genre that demands dramatic unity, and while *There
Will Be Blood* delivers a host of powerful scenes there remains a fragmentation
to the film, and a frustrating sense of key moments being missing. Plainview's
relationship with his adopted son is never convincingly developed and his war
with the church, in the form of the excellent Paul Dano's Eli Sunday (whose thin,
pallid appearance brings to mind Grant Wood's popular painting *American Gothic*),
never really demonstrates much more than that the pious can behave as badly as
the faithless.

Some have found in the movie a political critique of the oil industry, and that was certainly one element of the novel *Oil!* by Upton Sinclair on which the screenplay is very loosely based. But if there is a political dimension to the film, and it is more personal tragedy than political tract, it might be a dig at the rugged self-reliance and individualism that form a key element of America's founding narrative. Here these qualities initially lead to wealth and success, but then to bloodshed and self-destruction.

Despite all these reservations, consequences really of Anderson's grand ambition, *There Will Be Blood* is one of recent cinema's most memorable films: Day-Lewis's performance is captivating, his mellow, mellifluous voice (a riff on the late John Huston's cadences) in stark contrast to his fatally unbending character. And, after the tragedy is complete, the opening images of a man alone in a brutal landscape, carving out his destiny with every pick-axe blow, endures, haunting the imagination long after the film's flaws have been forgotten.

Man vs world: the ambition and obsessive self-reliance of Plainview (Daniel Day-Lewis) lead to tragedy on an epic scale.

Toy Story 3

2010, US, 108 mins, U (UK) G (US)

··

cast Tom Hanks, Tim Allen, Don Rickles, Ned Beatty, Joan Cusack, Michael Keaton *scr* Michael Arndt (story John Lasseter, Andrew Stanton, Lee Unkrich) *m* Randy Newman *dir* Lee Unkrich

And so finally it comes time to put away childish things. It's hard to credit now, but when, back in the mid-1990s Pixar, a company that only the real cognoscenti of the rapidly advancing field of computer animation had heard of, announced that they were going to produce a full-length, *digitally* animated feature, there was deep scepticism that audiences would warm to characters rendered on mainframes rather than inked on drawing boards. Now that traditional animation has all but vanished in favour of its digital successor, and the distinction between animated and live-action films has in some cases almost completely eroded, such worries seem almost quaint. But it turned out that as well as the colourful, effortlessly expressive animation Pixar's technology and artistry could deliver they also had a secret weapon in their scripts: precision-wrought little masterpieces that had not only compelling stories for kids but something of the snappy dialogue and the knowing, hip attitude (take those animated bloopers over the end credits) of the decade's favourite sitcom. This was Disney for the *Friends* generation.

Toy Story 3, made inevitably and somewhat pointlessly in 3D, continues this tradition of playing to the patrons paying full-price with as much care as it does to those demanding the toilet every twenty minutes. Andy is off to college and the future of Buzz, Woody and co doesn't look good. The attic, and a long wait until Andy produces kids of his own, seems to be the best of a set of bad options. But by a combination of skilfully plotted accidents the gang wind up confined in Sunnyside Daycare, a deceptively cheerful playgroup that turns out to be a kind of Stalag Luft for toys, a place – a cuddly hedgehog mournfully informs us – "of ruin and despair ruled over by an evil bear who smells of strawberries." Thus this third instalment reveals itself as a prison-break movie augmented by plenty of the sharply witty touches that are the series' trademark – Barbie's ascot-wearing boyfriend Ken turning out to be a moulded plastic quisling will, for instance, be of no surprise to anyone whose sister had one. Meanwhile director Lee Unkrich delivers enough in the way of breathless action – a nail-bitingly tense sequence set in a trash processor is a standout – to keep the kids' attention from flagging.

But this third movie's biggest surprise is how committed it is to the themes of abandonment, separation and the inevitability of change that have always been bubbling under its deceptively naive surface. Almost every character explores these deep ambivalences to some extent. Best pals Woody and Buzz must face the prospect of parting; at one point Andy's mother finds herself gazing round her son's newly empty room, the boxes marked "college" and bin bags marked "attic", a moment familiar to or secretly dreaded by anyone with kids; while Andy himself must of course face up to the fact of his leaving home. (Though wrapped up in all this there is an unmistakeable irony: the one thing that thirtysomething Hollywood executives have been signally unable to do is abandon their childhood toys, a fact evidenced by a summer full of the likes of *Transformers* and *Battleship*.) It all makes for a final instalment that is the very definition of bittersweet, a dayglo lament to childhood's end and a triumphant, irresistibly moving conclusion to the first true classic of the new age of digital animation.

Transformers

2007, US, 143 mins, 12A (UK) PG-13 (US)

∙∙∙

cast Shia LaBeouf, Megan Fox, Josh Duhamel, John Turturro, Jon Voight
scr Roberto Orci & Alex Kurtzman (story John Rogers and Roberto Orci &
Alex Kurtzman) *cin* Mitchell Amundsen *m* Steve Jablonsky *dir* Michael Bay

Michael Bay, Dark Lord of the Octane and purveyor of finest "Bayhem" since *Bad Boys* (1995), *The Rock* (1996) and *Armageddon* (1998), had cemented his reputation as whipping boy for the movie press with *Pearl Harbor* (2001), a dumb movie that made the fatal error of taking itself way too seriously. If nothing else, *Transformers* is a film that proves Bay is a man who learns from his mistakes: this is a dumb movie that revels in its own strident idiocy, cheerfully turning up the stupid at every opportunity. It's a film perfectly tuned for its adolescent male audience, an audience it's so puppyishly eager to please, it may as well sport go-faster stripes and a pair of fluffy dice hanging in front of the screen.

"There's more to you than meets the eye," Sam Witwicky (Shia LaBeouf) says, in a nod to the original 80s toys' marketing slogan, to his new beat-up yellow Camero. He's right. In fact it's a huge Autobot (good-bot) from outer space called Bumblebee, and it's not the only ultimate hybrid hiding out on planet Earth. Having comprehensively smashed up their own planet (Cybertron, since you asked), the bad-bots ("Decepticons", sporting a somewhat self-defeating name) are also here and both sets are searching for a mysterious cube which… well, plot isn't really the name of the game. Cue mucho smashing, bashing, grinding, clanking and screaming. Mostly accompanied by pounding rock music. Mostly at sunset.

Unlike his many imitators Bay has the vestiges of a sense of humour and the nerve, these days at least, to slow things down occasionally to indulge it. Okay, it ain't Woody Allen – government spook John Turturro gets pissed on by a giant robot, and when good-bot leader Optimus Prime is asked how he found out about a vital pair of spectacles imprinted with a code that will save the universe he replies in stentorian, auditorium-shaking robo-tones "Ebay!". (There's the odd nice detail too: when one of the Decepticons disguises itself as a police car, the legend "To Protect and Serve" is subtly replaced by "To Punish and Enslave".) LaBeouf works overtime to inject at least a little likeable regular-Joe humanity into the automotive cacophony, but the real stars of the show are the robots, who Bay and ILM render in perfect detail before flinging them about the screen like, well an eight-year-old and his toy robots.

To his many and vocal detractors *Transformers* was just another example of Bay's relentless assault on civilized cinema. But this was a movie with one audience in mind and for them it hit all the right spots – it's the cinematic equivalent of a giant Monster Trucks rally – and Bay, bruised after the twin more adult-oriented disappointments of *Pearl Harbor* and *The Island* (2005), seems to have known it. With typical modesty, at one point he has a fat kid running through yet another blasted landscape while yelling into his mobile phone, "This is a hundred times cooler than *Armageddon*, I swear to god!" It may not be the most ringing endorsement for the discerning cinema-goer, but for the average fifteen-year-old boy with a yen for fast cars, pulchritudinous female flesh, wanton destruction and an ocean of summer to fill, you know what, actually, he's right.

Robot out of disguise: one of director Michael Bay's metal behemoths about to cause citywide "Bayhem" in the hit franchise.

The Tree of Life

2011, US, 139 mins, 12A (UK) PG-13 (US)

....

cast Brad Pitt, Sean Penn, Jessica Chastain, Hunter McCracken, Tye Sheridan, Laramie Eppler *scr* Terrence Malick *cin* Emmanuel Lubezki *m* Alexandre Desplat *dir* Terrence Malick

British kids of the 1970s may remember a short film titled *Cosmic Zoom* that occasionally used to crop up on school projectors during wet lunchtimes. Made in 1968 by the Canadian Film Board, it began with an image of a boy rowing a boat across a lake. Slowly the camera begins to pull back, then more rapidly, and soon we are soaring through the solar system to the outer reaches of the universe. Then zooming back in just as fast, into a mosquito on the boy's skin and on to the intricacies of cells and atoms. Terrence Malick's audacious, ambitious, and for some it has to be said fatally flawed film takes the same theme and presents it on an almost infinitely grander scale. It attempts to set the minutiae of our tiny but (to us) important existences against the vastness of creation itself. "Life. The Universe. Everything." would have been a more than appropriate tagline.

Structured as a kind of Proustian reverie, *The Tree of Life* starts with Jack (Sean Penn/Hunter McCracken), an executive at some kind of architectural firm, wandering through a modern office's vast glass atriums; finally leaning back in his chair he is reminded of his childhood in the 1950s. Flashing back we see him growing up in a kind of idealized small Texan town (the Norman Rockwellesque perfection perhaps a function of Jack's reality-burnishing memory). He plays with his two brothers on the streets and riverbanks. Frogs are tied to fireworks, tears of guilt the result. Jack's mother (an ethereal Jessica Chastain) is graceful, sympathetic and loving. Dad (Brad Pitt) strict and unbending and disappointed by the turns his life has taken. In amidst this account of an ordinary childhood (though one tinged with our foreknowledge of a subsequent tragedy) are long, lyrical sequences concerning the birth of the universe. Giant gas clouds form nebulae, volcanoes spew, cells divide, life is brought forth. In possibly the film's most astonishingly bold moment we see a pair of dinosaurs involved in some Jurassic drama on a stretch of river very similar to the one on which the boys play millions of years later. As with *Cosmic Zoom*, this then is partly a story about perspective; there have been lives and events before us and there will be ones after.

The Tree of Life communicates for the most part visually; dialogue is scarce, uninformative and often mumbled. But the element of Malick's opus that will most surprise people is the intensity of its religious vision: the opening quotation is from Job, mother's whispers are often seemingly prayers. To American eyes and ears this might not be so unusual, but in more secular countries, and to some viewers, it may present an insuperable obstacle to accepting Malick's vision, as might its grand ambition. While making *Apocalypse Now* (1979) director Francis Ford Coppola said that the problem with attempting great art is that you will inevitably be accused of pretension, it goes with the territory. And so it was inevitable that a film that took as its subject human life and the totality of creation would appear to some critics as not much more than a couple of hours' vaporous ponderings. But even Malick's fiercest critics must admit that this luminously shot film leaves one in a strange reverie of one's own; musing like Jack on long lost friends, childhood streets and parents now understood through adult eyes. This tree's roots run very deep indeed.

Motherly love: the ethereal Jessica Chastain represents Grace against husband Brad Pitt's Nature in Terrence Malick's meditation on life, the universe and everything.

Twilight

2008, US/UK, 122 mins, 12A (UK) PG-13 (US)

· ·

cast Kristen Stewart, Robert Pattinson, Taylor Lautner, Billy Burke *scr* Melissa Rosenberg (from the novel by Stephenie Meyer) *cin* Elliot Davis *m* Carter Burwell *dir* Catherine Hardwicke

K.I.S.S.I.N.G. Grist to a billion tweenage girls' dreams, a vampiric Robert Pattinson woos his human main squeeze Kristen Stewart in the damp and drizzly setting of *Twilight*.

Way back in the 1950s Samuel Z. Arkoff, co-founder of drive-in teensploitation experts American International Pictures, came up with a formula to maximize his company's revenue. Sixteen-year-olds, he observed, generally could not be persuaded to go to movies that older people liked. The very fact that older people liked them turned them off. Similarly, he noted, while girls could be enticed

to go to films that boys liked, boys would under no circumstances go to a film that girls had identified as being for them. Zarkoff's remorseless logic led him to one conclusion: all his films would be narrowly targeted at sixteen-year-old males. It is a formula that Hollywood has slavishly followed for fifty years. Until, perhaps, *Twilight*.

Stephenie Meyer's novel, based, she has said, on a dream, had been an immediate sensation when published in 2005, but mainstream Hollywood's ignorance of this untapped audience was highlighted by the fact that what would become one of the most successful movie franchises of the decade was made by Summit Entertainment, a virtually unknown mini-studio. Summit's clear-eyed masterstroke was not to radically alter the plot, as had been mooted, but to stick to the fundamentals. Thus while necessarily condensed, Meyer's lightweight tale of a teenage Bella's move to rainy and, crucially, rarely sunny Washington state to live with her father, and her subsequent falling in with a group of vampires who eschew human claret in favour of animal blood, even though the result is equivalent to an eternal diet of tofu ("we like to think of ourselves as vegetarians," they explain), remains intact.

It is of course ridiculously easy to mock *Twilight*: horror fans rolled their eyes, for instance, at the unexpected news that when exposed to sunlight vampires do not burst into flames but sparkle gently like human glitter balls. But director Catherine Hardwicke delivers in the areas important to the novel's fans: her conjuring of the cloudy damp of the small Washington town of Forks, with its lush woodland and misty waterfalls, is pitch perfect (the film was shot in neighbouring Oregon). And if some of the action and effects are below par, the mood of adolescent yearning is nicely evoked. In any case, the screenplay is calibrated to romantic beats, a fairy-light-drenched prom dance or flight through an emerald-hued forest, rather than the car-smashing action of the giant robot movie playing next door. Even more vitally, the casting is spot on. Kristen Stewart's Bella is a heroine in the post-Judy Blume mould, ironic and laidback right up until she catches sight of alabaster-faced hottie Edward Cullen, whose cheekbones are sharper than his fangs and who Robert Pattinson pitches halfway between a consumptive Romantic poet and something out of an Abercrombie & Fitch catalogue.

Regardless of the critical brickbats *Twilight* did what no movie has done before: packed cinemas with adolescent girls in the way that George Lucas and Steven Spielberg's movies have with teenage boys for generations – a few of whom fall in love with the experience enough to become curious about that title "director" at the end. If, in twenty years' time, there's a healthy crop of female talent behind the camera, we might have a family of posturing bloodsuckers to thank. And with a box-office take of nearly $400 million from a movie that cost less than a tenth of that to make, Hollywood may finally have to rewrite Arkoff's depressing formula.

United 93

2006, UK/US/Fr, 111 mins, 15 (UK) R (US)

....

cast Khalid Abdalla, JJ Johnson, Ben Sliney, Christian Clemenson, Gary Commock, Trish Gates, Polly Adams, Cheyenne Jackson *scr* Paul Greengrass *cin* Barry Ackroyd *m* John Powell *dir* Paul Greengrass

One of the most striking photographs taken sometime on the morning of 11 September 2001 has a group of young people, a mountain bike propped up in front of them, chatting while across the Hudson River the World Trade Center is in flames. Thomas Hoepker's shot is a disquieting, almost surreal image of normal life colliding with unspeakable mass murder and there is much of that strange dichotomy in *United 93*, British director Paul Greengrass's quietly devastating record of the events of that day.

It was a full five years until Hollywood first tentatively approached 9/11, and when it did it was with this sober, gripping recreation of events aboard United Airlines' flight 93, the only one of the four hijacked aircraft not to reach its target, its passengers having become aware of their captors' intentions and deciding to try and overcome them. In the US Greengrass was best known as the director of the hyper-kinetic and highly commercial *Bourne* thrillers, but his previous career in the UK as a *World in Action* TV journalist and documentarian qualified him for this kind of potentially tricky docudrama. The danger, of course, is of exploitation, real or perceived, and it is one that Greengrass, with only a couple of minor exceptions, studiously manages to avoid. *United 93* seeks not to dramatize the events of that day, but simply to recreate them as truthfully as possible. Thus much of the first half-hour of the film follows the quotidian rituals of air travel: the checking of tickets, rigmaroles of security, the pilots' checklists and chat. At one point, as the jet sits at the gate, we see aviation fuel sloshing through a glass valve: it's impossible not to think of the vast blooms of flame into which it will soon transform.

But as events snowball we move between the plane and Federal Aviation Authority HQ, where chief Ben Sliney (played, as many of the roles are, by the real-life individuals themselves, their slightly ragged performances contributing to the film's *vérité*) tries to unravel what is going on as unprecedented reports of multiple hijackings come in. Similarly the military struggles to get fighter planes in the air after the first tower is hit (in a perfect example of the fog of war, permission is denied by the FAA before the jets scramble in the wrong direction, heading uselessly out to sea). But for the last third of the film the focus shifts to the aircraft: the hijackers (convincingly played, but surely roles the actors concerned must have thought twice about accepting) and the passengers, with their slow realization that they are about to die, and their heroic but doomed attempt to fight back (though of course their efforts may have saved many lives in preventing the plane reaching its target).

United 93 stands as an effective cinematic memorial, a remembrance of what happened that day, effectively capturing not only the events themselves but the strange amalgam of mundanity and drama that was so striking at the time (only one criticism: was the Hollywood score, subtly deployed as it is, really necessary?). But also somewhere near the heart of the central story of the passengers aboard the fourth plane is the troubling, unanswerable question that must have flickered across almost everyone's mind as they heard of what had transpired aboard the ill-fated flight: What would I have done?

Terror at 37,000 feet: the passengers of doomed United 93 (Daniel Sauli, David Alan Basche, Denny Dillon) plan their fight-back in Paul Greengrass's vérité-style 9/11 recreation.

Up in the Air

2010, 109 mins, US, 15 (UK) R (US)

∙∙∙

cast George Clooney, Vera Farmiga, Jason Bateman,
Anna Kendrick **scr** Jason Reitman & Sheldon Turner
(from the novel by Walter Kirn) **cin** Eric Steelberg
m Rolfe Kent **dir** Jason Reitman

"To know me is to fly with me," Ryan Bingham
(George Clooney) informs us at the beginning of this
smart comedy-drama from Jason Reitman. "All the
things you probably hate about travelling, the recycled
air, the artificial lighting, the digital juice dispenser,
the cheap sushi, are all reminders that I am home."
He's a "Termination Facilitator" – in other words,
he travels the US firing people for a living. It goes
without saying that, given the state of the economy,
business is good. His life is lived in an almost
perpetual state of transit: he exists in hotel rooms,
rental cars, in airport lounges or first-class cabins. His
lover, fellow corporate jet-setter Alex (Vera Farmiga),
demands nothing more of him than the occasional
rendezvous when their schedules are in alignment
("Think of me as you, but with a vagina," she tells
him). He is a man who, in the most important
respects, isn't there – and that's the way he likes it.

Reality intrudes on this anaesthetized idyll in the
shape of perky corporate firebrand Natalie (Anna
Kendrick), who proposes that Ryan's company
abandon in-person firings in favour of remote
termination via the internet. Horrified at the prospect
of losing his peripatetic lifestyle, not to mention
failing in his life's ambition to amass ten million

First-class lounge: high-flyers Alex (Vera Farmiga) and Ryan
(George Clooney) enjoy the chilled-out perks of a corporate
lifestyle on board a yacht.

JASON REITMAN
b. 19 October 1977, Montréal, Canada

"When I started my career I didn't want to make
a movie with him because I was dead set on
establishing myself as my own director," Jason
Reitman has said about his director-superstar father
Ivan. "I have ears. I hear the way people talk about
the children of famous people. The presumptions
are usually quite awful. So I tried to establish myself
with a couple of movies." The "couple of movies" in
question showed Reitman to be a hugely promising
director, not of the broad Hollywood comedies
that had been his father's staple – the *Ghostbusters*
(1984) and *Groundhog Day*s (1993) – but of smart,
sophisticated comedy, often with a glinting satirical
edge. His debut, *Thank You for Smoking* (2006), had
a superbly cast Aaron Eckhart as Nick Naylor, an
unapologetically cynical spin doctor working for
big tobacco "defending the defenseless, protecting
the disenfranchised corporations that have been
abandoned by their very own consumers: the logger,
the sweatshop foreman, the oil driller, the land mine
developer, the baby seal poacher," as he puts it.
(And it featured a brace of memorable cameos from
William H. Macy as an outraged congressman and
Rob Lowe as a sinister Hollywood agent.) *Juno* (2008,
p.149) and *Up in the Air* (2010) were both critically well
received, in *Juno*'s case winning an Oscar for best
screenplay for Diablo Cody. In 2012 he re-teamed with
Cody for *Young Adult*, a pleasingly tart tale of a youth
fiction writer returning to her hometown in order
to seduce her now married high-school ex, played
by Patrick Wilson. Charlize Theron's performance as
the self-obsessed drama queen conjuring a reunion
from hell was acidly funny and ultimately strangely
poignant. Whether or not Reitman ever does
collaborate directorially with his father (Ivan was
credited as a producer on *Juno*) remains a question for
the future: what's certain is that Jason has certainly
established himself as one of the thinking moviegoer's
greatest hopes.

frequent flyer miles, Ryan takes her out on the road to show her that ruining people's day is an art that cannot be digitized. Clooney leverages his movie-star persona to great effect; he deploys the megawatt smile and soulful eyes to the max and delivers the canned canning dialogue like a pro, but his heart is ice. He's got some pretty good tips for getting through airport security too. "Never get in line behind old people, their bodies are littered with hidden metal and they never seem to be aware of how little time they have," he cautions.

Reitman and Sheldon Turner's screenplay is deft, peppered with great dialogue, and in its third act takes a bracingly unexpected turn. Ryan's voyage of self-discovery might seem at first to be pure Hollywood boilerplate: the forced realization that his first-class cocoon must be shed if he is to be truly happy follows the schematic typical of studio comedies about men in need of a lesson on commitment. But in the final act, *Up in the Air* spins off into new, more rewarding territory.

The supporting cast is a joy: Vera Farmiga is sharp and sexy as Ryan's female alter ego, scenes fizz and sizzle when she and Clooney are on screen together; Jason Bateman is note-perfect as Ryan's oleaginous boss ("This is our moment," he smiles as the economic crisis hits); Anna Kendrick has energy to spare as a ludicrously young, inexperienced wannabe exec who has her entire future planned and is the proud progenitor of a particularly vile example of corporate-speak: "Glocal" ("Global *and* local," she explains). Watching *Up in the Air* it's easy to be reminded of the sophisticated dramas and comedies of the late 60s and 70s: movies such as *Five Easy Pieces* (1970), *Being There* (1979) and even *The Graduate* (1967), movies that had popular appeal but treated their audiences as adults. For a movie whose themes are so much of the present its tone is pleasingly redolent of the past.

WALL-E

2008, US, 103 mins, U (UK) U (US)

••

cast Ben Burtt, Elissa Knight, Fred Willard, John Ratzenberger, Jeff Garlin, Sigourney Weaver *scr* Andrew Stanton & Jim Reardon (story Andrew Stanton & Pete Docter) *m* Thomas Newman *dir* Andrew Stanton

WALL-E is the nearest thing to a perfect family film since Spielberg's *E.T.* back in 1982. As an example of the new craft of digital animation, it's like comparing early Disney classics such as *Snow White* (1937) to their hand-drawn counterparts: it marks a new and thrillingly promising art form's transition to maturity. Like these varied masterpieces it neither patronizes children nor panders to adults by stuffing itself with in-jokes to keep them interested. It simply finds a shared space where viewers of all ages can enjoy an art form in which the most advanced technology imaginable renders the simplest and purest of emotions.

Mankind, having drowned Earth in the detritus from its consumer lifestyle, has long departed on what seems to be an extended interstellar cruise, leaving miniature cleaning-bots to dig the planet out of the rubbish. Of these animated trash-cans, WALL-E seems to be the last working model, alone on a devastated Earth. (There's perhaps a nod to Douglas Trumbull's 1972 eco-tech tearjerker *Silent Running*, with its troika of squat droids endlessly tending the last vestiges of Earth's flora, in the set-up.) And so, every day, he leaves his home in order to continue his job collecting mankind's garbage, compacting it into small cubes in his tummy and stacking it in skyscraper-sized piles. His only companion in this Herculean task is a post-apocalyptic Jiminy Cricket in the form of an apparently indestructible cockroach. Every now and then he finds a new treasure – a Zippo lighter or sheet of unpopped bubble-wrap – and takes it back to his home, which is an Aladdin's cave of such treasures, illuminated by strands of fairy lights.

But one day something new arrives in this blasted, and beautifully rendered, landscape. A spaceship lands and deposits EVE, a sleek and obviously female droid who seems to be searching for signs of plant life. (It's no accident that EVE resembles something from Apple's R&D department – Steve Jobs had only recently become CEO of Pixar.) WALL-E inevitably falls head over wheels for his new iPal and accidentally departs the planet with her, finally finding himself aboard a giant space cruiser, the *Axiom*, where humans have become too fat to walk and scoot around on hoverchairs – the ultimate La-Z-Boys. On board the

Axiom WALL-E manages to cause a mutiny of rogue robots as well as finding himself in a battle with a crazed auto-pilot bent on preventing mankind's eventual return to Earth.

Aesthetically the movie is a wonder. For the first forty minutes or so it's mostly silent save for WALL-E's incredibly expressive beeps and pings, provided by legendary sound maestro Ben Burtt (he provided R2-D2's vocabulary). Like most of Pixar's oeuvre it is a work of beautiful, quirky detail: WALL-E repeatedly watches a salvaged videotape (Betamax!) of late 60s musical *Hello Dolly!* using a hubcap as a hat to mimic the dance moves. He stares with a mixture of curiosity and longing as Michael Crawford and Barbra Streisand hold hands. Of course we are in love with him within seconds. But Andrew Stanton and Jim Reardon's screenplay never takes a cheap shot by playing with our affection for these animated machines or exploiting a false sense of peril. And its satire of consumerism (offensive apparently to some American audiences who accused it of green propaganda) is softened by an appealing kindness and humanity. Earthlings aren't evil, just foolish: and in the end we are redeemable. But environmental concerns aside, at its heart *WALL-E* is a movie which, though populated by machines, is about that universal human trait, loneliness, and a fervent desire to connect. To dust down an old cliché that for once is apposite, it's a love story set among the stars.

FAMILY-FRIENDLY FILM

Ten movies for the matinee mob...

With a plethora of films no doubt appealing to kids of all ages – the recent *Spider-Man* and *Batman* franchises most notable among them – now attracting the 12A certificate (or PG-13 in the US), films that families with younger children can attend have perhaps been thinner on the ground than before the 12A rating was introduced in 2002. Pixar and DreamWorks have been key in saving the day with their superior digitally animated films, but there are still plenty of live-action efforts among this handful of the best 21st-century offerings, all with family-friendly U or PG certificates.

SHREK (2001, U)

DreamWorks took on Pixar at its own game with this digitally animated fairy tale about the eponymous less-than-jolly green ogre (voiced brilliantly by Mike Myers) who must rescue a human princess in order to rid his swamp of characters that seem to have wandered out of rival Disney's movies. Sharply written and full of pop cultural references for the adults and "swamp gas" gags for the kids. And adults.

THE SCHOOL OF ROCK (2004, PG)

Jack Black's finest hour has him as Dewey Finn, a failing musician who winds up at a posh prep school teaching uptight kids how to rock out. Think *Dead Poets Society* (1989) but funnier and with more drums. It's warm without being treacly, very funny and features great support from Joan Cusack as a ditzy headmistress. Stay around during the credits for an impromptu jam session.

THE CHRONICLES OF NARNIA: THE LION, THE WITCH AND THE WARDROBE (2005, PG)

Though not quite in the *Harry Potter* league, this adaptation of C.S. Lewis's timeless classic nonetheless boasts rich visual detail, a pleasingly old-fashioned story and is classic fantasy accessible to kids too young for Peter Jackson's *The Lord of the Rings* trilogy. And it sports a fabulous just-scary-enough performance from Tilda Swinton as the White Witch.

WALLACE & GROMIT IN THE CURSE OF THE WERE-RABBIT (2005, U)

Described by creator Nick Park as "the first ever vegetarian horror movie", this Oscar-winning outing for Gromit and his accident-prone inventor owner has all the charmingly off-beam wit of the previous movies – look out for a contraption that traps rabbits in a kind of giant Hoover – proof, if it were needed, that Park's clay can take on Pixar's supercomputers any day.

MARCH OF THE PENGUINS (2005, U)

Morgan Freeman's honey-warm voice narrates this chilly French-made documentary about the astonishing breeding cycle of the Emperor penguins, which every year march hundreds of miles to their breeding grounds in temperatures of more than 80 degrees below zero. Some purists might object to the extravagant anthropomorphism, but damn, those penguin chicks are cute...

HIGH SCHOOL MUSICAL 3: SENIOR YEAR (2008, U)

Well, OK. *Citizen Kane* it ain't, but this feisty big-screen outing for toothsome Troy, Gabriella and the rest is surprisingly pacy and has the requisite toe-tapping musical numbers. (It also had Disney studio execs rubbing their hands as it coined an astonishing $252 million from a paltry $11 million budget.) And at least mum can gaze at Zac and wonder what happened to all her old Donny Osmond posters.

FANTASTIC MR. FOX (2009, PG)

The Royal Tenenbaums (2002, p.202) director Wes Anderson brought some of his own eccentric, whimsical style to this beautifully animated version of Roald Dahl's classic tale of one fox's war against farmers Boggis, Bunce and Bean, but retained the sense of danger and darkness that was a key part of the book's appeal. The traditional stop-motion animation has a slightly ragged, worn-in feel. A delight.

UP (2009, U)

Grumpy 78-year-old pensioner Carl (voiced by the great Ed Asner) determines to fulfil a lifelong ambition to explore South America before it's too late and does so by tying thousands of brightly coloured balloons to his house, floating it away. Unfortunately he has a young stowaway. Along with the *Toy Story* films (p.236) and *WALL-E* (2008, p.249), this is among the best of digital kids' movies, its bright colours and bold animation great to look at, and supported by a funny script with an undertow of sadness and regret that is more apparent to older viewers.

HUGO (2011, U)

Martin Scorsese's homage to the days of Georges Méliès' silent pictures might sound a bit off-putting for kids, but the 1930s-set story, of a boy who lives in the clock of a Paris railway station and who searches for the heart-shaped key of a broken automaton, is pure magic and, predictably, 3D has never been more sensitively or skilfully used.

THE MUPPETS (2012, U)

Effortlessly proving what those of us who watched them on TV in the 70s already knew – *everybody loves the Muppets* – this first movie outing in twelve years for the furry gang has them attempting to save their old theatre with the help of some famous fans. Smart, funny, occasionally anarchic and then unashamedly heartwarming, this is unmissable whether you've known them for forty-odd years or are just about to meet.

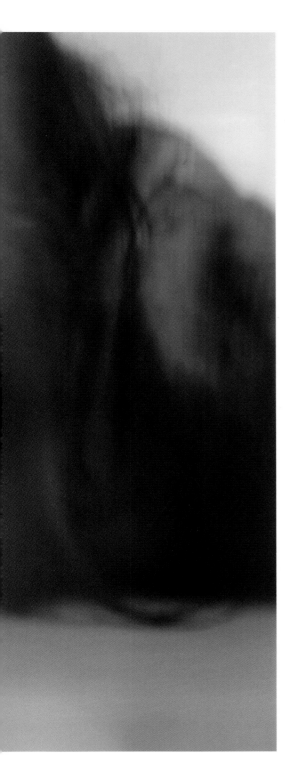

We Need to Talk About Kevin

2011, UK/US, 112 mins, 15 (UK) R (US)

....

cast Tilda Swinton, John C. Reilly, Ezra Miller, Jasper Newell, Ashley Gerasimovich *scr* Lynne Ramsay & Rory Kinnear (from the novel by Lionel Shriver) *cin* Seamus McGarvey *m* Jonny Greenwood *dir* Lynne Ramsay

Lionel Shriver had written half a dozen novels before she alighted on the topic and the plot that would rocket her to the top of the bestseller lists, her devastating tale of maternal ambivalence hitting some kind of nerve (perhaps as Ira Levin's similarly maternally themed *Rosemary's Baby* had 36 years before). But transforming this story of a reluctant mother whose child turns out to be a monster was something of a challenge, one of the key issues being that Shriver structured her book as a series of letters between Eva, Kevin's stricken mother, and his apparently absent father. Ramsay brilliantly solved the problem by shattering the narrative, replacing the epistolary format with a series of chaotic, intertwined flashbacks, a jagged, disorienting structure that reflects its tortured protagonist's state of mind and equally raises questions as to its reliability. It gives the story a sharper psychological insight and it makes for sometimes deeply uncomfortable, but compulsive viewing.

Early on we see Eva (Tilda Swinton) bathed in an almost amniotic red light lying on her couch. The colour comes from the paint that has been flung over the front of her tatty house by locals. Through a series of flashbacks of differing lengths we find that her son has committed some kind of atrocity at the local high school. Now, two years later, despised by her

Awkward reflections: a traumatized Eva (Tilda Swinton) ponders how her life with son Kevin went so terribly wrong in Lynne Ramsay's harrowing analysis of a malfunctioning relationship.

TILDA SWINTON

b. 5 November 1960, London, UK

Is it too strange to say that looking at Tilda Swinton's impassive, alabaster face one's thoughts tend to drift towards David Bowie during his *The Man Who Fell To Earth* (1976) period? She embodies the same intriguing androgyny and with it brings a curious, even slightly unearthly glamour to the roles she inhabits. She was born of distinguished military stock, her father having been a Major General. Initially she grafted in British arthouse fare, making her debut in Derek Jarman's *Caravaggio* (1986) and working with him again on *War Requiem* (1989) and *Wittgenstein* (1993), but she really came to notice in 1993 with the gender-challenging *Orlando* by Sally Potter, in which she played an eternally youthful seventeenth-century nobleman. The 21st century has seen her breaking through to more general audiences and working with Hollywood's biggest stars. She was ruthless as group leader Sal alongside Leonardo DiCaprio in *The Beach* (2000); mesmerizing and terrifying as the archangel Gabriel opposite Keanu Reeves in *Constantine* (2005); she bagged an Oscar for her performance as a agrochemicals lawyer in *Michael Clayton* (2007); and appeared with Brad Pitt and George Clooney as a cheating wife in the Coen brothers' *Burn After Reading* (2008). She was exquisitely cast as the White Witch in *The Chronicles of Narnia: The Lion, The Witch and the Wardrobe* in 2005. "I took it for Derek Jarman's sake, because of his great attachment to screen witches," she said, adding, "what Disney doesn't necessarily acknowledge is that little children love that witch – and most of them think the wrong side won." But none of this meant abandoning her indie roots. She played Ewan McGregor's lover in *Young Adam* (2003); was excellent as a booze-addled child-kidnapper in Erick Zonca's *Julia* (2008); and turned up in indie-king Jim Jarmusch's elliptical thriller *The Limits of Control* (2009). Her uncompromising, troubling performance as a mother whose son has committed an atrocity in Lynne Ramsay's nightmarish adaptation of Lionel Shriver's *We Need to Talk About Kevin* (2011) was critically hailed and heavily Oscar tipped, but it was not to be. To the academy's eternal shame the film inexplicably received no nominations at all.

neighbours, who are not shy about expressing their contempt, she works in a menial filing job but her chief occupation seems to be self-laceration. We soon see that she had never wanted to be married, let alone a mother. Presented with her bundle of joy, all she can see are her frustrated dreams, the life of a bohemian travel journalist now to be replaced with marriage and suburban boredom made flesh. "Mommy was happy before little Kevin came along," she yells at him early on. "Now Mommy wakes up every morning and wishes she was in France." And the infant Kevin (Jasper Newell) seems to return the hatred in kind. His shrieking caterwaul of a cry is so nerve-shreddingly persistent that Eva parks him in front of a pneumatic drill for some relief. Later he cunningly uses his bowels as a weapon of parental torment. And if Kev was a caution as a child, as a teenager (played with cold, sly menace by newcomer Ezra Miller) he is positively mephisphelean, the arrival of a sweet baby sister only revealing in him new sadisms and routes to inflict misery and fear on his mother. Dad (John C. Reilly) is distant and woolly, easily fooled and blithely unaware of the psychodrama being played out under his own roof.

We Need to Talk About Kevin is above all a smashing little horror film, which is not to dismiss the fundamental equivocations that its gruelling story mines for its undoubted power. Certainly in part it is a film about the endless debate on nature versus nurture, but its emotional power lies in Eva's initial ambivalence as it explores the uncomfortable idea that a woman may well hate her child. Swinton delivers a tour de force, her Eva is both haughty and brittle. Obviously in pain, and in need of sympathy, she's nevertheless not particularly likeable, while malevolent and cooly calculating Ezra Miller is capable of a superficial charm: *American Psycho*'s Patrick Bateman in his acne phase. The result is a queasily compelling study of every parent's darkest fears.

The Wrestler

2009, US/Fr, 105 mins, 15 (UK) R (US)

••

cast Mickey Rourke, Marisa Tomei, Evan Rachel Wood, Ernest Miller **scr** Robert Siegel **cin** Maryse Alberti **m** Clint Mansell **dir** Darren Aronofsky

The Wrestler is a film about Randy "The Ram" Robinson, a washed-up, half-forgotten championship grappler surveying the wreckage of his life and wondering if he can make it back to the big time with one last bout. Or is it a film about Mickey Rourke, a washed-up, half-forgotten championship *actor* surveying the wreckage of his life and wondering whether he can make it back to the big time with one last role? It's both, of course. Without Rourke this might well be a good film. With him, it's a great one. You'll have to watch the movie to see if Randy manages to resurrect his career; but by the end of *The Wrestler* there's no doubt that with *The Wrestler* Mickey Rourke has returned triumphant.

Randy, whose steroidal, scarred body looks not unlike one of the sides of beef that Sylvester Stallone pummelled in *Rocky* (1976), is a wrestler not of the Greco-Roman school but of the half-sport, half-circus variety where the pyrotechnics and dumb names – *Paul E. Normous vs The Funky Samoans!* – are as important as anything else and where the folding chairs get as much of a workout as the fighters. Back in the late 1980s he was reigning champ; there were posters, action figures and Nintendo games in his name. But that was nearing twenty years ago and things have changed. At his luckiest now he gets to fight in church halls and community centres, belting fighters as down-at-heel as he is. The one bright spot on the horizon is a possible rematch with The Ayatollah (Ernest Miller), a fight that had been the

DARREN ARONOFSKY

b. 12 February 1969, New York, NY, US

It's been very much a career of two halves so far for the Brooklyn-born Aronofsky. He started off as an indie darling; his first film, *Pi* (1999), was financed by loans from friends and family while marketing took the form of a spray-paint campaign in which New York found itself decorated with mysterious π symbols overnight. It was a cult hit and won Aronofsky the best director award at Sundance. His next, *Requiem for a Dream* (2001), was a beautifully acted if thoroughly depressing tale of drug addicts, featuring a standout performance from Ellen Burstyn and great support from Jared Leto and Jennifer Connelly. *The Fountain* (2007), though, was an infamous Hollywood debacle. A time-hopping examination of the meaning of life set in the fifteenth century, the present and the distant future, it was meant to star Brad Pitt who pulled out with just weeks to go (giant sets had already been built on location in Australia). A bad-tempered war of publicity releases ensued as the production rushed to find an alternative star and failed. Aronofsky described flying to Australia to fire the 400-strong crew as "the single worst day of my life". The film was finally resurrected with Hugh Jackman in the role, only to attract much critical opprobrium, "metaphysical codswallop" being a typical reaction. As a result Aronofsky seemed to consciously decide to pursue more obviously studio- and audience-friendly material. He had been hired to work on *The Fighter* (2011, p.95) but apparently found the story too close to his long-gestating project *The Wrestler* (2009), to which he transferred his attentions. A relatively conventional tale of a down-on-his-luck scrapper trying to make good, it nevertheless snuck up on audiences, winning a Golden Lion at the Venice Film Festival and gaining its resurrected star a best actor Oscar nomination. *Black Swan* (2011, p.28) was an outrageously entertaining melange of melodrama and ballet. His ambitious *Noah* is scheduled for release in 2014 with Russell Crowe in the leading role. Given that the biblical genre hasn't had a notable hit in decades (with the controversial exception of Mel Gibson's *The Passion of the Christ* in 2004), perhaps he's ready to take risks again.

highlight of his career. But after a heart attack brought on by a bout of "extreme" wrestling – a truly nauseating spectacle in which barbed wire, staple guns and broken glass are deployed by the fighters – he finds himself unable to continue in the ring. Terrified for his future, he tries to connect with the two women in his life, reaching out to stripper Cassidy (Marisa Tomei, giving what could have been a central casting tart-with-a-heart role depth and believability) and to his estranged daughter Stephanie (Evan Rachel Wood), a young woman whose memories of him amount to not much more than a string of missed birthdays.

Much of this of course conforms to the strict rules of the sports movie. But Aronofsky negotiates the tropes with skill and with Rourke he has an unbeatable card to play. Is it important that the audience knows that Rourke's story mirrors Randy's so closely? After all, having established himself as a bona fide A-list star in the 1980s with roles in the likes of *Year of the Dragon* (1985), the unforgettable *9 1/2 Weeks* (1986) and *Angel Heart* (1987), he vanished into a twilight career of low-level pugilism, an adventure responsible for his unusual appearance. Perhaps it does work as a marketing hook, but after a few minutes we're thoroughly immersed in Rourke's performance – one of incredible emotional subtlety from a body that looks like it shouldn't be capable of it. Randy's essential decency, and the painfulness of his situation, are revealed in the small moments: his return to his lonely cramped trailer from hospital, where he peers at his medications through reading glasses. His snoring, flat out on an unmade bed, a bottle of hot sauce inexplicably on the bedside next to his hearing aid. He aims for the most difficult of cinematic moods to get right: pathos, which is always on a knife-edge of icky sentimentality, and he does it with dazzling control. Maybe only Mickey Rourke could play this role – because he's been there. For a movie about a sport full of fakery and phoniness, *The Wrestler* doesn't have a dishonest moment.

A film about a wrestler or a film about an actor? Mickey Rourke throws body and soul into his performance as Randy "The Ram" Robinson.

Index

Numbers in bold refer to main reviews or biographical feature boxes.

Picture credits

The images in this book are from the archives of The Kobal Collection, which owes its existence to the vision, courage, talent and energy of the men and women who created the movie industry and whose legacies live on through the films they made, the studios they built, and the publicity photographs they took. Kobal collects, preserves, organizes and makes these images available. Rough Guides wishes to thank all the film distribution and production companies and apologizes in advance for any omissions or neglect, and will be pleased to make any necessary changes in future editions.

Page 3 Everest Entertainment; 7 Tree Line Films/Relativity Media; 8 Columbia Pictures; 11 Ugc / Studio Canal+; 13 Dreamworks/Apatow Prod; 16 Screen Australia; 18 Zentropa Ents.; 21 La Classe Americane/Ufilm/France 3; 25 Twentieth Century-Fox Film Corporation; 26 Millennium Films; 29 Protozoa Pictures/Phoenix Pictures; 33 Hunting Lane Films; 34 20th Century Fox; 37 Universal; 40 Alliance Atlantis/Dog Eat Dog/United Broadcasting; 42 Focus Features; 44 Marvel/Paramount; 46 HBO Documentary/Notorious Pictures; 48 SBS Productions; 51 Eon/Danjaq/Sony; 53 Globo Films; 54 Paramount Pictures; 57 Dreamworks/Paramount; 59 Warner Bros/DC Comics; 63 Kadokawa Shoten; 64 20th Century Fox; 66 Warner Bros.; 71 Key Creatives; 72 Flower Films/Gaylord/Adam Fields Prod; 75 Constantin Film/Ard/Degeto; 78 Bold Films; 82 Rollercoaster Films; 84 HBO / Fine Line Features; 87 Fidelite Films/Wild Bunch/Bug; 88 Focus Features; 90 Killer Films; 94 Quinta Comm.; 96 Mandeville Films; 99 BBC Films; 102 Dreamachine; 105 Fandango; 107 Miramax Films; 110 Wdr/X-Filme; 113 Warner Bros;114 Discovery Docs.; 117 Ardustry Entertainment; 120 Warner Bros.; 124 Beijing New Picture/Elite Group; 126 Sony Pictures; 128 New Line Productions; 130 Hostel Llc/Lions Gate Films; 132 Lionsgate; 135 First Light Productions/Kingsgatefilms; 137 Omega/EMG/Star Max; 139 Django Films; 140 Warner Bros; 144 Universal Pictures; 147 Marvel/Paramount; 148 Fox Searchlight; 152 See-Saw Films; 155 Universal; 188 Tequila Gang/WB; 156 Fido Film Ab; 161 Creado Film/Br/Arte; 159 20th Century Fox/Fox Searchlight Pictures; 164 New Line / Saul Zaentz / Wing Nut; 168 Focus Features; 170 Gravier Productions; 172 Focus Features; 175 Scott Rudin Productions; 176 Liberty Films UK; 181 Studio Canal+/Les Films Alain Sarde/Universal; 182 Paramount/Miramax; 185 Egg Films/Show East; 192 2.4.7. Films; 195 Canal+; 198 Ghoulardi/New Line/Revolution; 200 Chockstone Pictures; 203 Touchstone Pictures; 205 Big Talk/WT 2; 208 Paramount Pictures; 211 Weinstein Co.; 214 El Deseo S.A.; 216 Columbia Pictures; 219 Studio Ghibli; 220 Miramax / Senart Films; 224 Fox Searchlight; 227 Paramount Pictures; 229 Sidney Kimmel Entertainment; 230 Paramount; 234 Paramount/Vantage; 239 Dreamworks; 241 Cottonwood Pictures; 242 Summit Entertainment; 245 Universal; 246 Paramount Pictures; 252 BBC Films; 256 Saturn Films; vii Marvel Enterprises; viii Universal.

Cover image: Courtesy of Universal Studios Licensing LLC